WITHDRAWN
UTSA Libraries

D0745892

Green Mount after the War
The Correspondence of
Maria Louisa Wacker Fleet
and Her Family
1865–1900

Fred, Dr. Fleet, Mrs. Fleet, and Benny

Green Mount after the War

The Correspondence of
Maria Louisa Wacker Fleet
and Her Family
1865–1900

Edited by Betsy Fleet

University Press of Virginia

Charlottesville

THE UNIVERSITY PRESS OF VIRGINIA
Copyright © 1978 by the Rector and Visitors
of the University of Virginia

First published 1978

Library of Congress Cataloging in Publication Data

Fleet, Maria Louisa Wacker.
  Green Mount after the war.

  Includes index.
  1. Fleet, Maria Louisa Wacker. 2. Virginia—
Biography. 3. Fleet family. I. Fleet, Betsy.
II. Title.
GT275.F5827A4 1978 975.5'04'0924 [B] 77-24079
ISBN 0–8139–0730–6

Printed in the United States of America

LIBRARY
The University of Texas
At San Antonio

To those who live within these pages
and especially to
Reginald Scott Fleet
who happily is with us

Time is
Too slow for those who wait
Too swift for those who fear
Too long for those who grieve
Too short for those who rejoice
But for those who love
Time is eternity.

Anonymous

Inscription on a commemorative sundial on the Lawn in front of the Rotunda at the University of Virginia, placed by the Seven Society.

Contents

Illustrations

Preface

Among my first memories are those of the "Green Mount Girls" who used to spend a day or sometimes many days at Green Mount. They would look intently at my two sisters and me for some trace of resemblance to my aunts, Florence, Betsy, and Lou, and my grandmother, Maria Louisa Wacker Fleet, who had conducted the Green Mount Home School for Young Ladies. Invariably they looked away without saying anything and we could sense their disappointment. We wondered how anyone could be as talented and beautiful and good as everyone said our grandmother and aunts were. We never knew them, for they died before we were born, with the exception of Aunt Lou, whom we knew when we were very young.

On the occasions when the former "school girls" came, there was always a large dinner, and afterward we were allowed to come out of the kitchen, our accustomed dining place when there was company, and join the guests in the parlor. We found footstools and usually seated ourselves behind the chairs where "the girls" sat, as we were shy and didn't like being stared at.

About the same time Martha Ann Gaines Baylor arrived and was greeted by the former students as warmly as they had greeted the family. She was tall, spare, very dark and had the aristocratic bearing of some of her race. She always described herself as a "Green Mount family piece." Her grandmother, Milly, had been the mammy for Dr. and Mrs. Benjamin Fleet's children and her mother, Mary, had been the cook. They stayed with the family all their lives, even when Gen. Philip Sheridan and his men camped in the front fields and took their husbands, Joshua and Harry, away with them; the men escaped, however, and found their way back. Martha Ann put on a snowy white

cap for these occasions and innumerable starched white petticoats under her black dress. She always reminded me of a sym-
metrical cedar tree.

Then the reminiscences began about the absent ones, and
everyone contributed all she presently knew about them, some
of which was so sad that tears accompanied the recounting.
At that point Martha Ann, who had to a great degree that "peculiar gift" which an old Negro preacher referred to when he
prayed "O Lord, who hast given thy people a peculiar gift of
mimicry, teach them to mimic thy Son," would say, "You jes'
ought to seen Nancy get happy last Sunday at Morning Star
Church." Nancy had waited on the table when the school was
in session. Martha Ann, who had the most supple body, in
fact was double-jointed, would in imitation of Nancy get up
and shout and exhort; increasing in momentum, would show
how Nancy made a flying leap over the pews and how it took
six men to catch her. When one thought he had succeeded,
according to Martha Ann, he found his arms full of starched
petticoats.

The conversation inevitably turned to "dear Mrs. Fleet," and
one after another spoke of what she had meant to her. When
"Father sent me here just after Mother died," one said, "I
felt, and I am sure I saw, a warm glow of light and love radiating
from her; in fact, I still feel her comforting presence." Aunt
Lou was so overcome that she spread her handkerchief over
her face. Martha Ann got to her feet and with short, quick
steps walked the length of the room, saying, "As Old Miss
would say, 'Now girls, don't let the clouds obscure the sunshine!' " It must have been a perfect imitation, for everyone
in the room burst into spontaneous laughter.

Always we wondered what our grandmother was like. From
where we sat we could see her portrait over the mantel, but
the serene young girl in early nineteenth-century dress holding
a red bird on her finger gave little clue to the "dear Mrs. Fleet"
and "Old Miss" who dominated the conversation. Now she
comes to life for us in the letters and papers found in trunks
and boxes in the Green Mount attic.

Some of the letters written during the Civil War were published with her son Benny's diary in *Green Mount* (Lexington,

Ky., 1962; reprinted Charlottesville, Va., 1977); many of the remaining letters are presented here. The original spelling, punctuation, and abbreviations have been retained; but repetitious passages have been silently omitted. The letters show how "Ma," widowed before the war ended, on a plantation ravaged by both armies, with no money and little credit, kept her home, educated her six children, and held the family together by using her only resources—education, love, courage, and a firm and abiding faith in God.

Green Mount after the War
The Correspondence of
Maria Louisa Wacker Fleet
and Her Family
1865–1900

Jacob David Wacker

Introduction

Maria Louisa Wacker was the daugher of Jacob David Wacker, who was born in 1781 at Hildrenhausen in the duchy of Württemberg.[1] He was a page at the court of Emperor Leopold II and Maria Louisa in Vienna, where Gen. Lewis Littlepage, chamberlain of Stanislas II, king of Poland, and emissary to the courts of Europe, became acquainted with him. Maria Louisa entrusted young Wacker to General Littlepage with the entreaty and funds to take him to America and help him establish himself.

On October 3, 1800, they set out by coach from Warsaw, traveling through German and Danish cities, while General Littlepage attended to official and personal business en route. In May 1801 permission was granted "Lewis Littlepage & Family" to land in England. His "Family" included Wacker, a small dog named Crab, and a flock of game chickens which he called Suvarovs as a tribute to Gen. Alexander Vasilevich Suvarov, under whom he fought against the Turks and whom he considered invincible.

In London, Littlepage got a permit to purchase two pairs of horse pistols with which he armed Wacker and himself. He found a ship, the *Alexandria,* bound for Norfolk, procured passports for himself and "my servant, J. D. Wacker," and they sailed on September 24, 1801. The passengers landed on November 5 and proceeded by slow stages to Washington. Here Jacob Wacker delivered a note from General Littlepage to President Jefferson, who received the general the following day. Wacker remained with Littlepage until his death in July 1802.

In his will Littlepage bequeathed Wacker the "sum of five hundred dollars," which may have been the money entrusted to him by Maria Louisa; and in the fall Wacker entered the University of Pennsylvania. He studied medicine under Benjamin Rush and, after graduating *honorium* in 1806, came to King and Queen County, Virginia, established his practice, and on March 4, 1817, married Maria Pollard.

[1] Record in Fleet Family Bible, diplomas, family tradition, and *The King's Chevalier* by Curtis Carroll Davis (New York: Bobbs-Merrill, 1961).

Dr. and Mrs. Jacob David Wacker named their only surviving child, born in 1822, Maria Louisa, as an expression of his regard for his former patron. Since she was an only child, her parents were determined she should not be spoiled. Her mother said to her one day, "Stop crying, my child, you know you never got anything in your life by crying." "Oh yes, Mam, I have," she said, "a spanking many a time." Both parents died before she was eight years old, but she always said she never felt the loss of father or mother as she was so tenderly cared for and wisely educated by her aunt, Betsy Pollard, wife of Col. Alexander Fleet. Colonel Fleet was her guardian, and they both loved her as though she were their own child. One day her Aunt Betsy found her gazing in the mirror at herself. Determined to uproot any seeds of vanity that might be taking hold, Aunt Betsy said, "You are not pretty so you must be good." Taking another look at herself, Maria Louisa said, "I won't have to be so very good."

Maria Louisa grew up at Melville, across the county road from Goshen, the parental Fleet home, and about a mile down the lane. The same teachers who taught the young Fleets at Goshen came to Melville to tutor her. Later she was sent to Mr. and Mrs. Keeling's School for Young Ladies in Richmond, where she studied English grammar and literature, German, French, and music. After graduating in all these subjects, she spent a winter at Melville making preparations for her marriage to Benjamin, Colonel Fleet's youngest brother, four years older than herself.

When she was eighteen, they had become "firmly attached" and she wrote him at the University of Pennsylvania, where he was completing his medical studies:

Melville

My own dearest,   Dec. 4th 1841

Your welcome letter came yesterday and you see I have estimated your anxiety to hear from me by my own feelings; and so determined to write by the very next mail. Every day since you left us, I have counted the days which must elapse before the arrival of your first letter, and each night congratulated myself that I was one day nearer Friday. I had but one wish— one thought—that I should hear from you then. When the day came, how can I describe the feverish anxiety with which I counted the hours and rejoiced at the death of each one. Let me thank you again and again for not disappointing me. You never felt and heaven forbid you should ever feel as utterly desolate as I have felt for the last week. I fear I tried more to kill time, than to improve it. But my spirits are happily very elastic, and it is not my nature to be depressed very long at a time.

You need not fear I shall forget you if you knew how entirely every thought, every feeling of my heart was blended with your image, you could not but confide in my love. I think of you more than I ever wish to be thought of in return; for everything I see reminds me of you, every book, every flower, every piece of music I play brings to my recollection the many happy hours I have spent with you. Do you remember how short the moments would seem when you were by my side? But you have active and important duties to perform and I would not have one thought of me intrude, when your mind should be more profitably engaged. If you think of me, let it be to remember how much confidence I place in you, and that I not only hope but expect to see you eminent in your profession.

I have very little news to tell you, which must account for my talking so much about *myself,* that subject on which we all are eloquent. I received a letter from Betsy Fauntleroy last Monday, she said she expected I would be able to bear the separation pretty well if you wrote frequently. She tells me Mr. Hopkins had been to Col. Garnett's and staid several days, and it was thought he would succeed at last. She sympathized with Mr. Dew, in short, touched on everybody's love affairs but her own.

I received a ticket to Mr. James Jeffries' for next Tuesday, and I presume it will be a dancing party. If I had not lost all relish for parties I should go down to Uncle Robert's and get Cousin Sam [Harwood] to wait on me but I do not wish to go. I should not go to sleep that night with the sweet assurance that I shall dream of you as I do every night, how could I with my head full of music and dancing, "beaux" and compliments. Mr. Sydnor [2] came here last week and seemed more surprised at hearing you were gone to spend the winter in Philadelphia than I ever saw anyone. I am delighted to hear you intend having your miniature taken. I assure you I shall value it beyond everything—except the original.

[2] Thomas White Sydnor was minister of the Bruington Baptist Church.

Write very shortly and believe me to be through weal or woe, your own,

Marie Louise

Dr. Benjamin Fleet
No. 188 Chestnut Street, Philadelphia

Maria Louisa Wacker and Benjamin Fleet were married on Thursday, March 24, 1842, by William Todd at Melville. They bought a place in King and Queen County about thirty-five miles northeast of Richmond, called Pickle Hill, which was built before 1800 by the Roanes and was owned successively by the Campbells and Bentleys. The name did not suit Maria Louisa and she changed it to Green Mount; her husband always wrote it Green Mont.

Benjamin's medical practice grew, extending to a radius of about fifteen miles, which he traveled on horseback or in a buggy when the roads permitted. He expanded his holdings in land from the Mattaponi River to Clarkston, about three thousand acres, and ran ferries at Aylett and Dunkirk, the head of navigation. Here he built granaries to store his and his neighbors' grain until ships arrived to take it to Baltimore. He maintained an office in a wing of his home, and people were coming constantly to consult him on physical as well as legal matters, since he was also a county justice.

Maria Louisa assumed the responsibilities of running the house, training the servants, supervising the spinning of cotton and wool, and weaving the cloth for the servants' clothes. Their first child, Alexander Frederick Fleet, was born in June 1843. While on a visit to Melville, she received the following letter from her husband:

Green Mont, 6½ o'clock
My own dearest,   Febr'y 10th 1846
Here I am all alone, having just returned from Mr. Dew's where I took the tumor from his servant's lip. I am beginning to think that I have too much of the milk of human kindness about me ever to make a great surgeon, the most important requisites for one to possess are firmness, self possession and a lack of sympathy, to which I must confess I am now a total

stranger. But I am wandering away from my original intention to inform you that owing to my not having met with Mr. Chas. Harrison today at Aylett's as I had contemplated, I am faced with the necessity of leaving early in the morning for his home, as I succeeded today in getting the draft from Mr. Scott, I must take it to Mr. Harrison. I didn't know but that you might have expected me to meet you at Melville tomorrow, which I should be unable to do. Although we have received many newspapers and periodicals, I have not even glanced at them.

I pray you never again indulge even a suspicion that my love for you has lessened in the most remote degree, but let me assure you that I love you as deeply and truly and ardently as in the days of yore. And why should you ever doubt but that the child of our affections has cemented, as it were, us to each other? Kiss him for me and remember me affectionately to all at Melville. You see my devotion has caused me to detain you, I fear, quite too long but hope you will excuse,

Yr. ever affectionate,

B. Fleet

Happy, busy, child-filled years followed. Benjamin Robert was born in 1846, Maria Louisa in 1849, David Wacker in 1851, Florence in 1852, Betsy Pollard in 1854, and James William in 1856. There was a continuous round of dining days, parties, and visiting among friends and relatives, who were so numerous it was said one could travel for ten miles on the road from Dunkirk to Tappahannock without getting off Fleet land. But always the children came first, and their mother often said anyone who says children are no trouble is either neglecting them or is not telling the truth.

Their mother read to the children and started teaching them as soon as they learned to talk; and his father taught Fred the Greek alphabet by the time he was four. It was customary for one or more families to employ a teacher who lived in their homes and taught the young children. Fred and Benny went to school with their cousins at Goshen, taught by Miss Mary Chapin of Washington, D.C. As an expression of his admiration and affection, Benny named his colt for her. Later, Fred attended Fleetwood Academy, conducted by Oliver White, a graduate of Dublin's Trinity College, until his retirement in 1858. Then Fred and Benny went to John H. Pitts's Rumford Academy during the session of 1858–59. It was at this point that Maria Louisa Fleet drew up the following document.

We the undersigned hereby voluntarily pledge ourselves not to play any game for money as long as our hands are hereto signed.

A. Fred: Fleet   seal

B. R. Fleet   seal

There probably would have been more signatories had the other two boys been old enough to write. In the fall of 1859 James Calvin Councill opened Aberdeen Academy, near St. Stephen's Church, which Fred and Benny attended until Fred entered the University of Virginia the following year. In 1860 rumblings of war were beginning to be heard. Dr. Fleet, a member of the militia, was summoned to King and Queen Court House to plan for arming the county. Benny and David, caught in the tide of talk of war, went so far as to use their father's new mold to make bullets, "preparing for the Yankees."

In politics the Fleets were conservative Whigs and were bitterly opposed to the dissolution of the Union; but when war came and Virginia joined the Confederacy, the family devoted their time, energy, and resources to the Confederate cause. At a time when it was not considered proper for ladies' names to appear in print, or at best when they coyly signed only initials, Maria Louisa Fleet signed her name in full when on November 14, 1863, she wrote to the editors of the *Richmond Enquirer.*

Gentlemen:

I read with considerable anxiety an appeal in your last issue to the ladies of the country in behalf of our sockless soldiers. For the last two years I cheerfully gave all my surplus wool— about ten pounds—had socks knit, and distributed some with my own hands, feeling amply repaid by hearing some poor fellow say "thank you"; but now my tithe [3] of wool lies idle in the garret waiting the coming of the tax-gatherer.

---

[3] Tithes were an expedient of the Confederate Congress for securing subsistence for its armies. Since taxes collected in the depreciated currency were not sufficient, the levy in kind was adopted on April 24, 1863, to tap the resources of the Confederate farms.

Fred when he entered the university
in 1860

Fred during the war

If I could get permission, I would have the wool spun, doubled with my tithe of cotton (about five pounds), knit and returned to the government at Christmas—or soon after, in the form of comfortable socks for the army. Of course, I should expect help from my neighbors; but I have never seen the lady who is not willing to help the soldiers, and what I propose could be done by some influential, trustworthy lady in every neighborhood throughout our entire Confederacy.

One of my daughters asks what security I would give, and I reply: *My name,* and *word* of a *lady.*

Can't you help us in our "labor of love"? A word or two from you would have great weight. Can't you speak to someone in authority, and let me know as soon as practicable whether I may be allowed to do as I propose. By so doing, you will not only oblige me, but help our soldiers in the field.

The editors published her letter under the caption "socks! socks! socks!" and added the note: "We should be gratified if the proper authorities would furnish us with the information asked in the subjoined letter, from a lady well known to us for her unceasing labor and efforts in behalf of our soldiers. What she says can be fully relied on, and we invite the attention of the authorities to this letter."

On Jan. 1, 1864, she wrote again to the editors of the *Richmond Enquirer.*

Gentlemen:

I wrote a letter which you kindly published last November, offering to have my tithe of wool and cotton knit and given to the Government in the form of socks for the soldiers, promising to have them ready by Christmas. I have waited as patiently as I could till now, but have received no response, so I have concluded "silence gives consent," and intend to take the responsibility and have it done as soon as possible. My only object in troubling you again is to urge that others may do likewise. By just one lady in every neighborhood knitting up her tithes, with the assistance of her friends and neighbors, we can produce socks enough for our army, and I venture to say, we will not consume as much wool and cotton as would be otherwise wasted; and the soldiers would be sure of them. For, when the ladies undertake anything, you know they generally succeed. Gentlemen, my heart is with our army. If I were a man, I should be there, so don't deny me the poor privilege of doing what I can, though that be only knitting a few socks for our soldiers.— Let us work for them with our needles as long as they defend us with their bayonets, and then when our glorious cause triumphs, let us share with them the victory.

Very respectfully,
Maria Louisa Fleet

Dr. Fleet and Benny, members of the Home Guard, were called out frequently to meet the forays of the enemy. When on a scout, March 1, 1864, Benny was fired on by the advance guard of Col. Ulric Dahlgren, after his abortive raid on Richmond. Shot in the wrist, and bleeding heavily, Benny rode into the woods and lay down under a pine tree. In the early morning hours, his dog Stuart scratched on a Green Mount door and led a search party to Benny's body. At daybreak the fears of his anxious family waiting at home were confirmed when they saw his riderless horse grazing on the lawn.

This act set in motion a series of tragic events. The Home Guard, incensed at Benny's "murder," mustered and ambushed Dahlgren, killing him and capturing some of his men. In retaliation, those who escaped burned King and Queen Court House and several homes in the vicinity. The first break in the close-knit family circle was a devastating blow, separating them from Benny physically but never spiritually. The family put away his diary and the Confederate uniform which he planned to wear the next day to join Col. John S. Mosby, but they kept his loving, lively spirit in their hearts always. The many letters of condolence invariably referred to him as "a noble boy."

In May 1864 Fred returned from Florida when Gen. Henry A. Wise's brigade was ordered to assist in the defense of Petersburg. He was wounded there and, after leaving the hospital, was taken to the home of a cousin, Bernard Todd, to recuperate because he was cut off from his home by the Federal army.

On June 4, 1864, Gen. Philip Sheridan, with a column of cavalry, bivouacked in front of Green Mount for three days, using the palings of the yard fence to tether their horses. They drove off all the servants from the quarters except Milly and Mary, who moved into the house. Dr. Fleet was away visiting patients and did not dare return, knowing he would either be killed or captured. Ma and five children, ranging

in age from seven to fourteen, remained. The house was ransacked
by soldiers who took all the ornaments, silver, and food they could
find. Although dispirited, when General Sheridan came up to the
porch to call, Maria Louisa offered him a chair. Taking the largest,
he said, "A little man always likes a big chair." He asked if she would
like to hear some music. She requested *Dixie* and he ordered the
band to play it. She also asked for a guard and later wrote, "One
of the three who protected us was an intelligent, well-behaved man."

While Sheridan's cavalry was encamped in the front fields at Green
Mount, the soldiers searched the neighborhood for all the remaining
horses, cattle, sheep, hogs, and fowls and drove them into pens which
they had made by tearing down the rail fences on the farm. Mrs.
Fleet, realizing how utterly devoid they were of anything to eat, asked
one of the guards if she might have one of her cows so the children
might have milk to drink. He reported to General Sheridan, who
said she could have one if she could identify it. It was unthinkable
to send Lou, who was fourteen, or David, who though younger, was
tall for his age and might be captured. She wrote Fred, in a hospital
in Petersburg: "I can never tell you what it cost me to send little
Betsy and Willie and the anxious moments I had as I watched them
from the front porch. As they approached the headquarters' tent,
Willie took Betsy's hand and they held on to each other. They were
directed to a pen teeming with cattle. They were too small to look
over them and consequently couldn't see any of ours. But Princess,
a pretty Jersey, which they had petted, saw them and followed them
out of the pen and to our empty barns. It was with a thankful heart
that I held them in my arms again."

After Sheridan's troops moved on, the family were beset by strag-
glers who continued to force their way in and ransack the house.
Early in the war his mother wrote Fred: "We have never turned a
soldier away and the house is constantly filled with the sick, wounded
and hungry. Sometimes there are also Federal soldiers too ill to go
on, for I cannot but help even a Yankee if he is in trouble." But
after suffering so acutely from her own tragedies and those of her
friends, she had learned to hate and later wrote: "My heart is hard-
ened, if I were a man I would never take a prisoner but would consider
it my duty to rid the world of such monsters. God may have mercy
on them if he chooses but if I could I would rid Virginia of all such
brutes in human shape."

As the winter of 1864–65 approached, Maria Louisa wrote again
to the editors of the *Richmond Enquirer:* "Ladies of the country must
again re-inforce the army. There is a great scarcity of socks in the

Army of Northern Virginia. Gen. Lee has lately, we are advised, called upon the ladies of Richmond to aid him in procuring socks for his army. There is, we know, great difficulty in purchasing yarn, but where yarn cannot be procured, cotton is better than nothing. Let the ladies of Richmond meet together and take this important matter under their charge. Let all 'club dancing parties' cease, and knitting parties meet to ply the needles for the benefit of the soldiers."

The long, cold, dreary winter with its bad news from every front eroded the strength and spirit of those at home. They had taken all the doctors in the area and the care of the sick devolved very heavily on Dr. Fleet's shoulders. On March 8, 1865, he died, having ridden that day fifteen miles on horseback in the rain to visit an ill patient.

Then a month later came the dreaded news, "Richmond has fallen."

I

"We hear of nothing but hard times, want of money and chills."

1865–1873

In April 1865 when Fred Fleet came home to Green Mount, having walked most of the way from Appomattox so that his wounded companion, Ned Watkins, could ride his horse, he found the rolls of Confederate money and bonds worthless, the barns and stables empty, the fields grown up in weeds. His mother said, "I never thought I would see the day when I am unable to borrow two hundred dollars on three thousand acres of land." After Dr. Fleet's death, realizing she would be unable to pay the men whom he had hired, she had been forced to let them go. But Joshua Gaines, Milly's husband, who had been driven off by Sheridan's men but had managed to find his way back home, told her, "We all will get along together the best we kin." With his mule he put in a large garden; and when Fred came with his horse, they planted enough corn to last both families through the winter. Fred felt an overwhelming sense of discouragement, but his mother counseled: "I know the way is dim, but God will guide you through the tunnel to the light, with which you children can make your own way. I am determined that you shall be educated at any cost." Maria Louisa Fleet sold one of the ferries, the only disposable asset she owned, and Fred reentered the University of Virginia in the fall.

University of Va.
My dear Mother: Monday night, 9 Oct. 1865
   Mr. Jones arrived today and I went down to Dr. Broaddus' to see him and get your letter. He told me about Genl. Wise sending $20 along with your $30.[1] I assure you I was very

[1] Henry A. Wise (1806–1871) was born at Drummondtown, Accomack County, Va. He was graduated from Washington College in Pennsylvania and studied law under Judge Henry St. George Tucker. He was a member of the House of Representatives, 1833–44, minister to Brazil, and governor of Virginia, 1856–60. In May 1861 he was commissioned brigadier general in the provisional army of the Confederate States. A friend of Dr. Fleet and Fred's former commander, he advised Mrs. Fleet regarding the management of her estate.

much gratified. I am sorry to learn that Flossie was sick. I hope she may not have a recurrence of those miserable chills and that she will soon be out again. So it seems the "agers" are not confined to the indolent exclusively.

As you imagined I have been in much trouble about money matters, but now my mind is easy on that score and the only thing that troubles is the annoyance and inconvenience you will be subjected to at home this year in seeding the wheat crop and gathering the corn, but let us be thankful we have the corn to gather and hope that next year you will have a much easier time.

I found out on inquiry after I arrived that to take the medical ticket [2] required a deposit of $256 in advance, including one third of the board at $60, the rest to be paid in two equal instalments of $60 each, on the 1st of Jan. & March respectively. As I reached this place with only $175, and I had some books, a lamp & oil & some other little things to buy which took up about $23.00 leaving me $152. Well all last week I was quite miserable, and had delayed matriculating, but on Saturday evening I went over to see Dr. Maupin [3] and told him about the matter and he very kindly informed me that the professors could wait for their fees until it was perfectly convenient for me to pay the amount, (their fees are $115) so I matriculated, paid $150 gave him my due bill for $106 to be paid when convenient. I will hand him $50 tomorrow and any time in the next month or two, when you can collect some money from the ferry, you can send me the balance.

It gives me no little pleasure to tell you this. I find that books are from one half to two times as high as they were before the war when gold was in circulation, so you see how fortunate it was that I went to Smithfield. Pay Cousin Tom for the books before you trouble yourself about me again. He knows the amount & of course will give you a receipt. Tell him that I can use all the books, altho' one of them is some two editions behind the text-book now used here, but contains nearly every

[2] Students enrolled in classes by purchasing tickets from the instructors of those classes.
[3] Socrates Maupin (1808–1871) was professor of chemistry and chairman of the faculty of the University of Virginia.

thing the new editions have, and too they are much better bound than any of the new books.

I suppose I am indebted to Dr. Fauntleroy for the nice box of bones sent by Mr. J. Please thank him very kindly for them and the book and tell him the bones will be of great assistance to me. Dr. Davis has been kind enough to lend Walker and myself a pretty good assortment of all the bones in the body except the skull bones and these of Dr. F. came in very opportunely.

I called on Dr. Davis soon after I arrived and found his wife unwell with ague & fever but she is now up and Walker & Johnnie Bagby & I will accept the Dr.'s invitation to take breakfast with him tomorrow morning. He is a beautiful lecturer and makes anatomy, which I have always heard was the dryest part of the course, intensely interesting.[4]

When I arrived I had my choice of six houses on what is called Dawson's Row, & I selected the 2nd one and picked out a room for myself, reserving the others for my K & Q friends. Walker & I are in one of the four upper rooms, John Bagby & Warner Lewis adjoining, John Dew & Harvey, Marius Jones & a young man named Taylor from Richmond on the upper floor & Dejarnette & Broaddus on the lower, so we have a very pleasant crowd & I prefer this locality to any in College. There are now 160 students & Dr. Maupin says there will be 200 before the end of the month.

Give my love to the General and tell him I sincerely regret the necessity which forbids my being with him, but he must make himself perfectly at home. It is needless for me to ask you to do every thing in your power to make him spend his time pleasantly. Tell David to keep Alice in good trim for Genl. W. to ride and always to put a martingale & the "great bit" (Willie's expression) on her, for she rides a great deal easier with that than with any other.

Write me a full account of the Genl. & everything about home. I hope Mrs. Dunn may be well when this reaches you.

---

[4] Dr. John Staige Davis (1824–1885) was educated at the universities of Virginia and Pennsylvania and was professor of anatomy, materia medica, and botany. His second wife was Caroline Hill of King William County. Her sister, Evelyn Hill, appears later in the letters.

Fred after the war

Lou

Florence

Bessie

The drought is distressing in this section as well as in K & Q.

Best love to all the family & regards to enquiring friends,

Affectionately yours,

A. Fred Fleet

My dear Ma,   U. Va. Oct. 15th 1865

We have about 175 students who have matriculated and expect some 25 more during the present month. They seem to
be a nice set of fellows and seem to be studying as well as
anyone could expect after having been interrupted for four
years. The medical ticket is as much as I can attend to, I will
try to graduate but think there is little probability of it this
year. Charlie Fleet has done a more sensible thing than any
of us who are studying medicine. He has gone into a drug
store and next year he expects to go into business himself and
I have no doubt he will find it more lucrative and a less laborious
way of making a living than practising medicine.[5]

Let me know exactly what is going on on the farm. Please
try to have the wheat sowed and the corn gathered as soon
as possible. I received a check for $20 from Lucius Harrison
in payment for his medical bill, and also a check from the man
who bought Charley [horse] for $30 which I deposited. Dr.
Maupin said he could wait until it is convenient for the balance.

---

[5] Charles Browne Fleet (1843–1916) was educated at Columbian College (George
Washington University) of which his grandfather, Robert B. Semple, was a founder
and member of the Board of Trustees. Upon graduation he joined the Fredericksburg
Artillery, which was said to have fired the first gun at Gettysburg and the last at Appo-
mattox. He had planned to study medicine and follow the footsteps of his father,
Dr. Christopher B. Fleet, but impoverished by the war, he opened a drugstore in
Lynchburg. He developed a solution of sodium phosphate, which he called Phospho-
Soda; he also invented Chapstick and a compound which sobered people us instantly.
On Sunday mornings a diverse collection of men would be sitting on the long bench
in front of his drugstore in various stages of inebriety waiting for "Doc" Fleet to let
them in and sell them a potion to sober them up so they could go home and he
could go to teach his Sunday school class. His sons, Arthur and Paul, founded C. B.
Fleet Co., Inc., and wanted to use the formula of the instant soberer and develop it
as a new product. But their sister, Mrs. Dudley Diggs, was adamant, sure that their
father would have disapproved heartily; he would have said it would encourage drinking,
and *that* she knew he would have had no part of.

How is the ferry getting on now? and what is the prospect of any money from those who owe the small medical bills?

Love to all from your devoted son

Fred

My dear Ma,   University of Va. Oct. 26th '65

Willie Lee Broaddus just came in bringing your letter enclosing Genl Wise's. I was delighted to hear from you all and am very much interested in Genl Wise's plans. They read beautifully on paper and sound very fine coming from his eloquent lips, but I fear the practical part will be more difficult than one would at first imagine. Be it as it may, I am very much obliged to the Genl for his kindness to us all and his consideration of our interests and I wrote him to that effect.

I am getting on pretty well with my studies, only one of them bothers me, physiology under Dr. Cabell.[6] It is very difficult but I hope to get the hang of it after awhile. Under Dr. Davis, I am getting on very satisfactorily. He is the clearest lecturer I ever heard, & if we don't understand his subject— Anatomy, we had, I think, as well give the matter up. He lectures once a week on Materia Medica and makes that course particularly interesting. He seems to take an especial interest in me and I go often to call on him and Mrs. Davis and Miss Evelyn Hill and have such a pleasant time. Would go oftener and could have a charming time visiting if I could spare the time.

Love to all,

Fred

From Richmond, General Wise wrote Fred, his former adjutant general:

Dear Fleet: Nov. 10th 1865

I have had a very pleasant visit in your mother's home. I suggested to her that she sell her surplus timber. It is bringing

[6] Dr. James L. Cabell (1813–1889) was in charge of the military hospitals for the Confederate government during the Civil War. He was professor of comparative anatomy, physiology, and surgery.

an enormous price in Richmond, and standing in the woods, it is a costly investment for a future that can never want it as bad as the present does.

Johnny [Wise] left us Monday for the University and I beg you to have an eye on him, and try to stimulate him to study. You are all in danger, I fear, of rushing over your studies too fast. *Festina lente* in study, take no short cuts, be thorough and take time.

I am still uncertain what to do or where to go to live. The papers say my lands in Princess Anne are confiscated.[7] If so I

David at V.M.I.   Will

[7] In 1859 Henry A. Wise purchased Rolleston from his brother, an estate of about nine hundred acres located on the Elizabeth River near Norfolk. When Norfolk was evacuated, U.S. authorities took possession of Rolleston and established a school for blacks there. At the war's end large numbers of blacks were quartered in the house under the auspices of the Freedmen's Bureau. To General Wise's petition for the return of his home he was told that he had abandoned it to engage in rebellion, that he was a prisoner of war and had not been pardoned by the president. In 1868 his property was restored to him, but most of the timber had been cut and the household furnishings had been stolen or destroyed.

am wholly stripped. But if I can have my health, I will never droop in despair.

God bless you,
Henry A. Wise

My dear child [Fred], Friday night, Feb. 9, 1866
Sam Gresham came last week and tried to make me write Mr. Jones to legalize the ferry till I could put up a bridge. I told him I was not able to build a bridge. You need never expect that I will not have trouble as it is the lot of man, rather pray for me that I will have strength equal to my day and task. I never had but two children with energy equal to mine—Benny and Betsy. You and Lou work with a sense of duty, but it is reason you deserve all the more credit for it. I have come to the conclusion if I can get over this year, we will get along better hereafter, at any rate, I shall hope on.
I amused myself yesterday with writing some very polite duns [Dr. Fleet's outstanding bills] with what success, I will advise you. Dear child, don't take on the troubles at home. Let me do what I can and you do all you can at college.

Your affectionate Mother

Dear Ma, April 3, 1866
I'm trying to study and feel I am acquiring some knowledge of medicine [8] and I hope my taste for it will improve with time and study and practice. If I only had my father to advise and instruct me, how much I could learn from him.
I think you have made very profitable arrangements [to share the crops] and with thirteen men and horses at work planting corn, it really seems we ought to make enough to serve us and have about two hundred barrels to sell next year. You can do everything with the energy you showed while the war lasted because now you don't have the fear that any moment it might be taken from you.

Love to all,
Fred

---

[8] Fred entered the university with the intention of studying medicine, prompted by a sense of duty that he should carry on his father's work.

However, Fred's taste for medicine did not improve, and that summer when he came home his mother advised him against continuing an uncongenial course and urged him to take the subjects where his inclinations lay. The classics were his choice, and he elected to study Greek and Latin.

Department of Public Charities and Corrections
New York
Dear Fred,   Sept. 10th 1866

I don't believe you will regret giving up the study of medicine—just now I have confused feelings about the practice. When a patient recovers, I can't help feeling a satisfaction which almost repays me for what I have suffered when I lose one. Since I have been in this hospital I have lost three patients. I have begun to lose confidence in medicine & believe if nature were let alone, more cases would recover than when treated with drugs.

I have been unable to get home but Mother visited me for a few days—wouldn't stay because she said she was violently opposed to dying in N.Y. She had no idea of dying—but you know Mother.

Write often to your

Affectionate friend
Walker A. Hawes [9]

University of Virginia
My dear Ma,   Sunday night Dec. 23rd 1866

How I wish I could be at Green Mount with you all tonight by a large oak fire in the comfortable chamber, loving and feeling the love of all those around me. I am not permitted to spend this Christmas at home but I am with you in spirit and will think of you very often during the time.

[9] Walker Aylett Hawes (1840–1914), a veteran of the 9th Virginia Cavalry, was seriously wounded in the battle of Brandy Station. While recovering in a hospital in Charlottesville, he studied medicine, and he later practiced in New York and San Antonio. He married Virginia Sinclair and years later, when asked about her mother-in-law, said, "I loved her, but there was nobody on earth like her, and I hope there will never be another."

It is very comforting to know that an excellent plan has been adopted by which the girls can secure such a finished education at an expense which is comparatively nothing. Mr. Timberlake [10] wrote me an account of the excellent progress the sisters were making & the satisfaction & pleasure he took in teaching them. I will teach them some German next summer & I am sure they will like that language.

I have had a very bad cold and was confined to my room for three days, my friend, Miss Mary Minor [11] sent me a nice dish of blanc mange made by her own hand and you can imagine how Tunstall [12] and I enjoyed it. Miss Margaret Minor [13] invited me to spend the holidays at Gale Hill but I declined and have decided to spend two or three days at Castle Hill with young Rives,[14] who was here last session and is a particular friend of mine.

I hope money matters will be a little easier toward the spring. I saw Mr. Maupin about the sum we owe the University & he told me not to trouble myself about that. I have great reason to be thankful I am able to be here on any terms when so many poor fellows are denied that privilege and that my credit is still good.

I'm afraid I'll be greatly dispirited if I don't graduate on Greek this year. Such a Herculean task is rarely accomplished in one year and if I don't get through, I will have the gratification of knowing I'm learning what I hope to make a specialty, Greek and Latin.

Nothing more tonight but love to you all from

A. Fred Fleet

[10] Henry C. Timberlake, a graduate of the University of Virginia who taught at Aberdeen Academy, came to Green Mount when his classes were over and tutored the girls in mathematics, Latin, and French. Their mother taught them English.

[11] Mary Lancelot Minor (1840–1905) was the daughter of Professor John B. Minor; she never married.

[12] Richard Baylor Tunstall (1848–1919) fought in the battle of New Market and was graduated from V.M.I. and the University of Virginia. He practiced law in New York and later in Norfolk.

[13] Margaret Randolph Minor, daughter of William W. Minor of Gale Hill, married John Randolph Bryan in 1867.

[14] Charles Edward Rives was the son of George Rives of Mississippi, younger brother of William Cabell Rives.

My dear Mother,   Dec. 30, 1866
  I hope you have had a pleasant Christmas, but I fear you
were inconvenienced about servants. I suppose I should have
heard of it if Aunt Millie and Mary intend to leave. But who
is your cook? And what are your plans for another year? I
hear from Harry Dew there is the greatest difficulty in the neighborhood in making arrangements of the kind. I hope these
times can't last always. My friend Taylor [15] just returned from
Culpeper Court House where he spent the holiday. He tells
me the people there although as severely injured as those of
any other section of the country have recuperated very rapidly
and they are all making money, living comfortably and are
cheerful and happy. What a contrast that must be with the
people down in our section. It is true the land is better in
Culpeper and cattle can be raised at a comparatively small expense, but I think there is something lacking in our people,
some want of energy or fear to risk anything in an investment
and I am afraid it will take them a long time to get righted
again. Perhaps they are like the fellow who was graduated from
the University, a friend from South Carolina was telling me
about. He took the "grand tour" of Europe, returning at the
outbreak of the war. He fought for four years as a cavalry officer
and came home to devastation and desolation but got hold
of a mule which he hitched to a plow as best he could. "Proceed!" he shouted. Nothing happened. "Advance!!!" Again
nothing happened. Sinking to his knees, he said, "O Lord, why
wasn't I killed at the Second Battle of Manassas."
                          Love to you all and a happy new year,
                                                    A. Fred Fleet

                                              Fri. nt Jan. 25, 1867
My dear Fred,
  Mr. Timberlake seems more and more pleased with the girls'
progress. Only think of their reading Caesar already and getting
along very well. I don't know which of the three is most pleased,
the mother, the teacher, or the scholars. I have ordered a cook-

---

[15] Charles E. Taylor, D.D. (1842–1916), a graduate of the University of Virginia in
1870, was president of Wake Forest College from 1884 to 1905.

ing stove from Tappahannock for which I will pay 45 bus. of corn at $1.00 a bus. and I will send down for it just as soon as the roads will allow. With the stove and our help, Mary can do the cooking without my having to hire an assistant for her. Mr. Fauntleroy [16] now has a number of negroes, ten men, Joshua is the only one of his old ones, the others left him in the fall, they will finish his corn and get wood.

The people in King William are doing worse than in King and Queen. I fear the secret is the men for the most part are dispirited and are drinking very hard. I hear Ayletts [17] is worse than ever. Mr. Porter came yesterday for the taxes, instead of being $110, I was agreeably surprised to find they were only $81.50. I had enough to pay all of it, such a relief to me! He tells me he never saw money so scarce and Sam Gresham and Dr. Fauntleroy are the most low spirited men he ever saw.

Ethelbert Rowe is doing very well at the ferry, the river has not been crossable for some time on account of the ice. Mr. Longest says if I continue to let the heavy wagons and carts cross, I'll have to build another boat.

Lucy D. Stacy came to see me today—I always enjoy her. She launched into the indignities our poor state is suffering and ended by saying, "I hear it said Mr. Lincoln was a good man," tossing her head to one side, she added, "but so plain." I didn't inquire whether she meant in appearance or background, but I believe had he lived, the South would never have been treated so.

I got a letter from Dr. Goodall this week asking me to board his wife, himself, and nurse that he might practice medicine and attend to the farm, which of course, I politely declined to do. I don't see why he and his wife couldn't occupy a house [small overseer's house] at Old Hall but didn't suggest it as I suppose they are high flyers with clipt wings.

Your aff. Mother

---

[16] Thomas W. Lowry Fauntleroy of Holly Hill.

[17] Spotswood Pollard used to say his home, Mount Zoar, overlooked Sodom and Gomorrah (Aylett).

University of Virginia
My dear Mother,   Jan. 29, 1867
I never saw such a long continuous spell of cold weather
and snow in my life—certainly not since the terrible snow of
1856–7. I have often thought of the goodness of God during
the war in not sending very cold weather upon us. I really
don't think human flesh could have borne the bitter cold and
driving snows of this winter, as poorly provided with clothing
and fuel and as much exposed as most of our soldiers were.
I hope these snows will protect the wheat and a good crop
will be made and thus we can disembarrass ourselves in a measure from the debts which are oppressing us.

Several of the young lawyers here are talking about going
to California and Kentucky as they will not be allowed to carry
on their practice in the Southern States.[18]

Affectionately,
A. Fred Fleet

Green Mount
My dear Fred,   Feb. 24th 1867
David and another driver carried 47 bus. of wheat to Tappahannock last Monday and returned with a no. 9 Old Dominion
cooking stove. We got Sam Wilson to put it up and ever since
Mrs. Dunn,[19] Mary, and I—not to speak of the children—have
done little else but to cook and eat. Mrs. Dunn has fattened
perceptibly, Mary was fat enough before. Never had anything
I was so pleased with since we got the piano. We don't have
to have much but everything is "exquisite."

This morning when we waked up the ground was covered
with snow and Will got the hands and showed them how to
roll it up and put it in the ice house. They got along so well,
he went in search of more men. They filled the ice house within
five logs of the top giving promise of ice cream and cool milk

[18] Because the young lawyers were Confederate veterans, their civil rights had not
been restored. They were not allowed to vote or to hold office—a bleak outlook for
a lawyer.

[19] Mrs. Margaret Dunn had been at Green Mount for twenty years superintending
the weaving and general household duties.

next summer. Although I have enjoyed the delightfully warm weather we have had, I must confess it was a most lonesome feeling—an empty ice house. The thermometer is at four degrees tonight and we hope to fill the house.

Your affectionate
Mother

My dear Mother,

A delightful rainy Sunday! My mind reverts to home and the loved ones there. I must acknowledge that a large part of the poor merit I possess is due to you, for you know I was always a mother's child. I appreciate to the fullest the influence of my father upon my heart and mind and character for however he may at times have wandered from the path of right [20] he always taught his children to do what was honorable and noble and virtuous and few fathers had more of the love and respect of their children. Please have the palings around the yard nailed up and the turf levelled so that it will grow out at the first approach of spring. You know how particular I am about the matter. Are you not plowing this beautiful weather?

Aff. A. F. Fleet

My dear Brother [Fred],   April 19th 1867

We have been very hard pressed for milk & butter ever since that terribly snowy weather, but I have two fine calves now, named Harry and Caroline. They are mighty pretty and are great pets with me especially. Mr. Councill gave three days holiday & Mr. T. gave Sister and Si Florence some too but I won't have any, don't you think that is right hard? [Her mother was teaching her.] You recollect I told you Sister and Bro Will have a pig in a pen together, Si Florence and I are going to have one too.

Write soon to your little sister Betsy

[At the bottom of the page] Bess is as sweet as ever. Mr. Timber-

---

[20] At times he imbibed too freely, especially after he had performed an operation which was unsuccessful.

lake makes as great a pet of her as you do. You would be
amused to see her peeling his eggs for breakfast and treating
him like she does you.

Your loving Mother

Green Mount

Dear Fred,   June 7th 1867
    I hear Richmond has been beset by a fresh influx of Yankee
officers and carpetbaggers trying to register the negroes [21] and
influencing them to vote against us, drinking with them and
even promising them our homes. I will not dwell on this as it
is too dreadful even to contemplate. God grant our homes may
be spared to us. So thankful those with us are entirely loyal
and do not attend these meetings. When you hear of these
men associating with the negroes, you may be sure the *negroes*
are in bad company. Christ himself singled out hypocrites upon
which to heap particular scorn and I can think of no more
worthy candidate than the loathesome Hunnicutt.[22]
    When do you expect to come home, last time you came about
the 15th. Don't dread to come and take some of the burden
from me. You can help me so much and what is the good of
an education but to take you along this life wherever the path
may lead. I expect you to be more courageous than to shrink
from the battle of life after going through the war as honorably
as you did. Don't kill yourself studying for health is the first
consideration.

Your aff.
Mother

After graduating in all his subjects, Fred applied for a teaching
position in Judge John Coleman's school in Fredericksburg and asked
General Wise for a recommendation.

---

[21] The Civil Rights Act of April 1866 bestowed citizenship on the blacks.

[22] James W. Hunnicutt, a southerner who had lived in Fredericksburg since the 1830s,
became a radical Republican at the end of the war. Editor of the Richmond *New Nation*,
he was "an unprincipled rabble-rouser" who organized the blacks to demand not only
unrestricted suffrage but violent revenge against whites in Richmond (Virginius Dabney,
Richmond [New York, 1976]).

My dear Fleet,

I am of the opinion the depression of the times may turn out to your advantage. Nothing is so well learnt as by teaching it. The power of acquisition may be great and quick, but no knowledge is so well fixed in the mind, either for retaining it or for precision of definition, as by the exertion to acquire it for the use of communicating it to others. McGuffie is so well taught because he taught. I have received two letters from Mr. Coleman and will reply to them immediately. My only fear is that you have started your enterprise in a community too poor to support liberally a high type school and a lower one I would not engage in.

I would gladly run over through the sands to see you but Judge Meredith's Court commenced yesterday for a sitting of 30 days, and business, I am glad to say employs quite all of my time.

Say to your Mother I am glad she will have you so long with her and in September, perhaps I may be able to prove to her how I appreciated my visit to her when the chills overtook me at her house. I don't think I found them there but they caught up with me and did not make me think the less but the more of her kindness. Give her and your brothers and sisters my warmest regards. I am sending you a copy of the unconscionable testimonial I have sent to Coleman in your behalf, and tell your Mother I was made to pile up the falsehoods for her sake.

Believe me,

Yours truly,
Henry A. Wise

Dear Fred,   Richmond August 16, 1867

Your welcome letter came with your Mother's gracious invitation to visit you. Alas, I am left in sole charge of the house while my family have gone to the mountains and it is impossible for me to get away until my brother returns. I expect him before long and hope by then to conclude some business matters which must be settled; by which I have been worried and bored.

I don't know what I shall do next year. Times are very hard

and there seems but little prospect of making any desirable
arrangements here. Nothing can surpass the dullness and stu-
pidity of this town now; it has always been something of a
disappointment—not to say fraud; anyone expecting of it the
excitement and attractions which a place of its size and importance might be supposed to afford will be congratulated thereupon, on the principles of the German critic who pronounced
those nations happy whose annals are dull. At this season it
is flat in the extreme, and this is aggravated by the hard times,
whose miseries are constantly sung in your ears by the tribe
of grumblers and croakers whose name is legion. I steer clear
of them as much as possible and stay home most of the time.
My organ is in fine condition so I cultivate it with considerable
assiduity.

I have been thinking of a plan and since I have been home
my conviction as to its ultimate practicability has been confirmed. I am satisfied as soon as we recover from our present
depressed condition and prosperity is somewhat restored, there
will be an opening more favorable than ever before for schools
of high grade, and their establishment in proper and competent
hands will command success and reputation. All intelligent people recognize the fact that the great and only efficient remedy
against the evils that threaten us is to be found in a system
of education that insures the preservation of the principles that
have gained for us whatever is valuable in the past & which
alone can guarantee a future worth living & working for. To
put it plainly, we must prevent these Yankees from consummat-
ing morally & intellectually the victory their brute force has
gained in the field. I, for one, have not such contempt for our
people as to believe they will finally succumb to such *canaille.*
Proper encouragement & support will be given the effort when
it can be made. My idea is the establishment of an academy
here on a large & liberal basis, looking to its future enlargement
to a college of high grade, preparatory to the University, that
is as the University ought to be & probably will be in a few
years. Such a school as were some of the academies before
the war but without the nuisance of a boarding establishment.
This is, as yet, only an idea. I do not think of attempting anything till after I shall have gone to Europe & that may be two

years hence. I mention this matter to you for your consideration, because I know of no one whom I would rather be associated in such an undertaking. Think it over & let me hear your views.

As soon as there is a chance of my getting away, I will let you hear & if it is not too late, it will give me great pleasure to spend a week or two with you. Thanking you and your mother, whose kindness I beg leave to acknowledge, for your invitation.

I am, very truly yours,

Charles Poindexter [23]

The Grove
Dear Fred,   Sept. 17th '67

I am glad you have a fine school [24] & hope you will remain in it for some time as I think you are doing better than any other young man of my acquaintance. I shall think myself fortunate if I can make $800 by the practice of medicine next year. I have decided to settle at home as it is a duty to try to make Mama as happy as possible during the rest of her life. I got a letter from Old McClung who is rejoicing at having arranged his love affairs satisfactorily. I suppose you will not think of anything of the sort until you have established yourself.

Write soon to your true friend

W. Hawes

On September 19, 1867, Mrs. Wise wrote Mrs. Fleet: "Can't you come up this fall and bring your daughters and make us a visit. We can show you our once beautiful city, trying to rise from the ashes of the Civil War! but I feel Richmond is no longer Richmond to me."

[23] Charles Poindexter conducted a school 1873–77 and wrote several booklets about Richmond. Perhaps his major contribution was to save important documents which had been sold to a junk dealer by getting an injunction from the court to have them returned to the state.

[24] Fred was teaching at Judge John Coleman's Kenmore Academy in Fredericksburg.

                                              Aberdeen Academy
My dear Bessie,   Sep. 20th 1867
   I send you a song believing that you care more for me than
anyone else, for you sometimes express a small modicum of
affection for me, which cheers me for I wish to be loved and
the human heart, not withstanding its great depravity, fails not
to give vent to those out-gushings of love which have their
origin deep in the soul's pure fountains. We are so constituted,
and the principle of love being instilled into our hearts by the
hand of God, no wonder that we are continually seeking for
some object in which to center our affections. Oh, what a holy
theme is love! As falls the dew from heaven to nourish the
young and tender plant, so falls the endearing words of affection
on the spirit's ear, sinking deep into the heart, and cheering
it by the sweet anthems it is ever swelling. It elevates and purifies
our every thought, and softly, gently woos us from the contem-
plation of stern reality to that of the beautiful ideal in whose
fairy fields we may roam with ever new delight. It is a stream
from whose limpid waters we may quaff deep draughts, which
are so pure and sweet as to subdue the wildest nature and
cause the proudest heart to melt. What heart has not felt the
delightful throb, and what spirit has not been lulled to repose
by the soothing words of affection? That heart must be cold
indeed that has never felt its gentle influence and bowed before
its holy shrine. What a dark and dreary waste our life would
be, were it not for the halo shed around us by the beaming
star of love! We thank thee, Great God, that thou hast given
us hearts to cheer us on our way whose love "fails not with
the ebbing breath," but which are so entwined with ours that
naught can break the pleasing spell. Yours, Bessie, is one of
the hearts whose love will not fail me, though others may forget
and desert me. I will close with a piece of advice viz: when
you grow into womanhood never practice deceit towards those
who love you nor trifle with their feelings, for thus you will
destroy your greatest power and lose the esteem of those by
whom you may wish to be loved.
   Accept the song and learn it soon for the sake of your hard-
favored but warm-hearted friend,
                                              H. C. T[imberlake].

David entered Aberdeen Academy and Timberlake continued to tutor the girls. Fred wrote from Kenmore Academy to his sister Betsy a description of the girls whom he taught: "There's Miss Mary Coleman—to begin at home—just 16, 'sweet sixteen' a soft sweet girl with a gentle disposition and a warm and tender heart—much older for her years than most girls of her age, a child and yet a woman, a rosebud and yet almost a flower, a mind far above the ordinary and cultivated to an extraordinary extent for one of her years not exceedingly domestic in her turn of mind, yet practical enough for all intents and purposes. Not very pretty, but quite enough to make her attractive, and withal a charming girl." He continued in the same vein to describe Sue Scott, Mary Slaughter, Mary Gwathmey, Sue Bradley, Emma Towles, Charlotte Wolf, and Hattie Hall in equally glowing terms.

Dear Fred,   The Grove Nov. 22nd 1867

Your letter was received whilst I was in South Carolina & ought to have been answered, but there are so many things to do on a farm now that when night comes, I feel like doing little else but sleeping. There is nothing doing in medicine & prospects seem gloomy for the future. A letter from McClung said he was getting enough practice but no pay for it. I am bothered about what to do with the farm next year. Renting it is equivalent to doing nothing with it & hiring negroes will cost about what you make besides worrying the life almost out of you trying to get them to work.

I have no inclination to visit and have so far paid only duty calls in the neighborhood. Tonight I am invited to meet a couple of Misses Ruffin [25] at Dr. Wormley's.

My trip South turned out better than I expected & matters look much more favorable in that situation than formerly.

Alice has gone to Staunton with Hawes, she has had chills [26] nearly all fall, this is the most abominable locality in the state & if possible, I want to send Mama and Alice to the mountains next summer, I hope to be able to stand it by dosing with quinine.

I planned a course of reading for this winter but doubt that

[25] These were the daughters of Edmund Ruffin (1794–1865), a noted agronomist of Marlbourne, Hanover County, who fired the first gun at Fort Sumter. Preferring death to living under Yankee rule, in June 1865 he committed suicide.

[26] Malaria transmitted by mosquitoes breeding in undrained farm ditches.

I will get a tenth of it done. Don't trouble yourself about the money you owe, I don't expect to need it before next year. I know from experience it is hard to make proper calculations for the future in regard to expenses. I went over my allowance many times in N.Y. and can't make out how the money went.

Your true friend,
Walker

University of Va.

My dear Fred,   Dec. 5th '67

Your letter was doubly welcome, I appreciate the feelings of any young man, who after living for twenty-odd years, begins to see the folly of his way and determines to involve himself in the engrossing affairs of love. I hope you all success & if successful, believe it will do you good. It acts as the highest incentive to all that is good and honorable; to think that your success will insure the happiness of her, to whom you are to be partner of life, is enough to make the laziest man you know— even Dick Tunstall work a *little*.

Not to change the subject too abruptly, what do you think of my teaching next year? I am looking for the most lucrative & at the same time agreeable place I can obtain. I have already had a kind of offer of $1000 & board & if nothing else turns up, I think I shall accept. I hate the idea of being a teacher all my life & intend to commence the study of law, and hope in a year or two I will be prepared mentally and financially to come here another year & finish the course. The offer is from Gen. Kirby Smith to teach in Shelbyville College, which during the war was broken up & will have to be re-established which is a risk.

Ned Massie spends half his time calling Brock a humbug & the other half petting a cat he keeps in his room. Joe Bryan keeps a keg of ale with him.[27] Miss Mary Minor is campaigning (or in winter quarters) in Norfolk. I enjoyed looking at the opera from the gallery, alone of course—burnt child.

Your sincere friend,
Rich'd B. Tunstall

---

[27] Joseph Bryan had served with Col. John S. Mosby. He became publisher of the *Richmond Times* and that city's leading citizen.

One Saturday night Fred wrote his mother a desperate letter.

My dear Mother,   Jan. 11, 1868

   I am in a good deal of trouble—Miss Mary Coleman is the cause of the whole matter. I found out a month ago I was desperately, yes *madly* in love with her & I fancied she cared something for me, & as I didn't see any chance of anybody's coming in my way, I made myself quite easy about the matter & said nothing to her. Although just sixteen, she is superior in mind & heart to any girl in Fredericksburg or anywhere else whom I have met. Just before Christmas I found Watkins was falling in love with her too. Christmas night I made an engagement with her to go to a Christmas tree at the Presbyterian Church, just to get an opportunity of telling her my feelings toward her & to find out how she felt disposed to me. There was such a crowd of girls here, I could never get a chance to say anything to her. Later that evening I poured out my soul to her. She was dreadfully startled at first, as she hadn't looked for anything of the kind & it had come upon her like a flash of lightning in a cloudless sky. She told me she didn't love me & could hold out no hope she ever would. I couldn't sleep at all that night & for three days, I scarcely left my room. If I hadn't been sustained by religion & the thought of you all at home, I don't know what I would have done. If I could only go away where I couldn't see her again, I might be able to forget but if I remain here, I find it to be impossible.

   I try to go into society & forget her, but the other girls all appear dull. I agree with Moore, "The heart that has truly loved never forgets." I'll try to act like a man, stand the storm for six months more & then, separated from her, I'll be free. It is the first time I ever loved & perhaps it will be the last I can love as devotedly.

Love to you all,
Fred

   In reply to Fred's desire to leave Kenmore Academy because of his unrequited love for Judge Coleman's daughter, his mother wrote: "It seems a pity for you to leave your good position for the caprice of a child. You are too well educated to throw yourself away, and if you have talents for teaching, stick to it, you can be very useful. I want to assure you of our love and sympathy and even this sorrow, which looms so large, will pass away."

Dear Fleet,   Richmond, Va. Feby 3rd 1868

It is singular that I can offer the same excuse for not writing to you that you had for not writing to me—the presence of a felon on the finger. After lancing it and using the powerful linseed meal poultice, I have overcome the demon.

There is no news in Richmond except the continued harping about hard times—and that subject is too painfully present to everyone to be a novelty. Some of the principal houses are curtailing their expenses in every way they can—discharging clerks, etc. This, of course, is in a great measure due to the unsettled state of the agricultural affairs of the State and South—and somewhat owing to the political uncertainties of the times.

Johnny goes about among the girls and to the dancing school regularly—but I don't think he neglects the law by doing so. He attends to his business and so far has done very well.

Here closes this dull letter, let me hear from you,

                                        Yr. sincere friend,
                                        Rich'd A. Wise

My dear Fred,   June 16th 1868

I have just received your letter and hasten to say I am truly thankful you have decided to return to Judge Coleman's school for reasons which we can discuss when we are together. If you come to Tappahannock, I can send Flora for you to ride. She has improved since you saw her and I think will do for you to ride until Will can break the colt—a handsome creature which we have named Fleetfoot. If you were to hear as much as I have lately about the poverty of the people in the country, you would be very thankful to have no more privations when you come home than the want of a good horse. Mr. Wilson sends his love and says he has Fly in very good order for you to ride.

Certainly we thought of your birthday but we were all in a great hurry for the last two weeks. Miss Susan Crow was here making up the girls' summer dresses and we were helping all we could. I assure you, you are the same dear child to me you were *25 years ago*—at home, at school, college or the army— ever my oldest, best beloved and ever remembered darling.

Don't grieve over the failures at home to accomplish all the work laid out last fall. Do you ever think *contentment* is a duty? You will understand it better when you are older. Do you re- member what happened the 24th of June, seven years ago? You were mustered into the service, would you take a glance at the next seven years if you could. I prefer to put it in the hands of the Lord—and you too.

Your affectionate Mother

However, Fred was determined to leave and in the summer of 1868 he was selected to teach Greek and to assist Dr. Thomas Rambault, the newly elected president of William Jewell College in Liberty, Mis- souri, in reestablishing the college, which had suffered during the war. During the president's frequent absences to raise money, Fred was acting president. On his arrival in Missouri he found a letter from his mother, who wrote: "No matter how much distance lies between us, you can never be lost to us. Love obliterates the miles."

My dear Fred,   Oct. 13th 1868

I am heartily thankful you are so happily situated. I did not doubt that you would be benefited by the move but did not anticipate you would have a bit of pleasure except that arising from the performance of duty. All of your letters have given me such comfort during my sickness. I am much better now but very weak from a fortnight in bed. I really have no news to write you, everything moves along in the same old way. We hear of nothing but hard times, want of money and chills. I am glad you are out of it and will not object at the proper time to the whole family's moving out. The only trouble would be getting the value of our farms here. But after awhile the Yankees will come up the river with money and then—well, I wait and watch. I am thankful for your energy and a place wherein you can use it instead of sitting at home as so many are, waiting for something to to turn up.

I am tired and must stop, asking God to bless my son,

Yr. aff. Mother

A lively correspondence was kept up between Fred and his family. On November 9, 1868, his mother wrote: "You have no idea how well we get along without Mrs. Dunn.[28] Millie and Mary will remain with us and God helping us we can do our own work. Don't you think we will be ready for the West after awhile. Lou is all wound up to write to you—a loving farewell—my son."

My dear Brother [Fred],

Our "mail days" are emphatically days of rejoicing and your dear, long, affectionate letters add no small drop to our cup of happiness. Besides, we get regularly ten different papers. Ma takes the *Dispatch, Herald, Child's Delight, Little Gleaner & Burke's Weekly,* you see she has not forgotten to take some papers for the children. Since the last three cost just $2.50, it's the cheapest pleasure she could well give us. We owe a great deal to our Mother for supplying our minds with suitable food when we were young. Somebody is kind enough to send us the *Christian Examiner,* which is extremely poor but does very well for wrapping paper. Mr. Timberlake sends us *Godey's Ladies' Book* & *Woods Household Advocate.* We use them all as a bee would a flower; she steals the sweets from it but doesn't injure the flower.

We get along admirably without Mrs. Dunn and mean to continue to do so. We are too willing to help one another and bear each other's burdens for the work to fall heavily on any one. You could hardly find three busier, healthier, happier girls anywhere.

Your loving sister, Lou.

[28] Mrs. Dunn had offered her services to the Fauntleroys at Holly Hill.

My dear boy [Fred],   Nov. 12, 1868

The magazines you sent were a great and unexpected pleasure. How it expands the mind to see and hear from other parts of the country. I spent most of last night reading them and will have them bound when I go to Richmond. Our file of the *Eclectic* is complete.

You are right in thinking I would go to Mo. or to the ends of the earth with you & I think the sisters are coming over. Bess declared after reading your letter, she thought she would be "willing," [29] what effect the "90 fine young men" you mentioned, I leave to your imagination. The boys we write about haven't serious intentions towards anyone, they are just enjoying themselves generally. You know the boys from U Va have learned the peculiar art of love making better than anything else. The sisters very often thank their stars they have brothers or they might believe some of the sweet things they hear. I am glad "nobody's hurt," but gladder still you write as though you have come to your senses. I got a long letter from Mr. Taylor today. He mentions receiving a very "loving" letter from you. "Not that it expressed much love for *me,* but it revealed so much of his boundless love for a young lady." Don't be afraid to tell me all about it. You know I am not narrow minded nor narrow hearted either and love you too well not to prefer your welfare to any selfish considerations.

Last week Walter [30] took a load of corn and vinegar to Richmond which netted $26 and I shall send more next week. I am planning to pay some small debts and then get our winter clothes. Harry takes Willie's place in waiting on me and is proud of being of so much importance.[31]

Farewell dear child,
Yr. aff. Mother

[29] "When a man says he's willin'," said Mr. Barkis, "it's as much as to say, that man's a-waitin' for a answer." Charles Dickens, *David Copperfield,* chap. 8.

[30] Walter Pollard and his wife, Mary Eliza, built a house on a piece of land cut off from Green Mount after the war, and he remained with the family for fifty-one years, cultivating the garden and doing errands.

[31] Willie was attending Aberdeen Academy, as was David. Harry was Mary Gaines's son.

My dear Fred,   Wed. morn, May 5th 1869

I never had such a pleasant time in Rd. I carried some wine and butter to Gen. Wise and anticipated with great pleasure his coming to see me. When David went to deliver it, he found the dear old Gen. had been ill for three weeks. Mrs. Wise told David she heard we were in town and Richard and her daughter would call that evening. They came and were very polite. I was much pleased with Miss Wise. She told us John was to be married to Miss Douglas next Nov. Said she tried her best to catch you as her father and brothers were so complimentary of you but heard you were in love with a young lady in Fredericksburg and sent her love. The Doctor said he wished he had known we were in town he would have taken so much pleasure in showing the girls the city. He offered to take us to the opera but I declined, I knew he had been very much fatigued sitting up with his father.

Here, let me tell you what a gentleman David is away from home—here he is still the great big child but when he is away, he is the nice gentleman. I would like for you to take him with you in the fall of '70. I think it would be the best thing you could do for him but what about the trip to Europe?

We heard Cook & Treat have nothing to pay the other $400 with but there is still timber on the land, and all we have to do is wait 'til January and sell to someone else if they don't pay the balance. Everyone says money is scarcer than it has been since the war. The weight of responsibility is very heavy and hard to bear and nothing but my great love for my children and my trust in God sustains me. I shall hope on—what would we do without hope *and* money.

Lou wants to add a line. Florence and Bess send love. I will try to induce them to write next time.

                                        Your aff. Mother

Don't be putting notion's in Fanny's head, she hasn't had any experience yet and will be ready to attach more importance to trifles than you would wish. It doesn't make much difference what you say to an old girl, but these young things are ready to believe every word you say and a little more.

                                        Yr. loving sister Lou

My dear Fred, July 6th 1869

I haven't written because I have been prostrated by the heat, but it is cooler this morning. David was pleased with your letter and it did him good. He fancied he was very much in love with the Garnett girls [32] and planned to sell his young cow to take a trip to see them. But he has unbounded reliance on your opinion and is more disposed to take your advice than I ever saw him.

At this point, Mrs. Sterling [33] and "my daughter Lizzie" walked in. David was at the election keeping the polls and they stayed to tea hoping he would come in time to walk home with them. But David had a good deal to do, counting the ballots, sealing up the boxes, etc. and didn't get home until after sunset, so they stayed all night.

About the election—We had a Yankee Officer from Richmond in charge who was a strong Walker man.[34] The white people liked him very much, the negroes not at all. I never saw anything like the harmony and concerted action among a party (and you know I have seen a good many) as the whites displayed at Clark's. The blacks and whites were so equally divided that a majority of one or two was all we hoped for but 14 negroes voted for Walker and made a majority of 28. People dreaded disorder very much, but the Yankee was so strict in prohibiting liquor and firearms and had such good police, there never was such a quiet election at Clark's. The *Dispatch* will tell you about the State; we must thank God and take courage. People say if Walker is elected, lands in Va. will rise in 24 hours.

Everything looks more abundant around us than at anytime since the war. No rice, but we get along better than we expected without it.

Edward Garlick has disappointed his parents very much—didn't graduate on a single ticket. What a pity anybody so poor

[32] There were five Garnett girls, daughters of Dr. John Muscoe Garnett of Lanefield.

[33] Mrs. Sterling was Elizabeth P. T. Fauntleroy Winston Sterling, daughter of Dr. Samuel Griffin and Ann Govan Fauntleroy, who lived at the Mount.

[34] In 1867 Virginia became Military District Number One under Gen. John M. Schofield, with headquarters at Richmond. Gilbert C. Walker, a New Yorker who came to occupied Norfolk during the war, was elected the first Conservative governor of Virginia in 1869.

should be so lazy. Mrs. Dr. Davis is in King William. I shall send the girls to invite her to dine with us Sunday from Church. I must stop now for breakfast.

Yr. aff. Mother

[Written across the top] The Aberdeen School will break up Friday and the next day the boys will give a Tournament and party at Canterbury. David is practicing every moment in order to capture all the rings and crown the queen of his affections but is hard pressed to decide who that will be.

Yr. loving sister Florence

Dear Mother,   Missouri July 18th '69.

I was rejoiced to read the account of the election in Va. I hope the old state has clearly ridded herself of the filth & dirt which have covered her for these four years & that she stands "redeemed, regenerated, & disenthralled." [35]

I want to go to Europe & nothing less will satisfy me. Marrying must not engage a moment's thought for the present. Though I find myself involuntarily comparing all the girls I meet with Miss Belle Seddon and I haven't found the approximation to her yet.

What are the plans for the fall? Willie will go to school with David, I presume. The sisters will doubtless pursue their studies together as they did last year. They can learn more than if they were at boarding school if they will.

Yrs. aff. Fred

William Jewell College, Liberty, Mo.

My dear David,   Oct. 3, 1869

I want to touch on one point and that is visiting so much. You can't attend to that and school too and the lessons will go by the board (and not the blackboard either). Let the girls have a little rest and wait until next summer before you visit them any more. Life is too serious and earnest for us to fritter

---

[35] Governor Walker was believed to have redeemed the Commonwealth from the radicals.

away our precious school hours in visiting silly school girls (or sensible ones either). You haven't the remotest idea of marrying any of them, and the best thing you can do is to banish them from your mind.

The small number of students at your school this year will afford you the best opportunity of improving yourself, so go to work with greater energy than you have ever used before and do your whole duty to yourself and your teachers.

Please try to devote some of your time to general reading. If you do not you will often have to experience mortification from lack of information which every educated man ought to possess.

I feel anxious that you should be a thoroughly educated and useful man, and this can only be attained by hard, constant and close application. So go to work with more energy than ever before and see what you can do for yourself by next fall.

Everything works smoothly & quietly here. Ninety-three students are present, a fine set of young men and I hope they may continue to study as well as they have commenced. They seem to be perfectly satisfied with the way in which everything goes on.

I am invited to tea at Dr. Rambault's this evening. Of course I'll have to go, altho' I could be more profitably (& perhaps more pleasantly) employed at home. I wish you were here to take my place. I know you would like it.

How do you like the idea of coming out here with me next fall? Do you think you will be far enough advanced to enter college? Use all your efforts this year in your studies, so that I will not be ashamed of you.

Love to all,
Affectionately yrs, A. F. Fleet

My dear Fred,   Green Mount Nov. 16, 1869
My long and much dreaded trip to Richmond, dreaded on account of the cold, inclement weather, has been taken at last. David and I went in the buggy on Friday and returned next day. We started at 4 o'clock and reached Richmond at 12, put up at the Powhatan Hotel and had a good time generally. Dr.

Steele, Lizzie Garlick and Jeannette Ryland called before tea and told me of the safe return of Charles Ryland and his bride. After tea, Mr. Garlick, Mrs. John Temple and her sister Miss Sue Burnley called. I asked about Edward Garlick and was told he is at Mrs. Richard Gwathmey's doing nothing in the world. I told Mr. Garlick of my plan for Lou, and asked if he would take her as a boarder provided you approved it and what would be the expense. He thinks $150 would cover all the bills and thought it would be a fine thing for her in several respects besides the music, and will write fully after consulting his wife.

Now let me tell you about the weddings in prospect. Miss Emma Dudley will marry Spotswood Bird this week. Cousin Alice Hawes is thought about to consent to bless I. Sale with her hand after 14 years of courtship.[36] Mary Lewis Sale is said to be in Richmond having her wedding clothes made to marry a young man named Burke from Lloyd's, said to be very rich, but worse than nothing. Then there is a double wedding reported to be at Dr. S. Henley's. Mary Straughn to a very young man, named Carter from Fauquier where she taught last session and Becky to Bob Dew. Miss Virginia Ryland has a very nice beau, Mr. Winston from Richmond and she is said to be consoled for Tom Smith. I am glad poor girls don't die from love these times or feel they have to marry for a home for they can always study and prepare themselves to teach.

Milly was in here this evening and heard part of your letter read and sends you word, "the way belles do is to sift and sift, and get the husks at last and if you don't mind that will be your case."

Mr. J. H. C. Jones [37] has the management of Dr. Fauntleroy's affairs [38] and I sincerely hope they will be wound up soon before the interest accumulates any more.

Your affectionate Mother

[36] Alice Hawes, Walker's sister, married Robert Camm Campbell, rather than Irving Sale.

[37] Judge James Hawkins Claggett Jones (1823–1885), who came from Maryland, married Dr. Fleet's niece, Sally Smith, and lived at Roseville.

[38] Dr. Fleet had signed a note for Dr. Samuel Griffin Fauntleroy of the Mount, who took the bankruptcy law after the war, so that Mrs. Fleet was held responsible for paying the note.

My dear Mother,   Liberty, Mo. Nov. 23rd, 1869
I received a letter from Mr. Boulware [39] a few days ago, requesting me as Executor to see that his bond be paid and declar-
ing that he *must* have money. I enclosed it in a note to Mr.
Jones with the request that he send it to you, and you confer
as to the best means of raising money enough to rid the estate
of debt. I hope sincerely that you will try to sell some of the
land at least. Is there any sale of land in our section? Are you
afraid to have the money invested out here, so far from home?
We have just been compelled to exercise discipline upon
some of the students, and you know this always makes me feel
as badly as if I were the culprit.
                                   Very truly yours, A. F. Fleet

My dear Fred,   Dec. 4th 1869
I went to see Mr. Jones, he thinks you ought to write Mr.
Boulware and I think it will be well for me to write too. It
seems Mr. B. has been very pushed for money, had $1,000 to
pay for Dr. Hill and is irritated by the rumor of Dr. Fauntleroy's
being bankrupt and Mr. Sterling's making a deed conveying
all his wife's land to an uncle of his in Richmond to keep from
paying Mr. B. for a negro he bought from him during the war,
and I suppose he doesn't know who is safe or honest. I can't
think he will distress us so much as to sue us, if we are disposed
to do right. I'll do all I can to pay him a hundred dollars at a
time till all is paid, if he'll take it. If we ever have a constable
in this neighborhood I hope to collect some of our accounts,
and in one way and another I'll make it out. Mr. Jones said
he was much more uneasy about Mr. Fauntleroy's affairs—he
undertook the settlement entirely on our account. If he takes
bankruptcy, we will be liable for his debts. When I think of it
my feelings get the better of my judgment and words fail me
so I will change the subject.
In reply to your request to sell land, Mr. J. thinks selling
orphan children's land is a ticklish thing and may involve us
all in trouble.

[39] William Boulware (1811–1870), of Traveller's Rest, was minister plenipotentiary
to the Court of Naples during the Polk administration.

Mr. Councill is in grave trouble about the way people are not paying him and talks seriously of breaking up his school. You have no idea of the trouble in Va. & I can't begin to tell you. I heard yesterday Mr. E. Gresham had a sale and sold everything but the land and that will go soon. They say we are as well off in this part of the County as anywhere else but within three miles of us are ten stores. People who are too lazy to work set up a store without the first qualifications for business and you can imagine the result. For my part, I don't care how soon we sell and move away to a healthier state of things, but in the meantime let us be thankful it is as well with us as it is. Had I known about Mr. B.'s pressing us, I should not have said anything about Lou's going to Richmond this winter, but as it is, I think I best send her. I send Lou exactly as I did you to U Va. under difficulties, but believe it is for the best. I believe she will improve her talents to the best advantage, we can't tell what's before any of us.

David's hobby is shooting partridges, all his leisure time is employed that way.

All send love, Yr. aff. Mother

Mr. William Boulware, Esq.   Dec. 5th 1869
Mr dear Sir:
I received a letter from Fred urging me to see Mr. Jones and confer with him about selling part of our land to pay our debt to you. Mr. Jones thinks however desirable it may be, it is quite impracticable to do so at once. I write therefore to beg you for the sake of our old friendship to wait awhile longer with us. While your debt is perfectly good, it would distress us very much to be sued and I assure you we have met with the same difficulty everyone else has in collecting money—and to support and partially educate six children is no easy matter for a woman to do, even on a large farm. My children inherited their father's honesty and we have no intention of becoming bankrupt or deeding away our land to avoid paying our debts. If you will receive a hundred dollars at a time I may safely promise to pay you during the next eight or ten months, as

we have paid all the debts of the Estate except yours and one other.

Let me hear at your convenience,

Yours sincerely,
M. L. Fleet

My dear Fred,   Wed. morn. 5 o'clock, Dec. 15 '69

In answer to my letter Mr. Boulware wrote he did not wish to trouble me, but wanted money so badly, he thought perhaps you and Mr. Jones could arrange it, that he would sell the bond to someone who would wait with us. I then sent Willie down to ask Mr. Jones if he could not get it for you to buy, and he said he had written to Mr. B. on the subject & hoped to be able to manage it, so I leave it entirely in his hands and don't think we could be in safer human ones.

Christopher is to be married next Wednesday, a small wedding, none of our family is invited. The next evening there will be a "company"—not a party at Melville. Martha insists that all of us shall come so the girls and I will go down with Mary and some things in the morning to help prepare for it & the boys will come at night in the carriage to bring us home. Don't think I am deranged, Martha treats me like I was one of Uncle's children and I should be so lonesome at home by myself.

I think I could love that little Fanny for the encouragement she gave you, telling you your lecture was "excellent," but do great men care for the approbation of a child? or is greatness self sustaining? tell me. And did you tell her that her approval paid you for your trouble and set her little heart throbbing—take care, little girls have hearts even at 14. Be careful of what you say if you are not in earnest.

Yr. aff. Mother

Virginia Military Institute

Mr dear Miss Lou,   December 29th 1869

I had only one invitation, and couldn't decide which of you I would send it to, so I had to draw lots and it fell to you. I shall certainly expect you to attend and of course Miss Flossie

and Miss Bess will come to keep you company, while Dave
and Will act as escorts, and Mrs. Fleet must come to keep up
a flow of spirits (not ardent). I shall claim the pleasure of your
company and at the same time pledge escorts, the handsomest
and most attractive, to Miss Flossie and Miss Bess. Though
distance has spread her misty veil between, still memory often
bears me to your *happy* home where so many delightful recollections cluster though unseen. I often form one of your family
circle, and listen to the sweet music wafted upon the evening
breeze.

If not inconsistent with your ideas of propriety, I would most
highly appreciate a letter *twice* in awhile, if not oftener.

Unchangingly I remain, Your true friend,

Cadet M[iller]. A[ndrew]. Wilson

During the winter of 1869–70, Lou boarded in Richmond with Mr.
and Mrs. Joseph Garlick and studied music under Mrs. MacDowell
and Professor Thilow of Germany. Her mother wrote, "Have you
told Mr. T. how much German blood we have in our veins and how
proud we are of it? I hope you can get the things for Prissie and
Maria Louisa [Smith] but I doubt they will suit them as I don't think
they can suit themselves."

My dear Sister [Lou],   Green Mount Jan. 4th 1870

Sis Bess and I went to Aberdeen today to see them and kiss
the baby. Mr. Timberlake stayed in the chamber the whole
time much to our annoyance. He is just as lovesick as ever
but you needn't make yourself uneasy about my running away
with him; I am heartily tired of his foolishness.

All the flowers look beautiful, don't miss you a bit. It has
been cold enough to put coals in the greenhouse only once.
The ice pond hasn't broken at all and the ice house was finished
yesterday. All is ready now for a freeze but Ma says we must
thank God for every good day.

Yesterday we started out to study, we read and said our
Scholar's Companion to Ma. Read our French together and I cor-
rected Sis B's Latin and French exercises. Just then Martha
Ann came running in to tell us Uncle Robert was coming. When
we got to the door, he had reached the barn, unhitched his

horse and soon came in. He came to bring little Dudley to
Aberdeen and said he was glad of the excuse. The old gentleman hasn't fully recovered from his fall but his head has gotten
entirely well. He brought us half a bushel of excellent apples.

I had a very nice time at Melville. Maynard carried me in
to the meat and Ryland to the sweet supper. Then we went
to Smithfield one evening and to Mr. Berkeley's one morning,
have had very little company, but you know our happiness
doesn't depend upon visiting and having company.

We are very much obliged for the music, have nearly learned
mine and will help Sis B. with hers.

You must have your photograph taken and sent to us. You
know we want one very much.

Your affectionate sister, Florence

Dear Florence,

I return the flowers, the only gift I ever received from you.
Truly they are typical of your love wh. like them has faded,
tho' I fondly hoped it would be mine forever.

[Henry Timberlake]

My dearest Fred,   Jan. 14, 1870

I am glad to tell you that we got 45 loads of beautiful ice
last Tuesday, two inches thick. The next two days the weather
was so warm that we sat without fire all day. We had a good
many hands and got all there was by dinner time and if the
good Lord sends us more we will be thankful. You have no
idea how the last two winters have spoiled us. Do you think
we could stand the winters in Missouri? We are all very full
of moving, talk of it and make arrangements every day. I told
Grandma I had written you if I could sell I was willing to move
next fall. The poor old lady's eyes filled up and said she hoped
she might die first.

The visit to her is the only one I have made in weeks. I
find that staying at home and attending to my own business
keeps my hands full enough, for I find when I have anything
to do, I must do it myself.

As evidence of our warm winter, I found a violet blooming

in the garden which I enclose with our love and some more flowers Bess sends you from the greenhouse. She has the care of Lou's flowers and everyone tells her they don't know Lou is away. Can Lou have a greenhouse when we come to Liberty? Would you really like selling entirely out here or would you prefer to keep the home for all to meet in vacation.

Will you deliver another lecture this winter and will you bring them all home for me to read? David went to Richmond in the buggy & Bess wanted to go so I indulged her. They had a very pleasant time & delighted my little girl in Richmond. She is trying diligently to improve but Mr. Thilow has taken all conceit out of her. She says he plays a piece at sight better than she can after days & days of practice. They are as kind as possible to her but I'm afraid she's getting a little homesick. Have you sent her check yet? I have tried to help her all I can but it is as much as I can do to pay the insurance & taxes, for as to collecting money owed us, that is more than I can do—things get worse & worse. John Clarkson has been in Arkansas this last fall. He came home a month ago & carried back twenty young white men with him, among them Willie Walker, who was engaged to Betty Toombs' sister but she discarded him and so he goes to Arkansas. I don't think Mary is as anxious to see you as usual if you carry me away and leave her behind. All send love—white and black—

Your aff. Mother

My dear Brother [Fred],   Richmond Jan 17th 1870
    Thank you for the money, I will try to get along with this until the first of March. What have you done about your trip to Europe? Laid it aside until you get us settled? Then when you come back will you live with us? Have you thought of the struggle it would cost us to leave the old homestead? every spot of which is dear to our hearts? Would it cost you no pang to think it has passed into the hands of strangers? I know sooner or later the separation must come; and if we can keep together "the gems of our love's shining circle," I suppose they can be reset happily in another home—a fairer home perhaps, but never dearer. I trust in all this the Good Lord will guide us—

"And when that happy time shall come of endless peace and rest, We shall look back upon our path, and say: It was best."

Aff. yours, Lou

P.S. Mary says she is ready to move "out yonder" When we are.

My dear child [Fred],   Jan. 18, 1870

I dined at Smithfield & James Wm seemed to think my idea of getting a decree to sell or of getting a reasonable price for our land is entirely out of the question. He says half of Eastern Virginia is for sale if purchasers could be found. Mr. Jones sent me word that Uncle Robert thought it very unwise. My belief still is that a new country is the place for active, energetic young people, and I am willing to take the risk for my children's sake and to be with my son. I hope and believe old Virginia will, in the course of time, be a great state again but I fear it will not be in the course of my time.

We have decided that David is to return with you in the fall, tho' it is hard to be separated from my dear children. Last week I wrote Lou I would send Walter to see her when he carried the tobacco over if she would not cry when he told her good bye. She replied she was so full when she takes leave of anybody from home, she just cries a little to keep from bursting and asked if I wouldn't rather she cry away her clouds and clear up, than have her always cloudy. My reply to her was—"Don't cry enough to spoil your looks—a little won't hurt."

Yr. aff. Mother

Mr dear son [Fred],   Jan. 31, 1870

Just time enough to say we are now thankfully *Virginians* again instead of being the despised Military District No. 1, like common cattle.[40] Our men of education and principles are still deprived of the vote and we are ruled by the lowest types,

[40] Virginia was readmitted to the Union on Jan. 26, 1870, the federal garrison was withdrawn, and Virginia representatives were allowed to return to Congress.

but I have faith to know that even this shall pass away. The boys are waiting so good bye, dear child.

Your aff.
Mother

My dear Fred,   Feb. 23rd 1870

I told Florence she must write you an account of Charlie Fleet's wedding but she is a poor scribe, so I will write you all I have time or you have the patience to read. He is quite delighted at being married. He stayed at The Grove until nine o'clock, then found on getting to Queenfield, he had left his trunk and had to send for it. Don't you think it will be a wonder if he gets to his home without losing his bride? They had a small company but kept up the gayety for two days and two nights and all seemed to enjoy themselves. Three of the grooms-men were absent so David, Muscoe Garnett, and Dick Williams, took their places. The others were Norval Ryland, Mr. Goddin, Mr. Thomas, Mr. Carey from Richmond, Shaddoch from Lynchburg, and Winston from Hanover. The bridesmaids were two of Emma's sisters, Florence, Bet and Jeannette Ryland, Miss Lizzie Alsop, Sophie Wormley and Ruby Garnett. Walker Hawes and his wife were there. Jennie was very full of *"the baby"*—says unfortunately it is like her. But Mr. Timberlake, who likes her exceedingly, says the baby is like Florence, whom he thinks is the perfection of beauty. I have heard of love without hope but never saw it before. It would be very ridiculous if there were not something pure—almost sacred about it. Don't be uneasy your sisters don't think being married the greatest earthly blessing and I am glad of it. The care of this world will come soon enough.

Not a word from Mr. New about buying the land. I hope it will serve the purpose of teaching me patience.

Your aff. Mother

Mr dear Fred,   March 16, 1870

Our prospects are brighter than they have been since the war. I think I can see my way out of the woods at last and you don't know how thankful I am. Your uncle Robert praised me and the way I had disposed of some of the debts. I told him freely about our affairs because he is one of our securities and has a right to know how we are getting on.

About your coming home next summer, do what you think best. If I gave you up to go in the Army, I can bear any separation for your good and I love you as well as anyone can, or does, or will. I am so glad you are getting your salary—I never doubted it. Don't mention it or people would want to borrow it and I want you to make some good investments out West. I would much rather you should *make* your fortune than marry one.

Good night, dear son, your affectionate

Mother

Fred translated a letter to him from Professor Thilow and sent a copy home.

Richmond, Va.
Respected Sir: Apr. 10th 1870
I received your check for payment in full.

Your talented sister has made great progress in the study of music. Such talents as hers are very rare, and rarer still the taste for good classical music which she has shown. Such scholars are a rarity here, and afford great pleasure and reflect much credit on the teacher.

With the greatest respect,
C. W. Thilow

Va. Mil. Institute
Dear Miss Lou: April 26th 1870
I am thinking of spending next summer in Virginia and will be most happy to visit you all again. It would take something much worse than the chills to scare me from visiting King and Queen. I shall indulge the hope that I may come to see you all once more.

Say to David that he must come here and study Engineering

next year. We want him especially to lead the singing at our evening and morning prayer meetings.

Some of the pieces you mentioned I have been reading. The "Cotter's Saturday Night" is very superior—so nearly resembling one or two such scenes which I have met with in real life. I have taken a dislike to Byron's writings. It seems to me that the dark shadows which hung over him cast a gloom over all of his works. Perhaps my feelings may change when I have read more of him.

One of our friends, formerly Miss Ella Bowie, now Mrs. Pendleton reached here last week on her wedding tour. She paid me a call on Saturday after I had called on her first. She seemed much pleased with the V. M. I. and all its curiosities. Can't you all come up in July? it isn't much farther than Richmond.

I am beginning to feel a little homesick when I hear the boys talk of going home, and see preparations commenced for the closing exercises. We expect to have Dr. Curry [41] to deliver the closing address before our Young Men's Christian Association.

Remember me with love to all the home folks. May I hear from you many times before July. Ask Miss Flossie and Bessie if they won't put in a few lines.

Unchangingly I remain, your own friend,

Cadet Miller Wilson

My dear Lou,   Richmond June 1st '70
I thought of you and wished you could have joined us on Memorial Day in our trip to Hollywood with flowers to strew the graves of our fallen heroes.[42] Our party spent most of the day in the cemetery, but were fortunate enough to have reached home before the heavy rains fell which drenched so many per-

---

[41] Jabez Lamar Monroe Curry (1825–1903), member of the U.S. Congress, 1857–61, the Confederate Congress, 1861–65, and lieutenant colonel of the cavalry, C.S.A., was an aide on the staffs of generals Joseph D. Johnson and Josiah Wheeler. He was professor of English philosophy and constitutional and international law, 1868–81, at Richmond College.

[42] Confederate soldiers were interred in a section of Hollywood Cemetery in Richmond.

sons. The decorations were more beautiful than I've ever seen before, and even the top of the monument was crowned with a wreath of flowers.

Mary W. D.

In the summer of 1870 Fred returned from Missouri by way of Fredericksburg and became engaged to Belle Seddon of Snowden. While visiting at the University of Virginia, he wrote home.

My dear Mother,   Aug. 8th '70
I had not intended to write this morning, but the terrible accident to the train which passed here Saturday, bound for the White Sulphur, induces me to do so. From some cause, one of the cars became detached from the rest of the train and fell down a high embankment, killing eleven and wounding eighteen of the passengers. Among those killed was our old friend and neighbor, Mr. Wm Boulware of Traveller's Rest! The telegram said he was killed instantly. May God have mercy on his soul. I know of no man less prepared for death.

Aff'y, Fred

In the fall Fred took David with him to Liberty, Missouri, for a year at William Jewell College. He had completed the course at Aberdeen Academy, and Fred thought strict discipline in study was needed to prepare him to enter Virginia Military Institute. Mrs. Fleet continued the arrangement with Henry Timberlake to come to Green Mount and tutor her daughters. Tom Haynes, whose step-grandmother was Dr. Fleet's sister Sarah and whose mother, Mollie Hawes Haynes, had died, came to live at Green Mount and attended Aberdeen Academy with William.

My dear child [David],
I am so thankful to hear you are better, won't you try to take care of yourself hereafter? You must take your regular sleep or you will suffer for it. Nature requires us all to subscribe to certain laws, and if we do not, she makes us pay the penalty

and you will lose more time from your studies than if you did not try to steal the time from sleep.

Take care of my precious child,

Your aff. Mother

Dear Sister [Lou],   Liberty, Mo. Sept. 28, 1870

Have just time to thank you for your long letter. Please try and take care of Carlo [dog] & don't let him be bitten, you know he is one of my best friends. Love to all at home especially to Mary Eliza and Walter.

Yr. devoted brother, David

                                            Wed. morn.
My darling children [Fred and David],   Oct. 19th '70

The dearest name on earth to me, you must allow me to call you *child* as long as I live. You will never have that name applied to you by anyone else. I am glad my letters cheer you, indeed everything goes on well around us.

The girls are studying hard and progressing under Mr. Timberlake's instruction. Poor fellow! a colt kicked him the other day, nearly breaking his leg. Betsy thinks he gets kicked on all sides and is very curious to know which hurts the most.

Dr. Taliaferro [43] spent Friday night and finding no one here but the boys, came back again Saturday night. He offered to help in any way he could—offered to break Medea to his sulky. Farming is his hobby now. He is an enthusiastic about that as he was about practising medicine a few years ago. I hope he may not be as much disappointed.

We will talk about dear Belle's visit next summer when you come. My private opinion is, there will be no such thing as having a quiet time. Your friends will want to see you in your happiness and to meet your fianceé. After I take all the trouble

---

[43] William Taliaferro had been scouting with Benny Fleet when they encountered Dahlgren's advance guard and were fired on. His daughter, Mrs. W. Brooke Carter, said he never mentioned Benny's name afterward that his eyes didn't fill with tears.

I can to have things as nice as possible, I want you all to enjoy yourselves and I declare in favor of a *gay* time.

The boys are ready so goodbye, dear *children*. God bless you both.

Yr. aff. Mother

Dear David,   Nov. 9th 1870

I must tell you about the elections—Ben Taylor beat John Gresham for clerk which throws poor Uncle Robert out of office,[44] as he will have Lewis Tyler for his deputy, Col. E. Montague, Attorney for the Commonwealth, and Mr. Porter, County Treasurer.

Ask Brother if the college will help him in his trip to Europe? How will he make out for three or four years? The expense of having Belle along will be twice as great though I know the pleasure will be in proportion, but the money—the hard times with us and throughout this area are perfectly appalling. Walter hauled sumac to the amount of $21.00.[45] I gave him $11, and used $10 to purchase material for our winter dresses. Alfred Gwathmey has been ill, he was foolishly extravagant and the mill brought him so much in debt and is not making expenses, I hear. The people about here are getting poorer and poorer and I hope you will never think of coming back here to live—or starve.

Peachey[46] has another daughter, greatly to the relief of all the girls in the neighborhood, for we expected to go to two weddings this week and she was at church the Sunday before. Now she is cut short, for a time at least. Tell Brother to contrast the difference between her and Belle, thank God and take courage. Our reduced circumstances came about through no fault of ours, but it would be our fault if we allowed ourselves to be *blighted* by *poverty*.

God bless my dear boys,

Yr. aff. Mother

[44] Robert Pollard had been clerk of King and Queen County Court since 1833.

[45] The juice of the sumac root was used for dying wool and cotton and for tanning leather.

[46] Peachy Fauntleroy of Holly Hill, with whom Fred had been in love, married her cousin, Maj. Virginius H. Fauntleroy.

My dear Mother: Liberty, Mo. Nov. 22, 1870

Your letters all came today, thank you. I am exceedingly sorry to hear of the scarcity of money. When are the good times coming? Do you hear nothing of Dr. Fauntleroy's case? I can't help feeling uneasy about that bond and I wish the matter were settled. But I suppose Mr. Jones will do the best for us. Money matters are very tight out here, and for the next six months I shall be under a strain.

Last night all the professors and their wives had tea with Prof. Fox. Eaton and I were out in the cold, but we consoled ourselves it won't be so always. He marries in a year or two. I could but think Belle would outshine them all with perfect ease, Mrs. Rambault included!!! She is without exception the queerest old creature I ever saw.

I shall try to marry David to a rich girl—always taking care that the party shall be worthy of him. If he will only marry Alice Waddell, I know you'll be satisfied.

David will write a little to finish this. He has gone out with a friend of his to Liberty Landing & will soon be back. I am trying to keep him up to his studies, but he finds it hard to do. I have reason to feel encouraged at his progress so far & hope he may continue.

Love to all,
Yrs., Fred

My dear Mother,

Brother told me today I *had* to write as I hadn't written for some time. He has just gotten a letter from Mrs. Seddon & one from Belle together with her photograph. It is one of the prettiest little things I ever saw and he is just as happy as a figurative "June bug."

Will there be much gayety in our neighborhood this Christmas? I reckon not for the times are so hard.

They say they are not going to give us any Christmas holiday, don't think it is barbarous?

As ever your loving son, David

My dear Mother, Dec. 16th 1870

My letter from Belle has not come yet, but she sent me a beautiful photograph just before she left Richmond for Gloucester, and this has done a great deal to keep my spirits up. Today is her birthday—just nineteen. You have no idea how hard it is for me to bear the separation, with no hope of seeing her until next summer, it is far more trying than I ever thought it could be.

Our students are blue at the thought of having no holiday at Christmas, especially David. Sometimes I feel that David is so much of a child. He knows nothing scarcely about the English language and the mistakes he makes sometimes in his Latin and French exercises are "puffectly rediclus"; because he hasn't apprehended the English. I hope God will direct him the proper way and that he will do something as an engineer.

Love to all, aff'y, Fred

On March 21, 1871, Fred wrote his mother from Liberty: "I register today, the first time any rebel? has been allowed the franchise in Missouri for ten years."

Florence wrote David: "Mr. Alfred Bagby spent the night here and after praying as usual for the aged handmaiden (Ma you know) and all her children, he prayed for the grandchildren. Don't you think he's rather premature?"

My dear Mother, April 18th '71

We received your and sister's letters today, and am so glad to hear you all are so well. There is no news except the session is drawing to a close very fast, can hardly realize I'll be with you so soon. Brother says we will leave here on the day of commencement which is the 7th of July, in order that he might get to Fredericksburg on the following Saturday night. I tell him to stay here until about Thursday or Friday & that would be soon enough to see Belle, and then I would not have to stay in Baltimore from Saturday night until the next Tuesday evening as the boat only runs from Norfolk on Saturdays and Wednesdays. Don't you think that would be best? I could stay to the commencement and a day or two after and have a nice time after studying so hard. But I will do what *he says.*

I went to an exhibition of one of the female schools here last Friday to hear them speak, debate, &c, &c—think it is a horrible custom. The President was very pretty little lady indeed and the whole thing would have passed off very well but she, when the thing was about half over, had one of the most terrible fits I ever saw. Suppose it was from tight lacing and fright together.

I won't write anymore as I am so busy, & am afraid I will not have anything to tell you when I come home.

Your loving son, David

My dear Mother,   Liberty, Mo. May 9, 1871

Your letter enclosing dear little Belle's has just come. Doesn't it confirm what I told you that she is the loveliest girl in the whole country. Don't you love the little creature almost like a daughter already. I have just talked to David and we came to the conclusion it will be better for him to go into business right away, just as soon as he can get a position on some railroad. The facts are, it would take him at least 4 years to graduate as a Civil Engineer. He says he is tired of books and all his studying this year as well as all the years before were a bore and burden to him. He feels all of us have done as much as we could for him now. There is a possibility of his getting a position in Arkansas & if so, don't you think he had better not come to Va., but go to work right away?

I'm not so ardent a Missourian as I was a year or two ago and some day I would like to land in Va. again. It may be best after all that we could not sell when we wished to and land, even in King and Queen, may bring something after awhile.

I don't regret for an instant the step I am taking, for I rather have Belle than a lifetime in Europe.

Love to all,
Yours, Fred

Mrs. Fleet,   June 17, 1871

Mr. Basket refused to pay his account of $16 & I thought it was a good case to try & did warrant him today at Walkerton. Mr. Walker gave judgment vs you for the cost as he proved that Dr. Fleet said he would not charge him or any other soldiers anything for services rendered during the war. I write this note to let you know if you want to get an appeal to the County Court, you can do so by letting me know at once. If you don't succeed in this case you won't get much from the rest, they will all say the same thing.

Respectfully in haste,
W. R. McGeorge, Constable

Alexander Frederick Fleet and Belle Seddon, daughter of Mary Alexander Seddon and, the late Major John Seddon were married Thursday evening, July 6, 1871, in Fredericksburg at Little Snowden, for the main house, Snowden, had been shelled and burned by a gunboat dispatched by President Lincoln, who believed it to be the home of Major Seddon's brother, James A. Seddon, secretary of war in the Confederate cabinet. Although space was limited, there were seven bridesmaids: the Seddon cousins, Ella, Rosa, and Sallie; the Morson cousins, Alice and Minnie; and Lou and Florence. Belle's brothers, Tom, Sawny, John, and Will; her cousins, Arthur Seddon and Seddon Morson; and David served as ushers. Maria Louisa Fleet remained at home to welcome the couple. After spending a month at Green Mount, Fred and Belle visited her relatives, the James A. Seddons in Goochland and the Charles S. Bruces in Charlotte County, before returning to Missouri by way of New York, Niagara Falls, and Canada.

Snowden

My dear Mother,   Monday morning Aug. 7, 1871

We had a very pleasant visit to Sabot Hill. They are all devoted to Belle, and of course treated me with great kindness and affection. I enjoyed Mrs. Seddon's music and Mr. S's conversation in the highest degree.[47] Mrs. Seddon is the finest pianist and singer I ever heard except professionals, and is so fond

[47] Mr. and Mrs. James A. Seddon, Belle's aunt and uncle.

Belle Seddon when she married   Fred
Fred Fleet

Belle Seddon Fleet

of music that she plays just as soon as one asks her, and as much as we wish. I found Mr. Seddon very intelligent and amusing, Miss Ella charming, Misses Alice and Minnie Morson very pretty and pleasant, and the younger girls, Rosa and Sallie, as sweet girls as I ever saw.

We left Sabot Hill Thursday night at 2 o'clock and reached Richmond at 7! Distance 21 miles by the Canal. Here we stayed at Dr. Wellford's, spent the day & night & started for Staunton Hill [48] Thursday morning at 4 o'clock. We got there to dinner or rather by 12 o'clock, after some four hours' ride in the cars & the same time in a carriage.

The porch is of marble, the pillars beautifully carved and fluted, with a black and white tessellated floor. The grounds are beautifully laid off around the house with walks and shrubs. Within the sixty acres inclosed within a stone wall as the yard, is as wild and beautiful scenery as can be found in the depth of the woods. But the library attracted me most. It is more carefully selected and more fully up to the times than any private library I ever saw, I felt I could gladly have spent four or five years there.

Mrs. Bruce is the most beautiful woman of her age I ever met, and certainly one of the most intelligent and affectionate. She has six sons and two daughters, and trains them as such a mother would. The oldest is spending a few years in Berlin, studying & travelling. His mother wants him to be a teacher & says she will be delighted to have him a professor of Modern Languages in some college.

Mrs. Seddon has just come in to tell us we must get ready to go to Chatham to dinner.

Goodbye and best love to you all,

A. F. Fleet

---

[48] Charles S. Bruce married Sarah Seddon, sister of Maj. John Seddon and James A. Seddon, and lived at Staunton Hill, one of the largest tobacco plantations in Virginia. The crenelated mansion was designed in 1848 by John E. Johnson, a West Point graduate. Captain Bruce raïsed and equipped the Staunton Hill Artillery and served throughout the war in Virginia, North Carolina, and Georgia. His home was used as a refuge for Confederate officers recuperating from wounds.

David entered Virginia Military Institute as a third classman but still had to undergo his first year as a "rat." "Rat bucking" was a form of physical hazing designed by the upperclassmen to put a "rat" in his place.

My dear Mother: V. M. I. Sept. 2nd 1871

I am here all safe and sound as you see. The train got to Goshen Bridge about sundown on the evening I left home. I had quite a lonesome time, as I knew no one on the train at all. In about half an hour we took a stage for Lexington, and after travelling 22 miles over the worst and rockyest roads I ever saw, we reached this place about 4 o'clock Thursday morning. Of course I couldn't sleep a wink as travelling on a stage is the roughest in the world.

I took breakfast at the hotel after which I went to the post office to get the letter which I expected from Brother. I was very much disappointed when I was told there was nothing for me. I determined however to go up to Gen. Smith [49] and report. After I thought he had finished his breakfast, I went & told him the whole story. He said it was all right and introduced me to one of his clerks who fixed me up. The Gen. remarked that my brother had married since he heard from him the first of the summer.

When I came down to the Barracks, I was hailed on all sides by "Hello Rat! Hello Rat!" I said nothing but laughed a little and one said "Rat has the grins." I then went to the tailor, and he cut me out a suit of clothes. About one o'clock we had to "fall in" for dinner. I went but didn't eat much because I was right much frightened. We had beef soup, stew hash, corn and loaf bread, and wound up with coconut pie and milk.

Immediately after dinner the corporal of the guard came to me and said it was my turn to stand guard, so I have just come off post. They are just as strict as they can be. That evening one of the cadets told me he had a letter for me. I was expecting them to play a trick on me but sure enough there was the

[49] Gen. Francis H. Smith, a graduate of the U.S. Military Academy, was superintendent of the Virginia Military Institute from 1840 to 1889.

letter from Brother with one for Gen. Smith. I took it to him the next morning and he said it was all right.

Monday: Yesterday I went to the Presbyterian Church and heard a most excellent sermon by Mr. Pratt. His sermon was chiefly to the young men of the Institute and Washington College. His text was, "Can the Ethiopian change his skin, or the leopard his spots? then may ye also do good, that are accustomed to do evil." Jer. 13:24. I hope it did some good. I know it did me good.

Today the exercises were suspended in order that we move in certain rooms that belong to the company which I am in. I am in a room with three young fellows who seem to be very nice young men. One is [Shirley] Bragg from Mobile, Ala., a nephew of Gen. Braxton Bragg, and Wright and [Charles Stuart] Spann, both from S.C. I couldn't get in with [Benjamin Junius] Saunders as he had made other arrangements. I will close in order to put this in the mail in time. You must direct your letters to Cadet D. W. Fleet, as I will get them sooner.

Affectionately, your son
David

My dear David,   Sept. 5th 1871
Thank you for your sweet letter we were so glad to get it. Read Fred's letter over and take all his advice. Everything just as usual at home. I will tell you everything I think will interest you but you have a great deal more to tell us because everything is so new with you. Be sure to tell us how they treat the "Rats" and how you like everything. Only one letter came for you which we have forwarded. Try not to waste any more time writing to ladies if you can help it.

Your aff. Mother

My dear Mother,   Sept. 15th
We have been subjected to considerable hazing and the old men have been threatening us all week with what would take place on Saturday night. After supper we were marched over to Barracks and crowded together at one end of the hall. The

old men lined up on either side of the long hall armed with paddles (newly cut), sticks, and even clubs. One of them stepped out and shouted "Sing" to a small fellow whom I knew stammered. He stood there with his face getting redder and redder, his mouth open but not a sound coming out. Before they could make him "run the gauntlet," I stepped forward and sang "Seeing Nellie Home." When I stopped they shouted "Sing, Rat, Sing." They put down their paddles and many of them sat on them. I was mighty glad of all the songs you and my sisters taught me because I think I sang all of them, knowing I had to save my classmates' hides as well as my own. They made me sing "Lorena" twice. When I got to "Tenting Tonight," everybody joined in and then a mightly welcome tattoo was sounded.

Your loving son,
David

My dear Bro: David,   Green Mount Sept. 19th 1871

Yesterday morning Sis and I went down to see if Mrs. Toombs had gotten a teacher, she had not, so Sister asked if she would take her, telling her she would take $250, her board and any day scholars she could get. Mrs. T. has not decided yet. If Sis does go there, we will try to get Mr. Shackford [50] to come up Friday and some other evening in the week and teach all three of us Latin and Math (didn't know how to spell it so stopped there).

Tommie came back this evening and brought 1500 Chinco-pins (if this isn't the right way to spell it—you do it better) which I have been enjoying very much.

I think those Cadets must be a terrible set of men and I hope and pray you will not be injured in any way by them. Do they make the others sing now or just you?

Hoping you will take more notice of this letter than you did of my last, I remain your very affectionate sister

Bessie

---

[50] Joseph Shackford was the son of Rev. John Shackford, who came from New Hampshire to live in the county. Also a preacher, he replaced Henry Timberlake at Aberdeen Academy and preached at Shepherd's Methodist Episcopal Church on Sunday.

My dear Boy [David],   Wed. morn Sept 20th 1871

We were so thankful to get your letter and to see the humble Christian spirit it displayed. Do you remember when Christ told Peter that Satan desired to have him that he might sift him as wheat, but He prayed for him. Now always remember that "He ever liveth to make intercession for us," and we are praying for you and you must pray for yourself more than you ever did before that your strength fail not, and He will not allow you to be tempted more than you are able to bear. You are a man and have to go out in the wicked world, you cannot stay at home and lead a quiet life, but you can so live that others may see that you honor the name you profess to bear.

My dear child, if I had but one word to say to you all in this world, it would be, my children, love one another. The more I see of other families, the more I cherish love in mine. Bess has written you all the news. Milly and Mary send love so do Tommy and Will.

God bless you dear child,

                                        Your aff. Mother

My dear Miss Lulie [Lulie Belle Lyne]

I received your sweet little missive and now I have a little time to pour out from the bottom of my soul, the thought and feelings which are there hid. I would give almost anything to see you. There is no one here to whom I can go and make known my sorrows and joys and meet with the same sympathetic heart as I would meet in you.

I know very few ladies in this place, and those whom I do know, I would almost as lief not, for the Cadets have a very bad name here, and there is no distinction made among them by any of the ladies. This place is carried almost entirely by the Presbyterians, who are the most bigoted people in the world, especially those here.

Then I am surrounded by those, most of whom curse, get drunk and even play cards on Sunday. All my roomates though are steady fellows, for which I am very thankful. Please don't mention any of the above to anybody. I am looking forward now to the time when I will go to my "sweet home," there to meet a loving Mother and sisters, free from all this wickedness and unpleasantness. Then too, I am looking forward to next summer two years, when I will probably make the West my home. These are thoughts which comfort me.

You will doubtless graduate this session and what will you do after that—like most young ladies—enter in the marital state?

Please pardon me for imposing on you my picture, for knowing how much I would like to have yours, I cherish the hope the compliment will be returned on your part.

I am your sincere friend,
D. W. Fleet

My dear David,   Sept. 27th 1871

Last Wednesday Willie and I went to the Court House and dined with Uncle Robert. The old gentleman was delighted to see us and kept bringing in fruit all day. He sent Florence a beautiful bridle which came from Texas, to use when she rides horseback and gave me fifty nice salted shad to bring home.

Now I will tell you about the Fauntleroy affair, the lawyers arranged it all that day, ready for the judge's sanction. We are to pay their debt to McConkey & Parr [commission merchants of Baltimore] for $900, give Mrs. Fauntleroy $1,-000—$500 in six months and $500 in twelve. Then give Ella all of Glenwood and our interest in the Mount and $100 a year for five years—then we will be free!! I don't know how we can manage except borrow the money, we have so little time allowed us to pay it. Now, my dear boy, won't you try to work as hard as you can so that you may be able to help bear your part. The sisters are nobly bearing theirs—and you well know I don't sit and hold my hands. I do hope you and Willie will never have to regret your "lost opportunities" as so many young men have to do, but you must remember it is no disgrace and you must stand on your own merits and it is far more noble for us to pay our debts than for other people to have to pay them for us.

They say George Croxton and Miss Mollie Jeffries are to be married, she furnishing the blood and he the money. She is, I don't know how much, older than he.

Yr. aff. Mother

My dear Brother David, Oct. 3, 1871

Sister started out Monday morning for Mrs. Toombs' and commenced with five scholars; Sallie Brooke & Lelia, Sallie Browne & three of Mrs. T's children. Mrs. T. & all her family are very kind to her & you know she will come home every Tuesday & Friday, so she is delighted with her place.

We heard of a pretty little romance yesterday. Dr. George William Pollard of Hanover got a letter not long ago from a Texas soldier who was sick at his house during the war, asking his permission to pay his addresses to his daughter Fannie Peachey, who at the time he knew her was only nine years old. She is in Kentucky with her sister Ellen. He has been to see her there and they are to be married!

Now I must close as the boys are ready to start.

Your affectionate sister
Florence

My dear David, Oct. 8, 1871

I am pained at what you write about the irreligious character and conduct of the students (Cadets, I believe you call them). I was led to believe that a decided improvement had taken place in the students at Washington College & the Institute, especially at the latter. Remember, my dear David, you are building your character at this period of your life. How very important that your heart should be pure, your mind elevated and your aspirations noble. Read your Bible and pray morning and evening, asking God's direction in all things until it amounts to "unceasing prayer." Try to keep the best company and avoid the wicked and profane fellows.

College goes on well with a larger enrollment than ever before. I have 160 in Latin and 50 or 60 in Greek. I am teaching

Belle Greek and she is responding very well, such a contrast with one of the young professors, whose wife's head is empty as a gourd, please avoid that kind.

Write soon and fully to your aff. bro.

A. F. Fleet

When Belle and Fred "went to housekeeping," they took Mary Moore to Missouri with them. Lou had taught her to read and write while she was a maid at Green Mount, and Mary Gaines had taught her to cook.

Dear Miss Lou,   Liberty, Mo. Oct. 16, 1871

Mr. Fred gave me your two sweet little notes and I can't begin to tell you how glad I was to get them. I don't bleve anybody in the world can write half as sweet a letter as you can, Miss Lou. I have been waiting to answer them for so long so I could think up a lot of things to write you about but I have been so busy all the time I haven't had time to think. I am getting along furstrate, I do everything I can for Mr. Fred and Miss Belle but every time I think about home, I want to be there so bad I don't know what to do. I wish next summer would make haste and get here. I have been going to Church almost every Sunday night with Mr. Fred and Miss Belle and sometimes when Miss Belle don't go I go along to take care of Mr. Fred. I have to take care of Miss Belle too and I walk around to Mrs. Lannos [Lanneau's] sometimes in the morning with her because she is afraid something will catch her if she walks about by herself in this strange place. Next time Miss Lou won't you send me a little bunch of minonet and rose geranums I love to smell them they remind me of how I used to help you tend your flowers and what good times we had. Now Miss Lou I must stop, tell Mary and her Mother to write to me. There is not a day that passes I don't think of them. Tell her just wait till she get out in a foren country and see if I don't treat her better than she do me. Give my bes love to all my friends and to Miss, Miss Florence, Miss Bessie and

Mr. Willie but most to you dear Miss Lou for being so kind and good to Mary.

My dear Sister Florence,   V. M. I. Nov. 4th 1871
   I have just about 10 minutes before "tat-too" to commence a letter to you. I am so much obliged to you for writing to me as I know you had to work harder the next day. Now about the box (which was a very interesting part of your letter). I will be very much pleased at having a turkey and beaten biscuits, they will be very acceptable. Please send my boots in the box, you will find them in the wardrobe in the office, they allow us to wear them.
   Sunday evening: Everything goes on as usual here, no news except we stopped drill last Friday evening until next spring. The Cadets heard about three weeks ago, that Gov. Walker wanted them to come down to Richmond to the Fair, but I heard the reason Gen. Smith wouldn't let them go is because he was afraid they would all or most of them get drunk, and do the Institute a great deal of harm. Yesterday as we didn't have drill and it being Saturday, and a rainy evening, (for there was not so much chance of their being caught) a good many Cadets went up town and came back deadly drunk. Two of them have since had fits. Such a pity that they should be throwing themselves away so early in their youth. I feel so sorry for Gen. Smith, he is such a good man and his face bears the appearance of seeing so much trouble.
   My uniform is very becoming and makes me look very tall and slender. They say I am a very fine figure & stand a chance of getting an office next year.
   You can't imagine how thankful I was at hearing you were all so well and *cheerful,* for really I have been deeply troubled thinking about your troubles at home, and whether I was doing my duty in staying here and spending money. But I hope the time will come when I can help you, and am working with all my might. I hear they are going to introduce Greek and German here next year and compel the 1st & 2nd classes to study them, dropping one of the lesser important studies on artillery tactics.

So you see we will be better prepared to meet the difficulties of the world.

Tell Mother the sweet potatoes will come in very well provided they are cooked, for we have no way to cook them. And could she send me some cotton socks as most of mine have been lost.

Love to all, David

Dear Brother David,   Green Mount Nov. 7th 1871

Ma starts up with something new every now and then to put in your box. We all anticipate a great deal of pleasure fixing it up and hope that won't be lost, also hope you won't make yourself sick *feasting*, after your long fast. I don't mean you haven't had anything to eat but that you haven't had things as good as those from home. I hear Mr. Henry Robinson (youngest son of the major) will be married to a Miss Goldman of Essex.

There was a Tournament at Tappahannock a few days ago. Muscoe Garnett crowned the queen, Miss Mollie Wright. The Dillards rode but didn't get an honor. Mr. Newbill got the bouquet for being the best rider.

Cousin Mollie Hawes, in reply to a letter I wrote her last February, said she is teaching again this year, says this seems to be the general resort of old maids in Kentucky—and in Virginia too, I think.

Mr. Timberlake is Prof. in a college at Clinton, Miss. now and gets $1000 a year. Edward Garlick is in the same college and gets $800, that's good for him, isn't it?

Ma says what will it cost to have your photograph taken in your uniform? She expects to sell some staves soon. She says you must put on your sweetest smile and best looks generally as she wants it to be better looking than Brother's was when he was a soldier and she wants to send one to Sis Belle. If you get this letter, please answer it, if you don't, let me know and I'll write again.

Affectionately, Bessie

My dear Mother,   V. M. I. Dec. 2nd 1871

Thank you for your very interesting letter, it cheered me up so much. I started this when I was on quarter guard. Every day three of us have to be detailed from a company to stand guard about 6 hours out of 18, to see that everything is carried on properly, no noise in barracks, to see that each man has his coatee buttoned when he leaves his room, to salute all of the Profs: with a "present arms" etc. It fell to my lot last Sunday, the worse day in the week as it was so lonely and you can't go to church or out of the guard room. One's turn comes around once in two or three months.

This evening one of the Cadets came in and asked if I would go to the Episcopal Church and practice singing and sing in the choir. I went and sang a little, but don't know whether I will try it in the choir as I won't have time to practice except Saturday evenings. There was only one lady, Miss Maury, daughter of Commodore M. She seems to be very intelligent but is very ugly and about 25 or 26, I suppose.[51] This evening one of my roommates went up to the Lees and Miss Mary told him they were trying to get me to sing in their church Christmas as she heard I had a very sweet tenor voice.

Mr. Wilson is principal of an academy in Tenn., which pays him pretty well, but don't know what his salary is. He said he was going to write to little Sis—give my love to her.

I will stop now and if I don't get my lessons before "tatoo" I will get up before day to study.

This morning when we went down to "rev" it was snowing as hard as possible and the snow was 3 or 4 inches deep. All of us were very much surprised as yesterday was one of the most beautiful days I ever saw.

Good bye, love to all from your affectionate son, David

[51] Mary Herndon Maury (b. 1844), Eliza Hull Maury (b. 1846), and Lucy Minor Maury (b. 1851) were the daughters of Commodore and Mrs. Matthew Fontaine Maury. On Aug. 4, 1870, Eliza wrote, "Mary and I keep house for Mama—she one month and I one month—on opposite months we take turns writing for Papa." (Maria Williams, *Ocean Pathfinder: A Biography of Matthew Fontaine Maury* [New York, 1966]).

My dear David,   Dec. 5th '71

No letter from you last week or today. If you are sick, do let me hear, for anything is better than suspense. The weather is severely cold, I often wonder how you stand it. If you would like some flannel shirts, I will have Willie buy some in Richmond and put them in your box.

I enclose Ellen Browne's marriage invitation. The groom's name is Garnett—plenty good enough for her I reckon. She is just 18 and her father did not wish her to marry so young, told her she might travel all over the U.S. and even to Europe but the young miss must be married.

Mrs. Seddon wrote me a very sweet note last week, sent her love and asked how you liked the Institute. Write me what to tell her.

We have made all our arrangements for next year except for one man. All that were here this year will remain except Lawrence and I wouldn't have him. We are exceedingly fortunate for so many of our neighbors have to change every year.

What is the reason I have never received but one report from you and you have been there three months. I feel very anxious about you, dear boy, and earnestly pray you will come out of your temptations and trials like pure gold refined by fire. Into each life "some rain must fall" but what would we be without rain! The boys are waiting so good-bye,

                                    Your devoted Mother

My dear boy [David],   Dec. 12th 1871

I know you read my letters because you answer them and I am encouraged to write often. I hope you will sing in the Episcopal Church at Christmas. In the first place, be accommodating— it will give you a good name—we should do all the good we can with the talent God has given us and you have that talent. Then too, you will learn some anthems to teach the sisters. If the ladies are not young and pretty, they are agreeable, no doubt, and will appreciate your tenor voice and you couldn't *marry them all* you know.

I wish you would inquire about Prof. Brooke's wife, she was an old playmate of mine. I don't ask you to neglect a single study, but sometimes you would like to have a friendly word spoken to you, it will do you good so don't lose such an opportunity. When I write again I will tell you I have sent the box and when to look for it. God bless my dear child,

Your aff. Mother

My dear brother David,

Ma says I must tell you about a molasses stew I went to at Smithfield. I "opened the ball" with mine, and last Friday night Grandma gave Sallie Brooke one. Brother Willie, Tommie & I went. I had just gotten in when James stepped up and asked me to pull with him. It seems that Jimmie Jones, Claggett & Bathurst had been arguing about who should pull with me. James didn't say a word but as soon as he heard us knock, came to the door & engaged me on the spot. Uncle & Aunt Martha were there, and about 11 o'clock Uncle came in to have prayers, we stopped playing and seated ourselves. He read and then said, "We will sing" which very few of us heard. As prayer generally followed the reading, all who didn't hear (I among them) knelt down and bowed our heads. We didn't know any better till those who didn't kneel commenced laughing, at which we, feeling very sheepish, got up, each one thinking he or she was the only one who knelt. Altogether though, we had a splendid time and I am glad to hear there will be one at Aberdeen & Mrs. Toombs' after Christmas. Every dog must have his day, you know and now the pups are having theirs. Yesterday in arithmetic we had a problem Mr. Shackford couldn't do. He seemed very much mortified & took it home with him. I was amused and a little sorry for him too. Mammy & Mary send love, Mammy says she knows if the ladies saw such a fine looking gentleman walking about they would want to meet you. It's just before breakfast & as usual I'm very hungry.

Lovingly, Betsy

My dear brother David, Dec. 19th 1871

Last Friday morning it commenced snowing about seven o'clock and until three, I don't think I ever saw it snow harder. The boys didn't go to school so at half past eleven, we started

Willie in the buggy with Alice to get Sister, thinking he would be back by two. When four o'clock came and they hadn't come, Ma became so uneasy she sent Walter to look for them. He soon came back, saying he met them at Clark's. Nothing was the matter except Sis spent the night at Melville and was caught there by the snow. Aunt Martha sent you some apples, which Uncle dug out of the snow especially for you, you know we haven't had any at all this winter.

Our lessons were quite hard and troublesome Friday evening and it was nearly supper time before we finished so we persuaded Mr. Shackford to stay to supper and have some snow cream, though he said he ought to go back because he had Mr. Councill's mail. After supper we were all sitting around the parlour fire when Mr. Councill walked in, said he had come to look for "Joseph." Said Cousin Mary had become uneasy, thought his horse, which was a wild colt, had thrown him and left him to freeze in the snow! Mr. S. looked abashed and said they must go back at once to relieve Cousin Mary's mind, but Mr. C. said he told Mary if he found Joseph sitting by the fire like any sensible man would on such a night, not to look for him until ten o'clock.

The other day one of Mr. Edwards' little boys about seven years old, fell down the well. Someone heard him calling and ran for Mr. Longest, who lowered the bucket, the little fellow got in, and was pulled up without a single bruise.

Mr. Aleck Acree and your old flame, Miss Lucie Dew, were married last Wednesday. Bettie Payne Falconer and Charlie Bray will be married next Thursday. We hear she said she was engaged to three gentlemen and would marry the first who came! It rained and hailed nearly all of yesterday but Willie went to Ayletts and got your box. Ma has just come in and said your turkey is ready. Tomorrow Willie & Walter expect to start to Richmond with it and we hope it will reach you by Christmas Day. We'll send three pairs of cotton gloves and one pair of yarn—hope they will fit.

Affectionately,
Florence

My dear Sister Florence,   V. M. I. Dec. 23rd '71

Yesterday your sweet letter came, as this is Saturday night and as we will have holiday Monday (Christmas Day) and as I have so much to tell you I will commence to-night.

Last Thursday was one of the coldest days I ever felt, and I thought of poor little Willie having to go to Richmond to carry the box. I was thinking about him all day, hope he didn't suffer much. Thank him very much for doing it for me, he is a noble little fellow. Good many of the Cadets are getting boxes for Christmas and I heard there were about 200 at Goshen waiting to be brought over to Lexington. Don't you know there will be feasting.

I was very much amused at Mr. Councill's having to come to look for Joe Shackford and had a good laugh over it. The people down our way must be in a flourishing condition from the number of marriages you wrote me are going to take place.

I wish very much I could be with you this Christmas. The other day my friend and room mate, Mr. [John Enders] Robinson, was invited to Commodore Maury's to dinner. They told him they were going to have a Christmas tree at their church today and invited him to come and help them put the tapers on so they wouldn't fall off and burn it up. He told them he had heard me say I had fixed a tree in Liberty and was sure I would help them and was tall enough to reach the top. Next day he received a note from Miss M. asking him to come over. She said she didn't know me well enough to write to me so she told him to ask if I would come and fix the tree for them. So he and I went up to Gen. Lee's to see Miss Mary (who was boss of the thing & one of the pillows of the church) to get the tapers and say we would take great pleasure in fixing it for her. They live in the house built for the Pres. of W. & L. University, which is very large and beautifully furnished, pictures of every kind. Miss Mary came out and said she was very glad to see us and particularly glad if we would help them. She is right old and ugly, but is one of the most pleasant ladies I ever saw. We told her we would come up after dinner and fix it. When we got there Miss Mary was not there, but left word with Miss Letcher (a daughter of the Gov.) [52] to introduce herself to us and tell us what to do. She didn't exactly introduce herself, but asked a young man to introduce himself to us and then us to her. He did so and she carried me in and introduced me to Miss Pendleton, daughter of Gen. P. rector of the church,[53] so you see I was in a swarm of really nice ladies. I felt perfectly at ease and fixed the tree prettier than it ever had been fixed, so they said.

Saunders and I got a permit to be absent from barracks until tattoo to attend church and sing in the choir. I could hear everybody admiring the tree and especially how nicely the tapers were fastened on.

Sunday evening: After all the people left the Church, Miss Maury, Saunders and I staid to practice the hymns and chants for today and tomorrow. I forgot to tell you, yesterday Miss Letcher handed me the tapers as fast as I could put them on and talked like a wheat-fan. She is really one of the nicest ladies I ever met but she too is rather aged and not very pretty. When we had finished she told Miss M. and Saunders and me to come in the vestry, that her mother had sent her some ice cream and cake and we must help her eat it. There were four spoons so each of us took one and we ate out of the same bowl. My friend, Mr. Robinson, had gone up town with Miss Mary Lee and missed it. I crowed over him right much but he countered by saying he was with Gen. Lee's daughter, holding an umbrella over her.

I went to the Episcopal church this morning and sang in the choir. I have been several times and Miss Maury has insisted on my joining the choir. The only objection I have is Gen. Pendleton is the most boring & uninteresting preacher I ever heard & bores me nearly to death in about half an hour. Mr. Pratt, the Presbyterian minister is one of the finest preachers

[52] John Letcher (1813–1884), Democratic lawyer and editor of the *Valley Star* in Lexington, was a member of the House of Representatives from 1851 to 1859. He opposed secession but served as governor 1860–64.

[53] Gen. William Nelson Pendleton (1809–1883), rector of the Episcopal Church, was a graduate of the U.S. Military Academy. During the war he was chief of artillery of the Army of Northern Virginia. Whenever he gave the order to fire, he always added, "and may the Lord have mercy on their souls."

I ever heard, & I can listen to him for an hour & half with ease.

Miss Letcher made herself very agreeable & kindly invited me to come to her home. They say Gov. L's family is the kindest of any in town to the Cadets. Robinson told me Miss Mary Lee praised me very much, & said I seemed a gentleman of such refined manners. Tell Mother I am passing that compliment on to her because she deserves the credit. I promised Miss Maury to come up tomorrow and sing in the choir.

Good night and a happy Christmas
to you all, David

My dear Mother,   V. M. I. Jan'y 6th 1872

You don't know how thankful I was when I rec'd your cheerful letter and to hear of your and little Sister's good health. It is my daily prayer that you all may have strength equal to your day and task. I got a letter from Brother with a check today and went right over and gave it to Gen. Smith. The box arrived in good shape. The boots were excellent but a little too large so I took them up town and traded them off for a pair of very good shoes. The gloves are plenty large and are a great comfort these nights when I am on guard. The pickle was excellent and arrived in good condition. It is hard to tell which of the good things we ate first, we ate a little of all at the same time.

Now to answer your questions—I have never seen Miss Madison but have heard a great deal about her. Her father teaches me Human Physiology and makes it very interesting. She stays with some of her relatives in Culpeper as she and her step-mother can't get along very well. Prof. [John Mercer] Brooke lost his wife some years ago, I don't know how many. He is married to a lady from this county. He has a daughter about 14 and she has one about the same age—she was a widow. They are the prettiest and most affectionate little sisters I ever saw.

Did the girls skate any this winter? The ice up here is splendid and a great many ladies skate first rate, some better than I do. The river is about half a mile from barracks and is frozen for miles some six or ten inches. We skated about an hour and half this evening and I never had a better time. I skated around considerably with all three of the Misses Maurys.

Time goes quite rapidly and the term is nearly half over. I am more closely occupied than I was even before Christmas. My birthday comes in about a month, I can't realize I am almost a free man.

Love to all from your son.
[David]

My dear Mother,   V. M. I. Jan'y 14th 1872
Please tell sister Florence to look in the office library for Lincoln's Livy and send it as we commence it tomorrow. I will send Willie the Sallust.

I was invited to Com. Maury's last week to a party and had a very nice time. The three Miss Maurys are the smartest ladies I ever met.

Our marks were read out yesterday. I had 30th on drawing, 13th on Math, 8th on Latin and 3rd on French and everybody told me I had taken a splendid stand. They will not make out the general stands until July.

Excuse brevity, Your aff. son David

My dear boy [David],   Jan 30th 1872
Little Betsy has been very sick, sicker than I ever saw her, I am very thankful for the little knowledge I have of medicine and that I haven't had to call a doctor for years—but I was very near it this time. The little one looks quite delicate and interesting but is better and was able to say her lessons this evening. We had a very cold spell for a fortnight and everyone has gotten ice. We filled our house last Friday. Won't you enjoy it next summer, the nice milk and ice cream. I am afraid you have suffered greatly on guard and generally without *seeing* the fire. We have such good oak wood and enjoy its warmth and seeing it burn. Little Sis has such cold rides to her school but she says it will make a woman of her and a man of you.

Mona Berkeley has left her school, says "it was too lonesome"—something behind the curtain, I'm sure. Any one would think we would have a lonesome time if we were not so well employed for we have so little company. It is seldom anyone comes from one week to another—except Mr. Shackford, but we never know the meaning of the word.

Your aff. Mother

My dear bro: Dave,   Green Mount Feb. 18th 1872

As this is the first time I have written this year, I wish you a happy new year and a happy birthday too. How do you feel now that you are 21? more like a man or the same childish boy? meaning no disrespect—Cadet Fleet, but if you were anything else you wouldn't be like the bro: David we know. Last Friday was a beautiful day but that night it commenced snowing & now it is six or eight inches deep. This evening we had some excellent snow cream, I wished you could have some too, then about twilight around a bright oak fire, we sang our favorite hymns. All the while wondering what you were doing and wishing we could hear your sweet voice mingling with ours. But it will be all the sweeter next summer because we haven't heard it for so long. I expect to enjoy my vacation more than I ever did before because I am working harder than I ever did before.

We received your letter and Ma said it was very satisfactory to her, for it told her you had gotten the money and had your photograph taken. I never saw anybody so anxious to see a picture as she is to see yours. Says she knows "the man couldn't possibly flatter her *Dave.*" Now don't be vain and conceited, but make all due allowances, for it takes a Mother to be so blind, you know.

Dr. Taliaferro, his wife and sister dined here Sunday a week ago, he is the same old thing and I don't think his wife *looked* at him like she loved him much. Tommy has had the measles for the last 14 days but Ma says its the mildest kind she ever saw, hasn't been sick much.

All send love—Ma says she has written herself out this week, eight pages to Mrs. Seddon.

Write soon to your affectionate little sister, Bess

My dear brother David,   Green Mount Mar. 12th 1872

We have just finished our lessons and Ma says I must write to you as she has to write to Brother. We are so thankful you are well again. I was so much afraid from the symptoms you wrote of that it was scarlet fever, and yesterday when I was practising I thought so much about you I got very nervous. We have had so much trouble in March, you know, I reckon that was the reason we were so uneasy. Mr. Land told us Cousin Sarah Pollard was dead. Ma wrote Uncle Robert and asked him to come and live with us, I don't know what he will do.

Maj. Douglas came to see Ma Saturday and told her he didn't apprehend any trouble in getting through with the suit. Won't you be glad if we can get out of that scrape without losing much. Major Douglas [54] said we would have to pay about $1,000 but Ma says that is much less than seven or eight thousand and we ought to be thankful to come off as well as that.

We are very much obliged to Miss Maury for her kind attention to you. Did you write her a little note or will you call in person to thank her? Is she young and pretty or the reverse?

Your most affectionate Bessie

My dear Mother,   Liberty, Mo. Mar. 15, 1872

Dr. Rambault's health is so bad that he has resigned his pastorate and received an indefinite leave of absence from the College and will probably go to Europe in April. Meantime the Trustees have conferred the honor of Chairman of Faculty on me, it will increase my duties and responsibilities but not my pay. I am in hopes we can have Dr. R's house in his absence and if so, we propose to enter upon the duties of housekeeping. This means I will be unable to come to Va. next summer as I will have to travel in order to build up the school.

Love to all, Fred

---

[54] Maj. Beverley B. Douglas (1822–1878), a King William County neighbor and friend, was educated at the College of William and Mary, the University of Edinburgh, and Harvard University and read law under Judge Beverley Tucker. During the war he fought with Lee's Rangers.

My dear David, March 22nd '72

Last Wednesday we went over to see Grandma, who is looking better and more cheerful. When we returned we found Uncle Robert here. The dear old man seemed more distressed than I ever saw him. I think he came up to avoid seeing so many people, it was a three days' court. He told me Cousin Sarah was very well and cheerful on Saturday, that stormy day. The next morning they waked up about day, he proposed getting up to make the fire. She said it was not necessary to get up so early and they went to sleep again. When he woke up, he spoke to her, she didn't answer but he thought she was asleep. On going to the bed, he found she was dead. Shocking, wasn't it? He told me he could not tell me whether he could come to live with us, doesn't know what to do but hardly thinks he can give up his old home and everything he has been accustomed to for nearly 70 years. I feel so sorry for him. He stayed until Friday evening, then went back to his lonely home.

I enclose Fred's letter, I have given up all idea of seeing him this summer. Don't you think it's an honor to take Dr. R.'s place. You know "the Mother" thinks he can fill any place he is called on to occupy.

Goodbye, dear child, yr. aff. Mother

My dear Mother, Liberty, Mo. Apr. 12, 1872

We are rather inclined to start a small house this summer on a corner of our lot. Later when we can afford it we plan to build a larger house. Could Caroline cook for Belle and me? Begin now and train her in your best recipes so she will be ready to come in the fall. You suggested Mary, it is true she is the best cook I know but Mary, we would not have, as she would not only manage the domestic department, but *us* as well.

Aff. Fred

My dear Mother: V.M.I. May 18th 1872

I haven't heard a word since your letter of the 26th of April. I hope none of you is sick or have so much to do you can't write. I think though there is some irregularity in the mails, for I know how it has been in the past. It has been raining since Friday, so all together I have been right low spirited but will try to look forward to the time when I will go home, only 7 weeks off.

Last Wednesday, the 15th was the anniversary of the Battle of New Market, in which the Cadets performed so noble a part. We had suspension that day in commemoration of it. In the afternoon Dr. [Robert Lewis] Madison made one of the finest speeches I ever heard at the mess-hall, from whence a great many of us went to decorate the graves of those who had fallen in the battle, seven in number. Genl Smith has had an arsenal made and the bodies were placed in metallic coffins & then in a painted box and placed in the arsenal unburied. I went and everything was beautifully arranged and decorated.

I will stop now and add more tomorrow after church if I have anything to say.

The weather has cleared, clouds have lifted and so have my spirits.

Be sure and write by Friday—

                                          Your Affectionate David

My dear Mother,   V.M.I. June 22nd 1872

Your letter together with the check came all safely yesterday. Surely I am very much obliged to you for it, but particularly so to "little sis" [Lou]. Indeed she is a great help and I don't know what we would do without her.

I shall (D.V.) start from here on the night of the 4th and be in Richmond on the evening of the 5th. So if I don't write any more you needn't feel uneasy. Things are drawing to a close I had my examinations on Mathematics Thursday, the one I dreaded most. I am through all right but didn't do as well as I hoped. My physics & Latin are to come off next week, I hope to be a "second classman." The College exercises commence tomorrow and the commencement on Thursday. People are coming in very rapidly, particularly pretty ladies. I saw a good many on the parade ground yesterday evening while we were at drill. It is very warm, & drilling these hot evenings almost kills us. I am burnt nearly as black as a nigro.

I am so full of coming home I can hardly think about anything else. Only one week and four days more.

I went to the College chapel today and heard a very fine sermon from Bishop Atkinson. None of the churches had services this morning.

Goodbye till I see you dear Mother

Your aff't son

David

In the fall Tommy Haynes returned, and Willie Garlick joined him and went to Aberdeen Academy with Will. Lou went to Waterview in Middlesex County to live in the home of a cousin, Browne Evans, and teach his children.

My precious child [Lou],   Sept. 25th 1872

I went right to work as soon as you left though my tears fell in the watering pot and helped considerably to water your flowers. I cried them all away and we have had clear weather since.

Mr. Shackford came and taught the girls this evening, then took supper and stayed til 10 o'clock. When he got down to the yard gate, he came back and called Betsy to show her the North Star and gave her the first lesson in *Astronomy*. Florence seemed so amused to tell me Sis Bess & Mr. S. were out star gazing.

You don't know how many thoughts and prayers I sew into your dress as I make it and how I wish it were in my power to give you so much more.

Your devoted Mother

Lou replied, "I have everything I want because I don't want anything I can't have and I love my work and the children so much, it's a joy just to be alive."

My dear brother David,   Oct. 4th 1872

Last Monday week Sister [Lou] & I started out to our respective schools. We rode in the carriage together as far as Watkins' where I turned off to Mrs. Toombs with a heavy heart and had to work very hard all day to divert my mind and keep from breaking down. I have the same scholars Sister had last session. I like teaching so far very much and hope the children will improve very fast. They are very kind to me and seem disposed to give me as little trouble as possible.

Mr. Councill has a very good prospect for a school this session, about six or seven boarders and fifteen day scholars & the free school besides. Willie Garlick seems to study quite hard and is very much of a gentleman. I think he is very much in love with Si Bess already and would go through fire and water to do her bidding. He, Tommie and Willie are firm friends and get on finely together.

Last week Miss Nannie Temple and Alpheus Lyne were married; and the week before, Miss Mary Temple and Dr. Warner Lewis, Miss Lulie and Catesby Lewis—two sisters married together.

Write soon to your affectionate sister,
Florence

My dear child [David],   Oct 8th

Lou says she is reminded of our table before the war—they live so well and at first she would almost choke when she went to dinner to think of Bess and me sitting down alone to our little one. I told her not to choke any more for we have a plenty and it is all seasoned with love, and that is the best after all.

We soon got up the pitiful little crop of corn here, nothing but nubbins but at Old Hall and Glenwood the corn is much better and we think we will have enough to serve us until next year. That is a great deal more than many have and we are very thankful our taxes are less than last year by twenty-two dollars—ninety-four dollars and we have till March to pay them, so the sisters can have a chance to collect some of their money to help pay them.

Lou says she can get chestnuts for three cents a hundred and we sent fifty cents apiece to get some and I will send mine to you.

The boys are ready to take this—

All send love, Yr. aff. Mother

My dear son [David], Oct. 30 '72

I got your letter last week with the aristocratic likeness and was so pleased to see you in good health & spirits and that ambition has taken a good hold at last, but you need not think I can't read you. I like for you to visit the ladies occasionally, it is so refreshing and polishing—and we are all amused at the symptoms of an old fever cooling off and looking for signs of another, who is it now?—for as to your being indifferent to the whole sex—I don't believe a word of it.

I am up as usual very early, going to Old Hall to divide the corn today. Will write you all about what we have gotten from the tenants next time, I hope I have rented all of Stewart's and Butler's and made my arrangements for next year.

Where will you go at Christmas? I need not assure you how glad we should be to see you at home if they give you time enough, tell me in your next.

Your devoted Mother

Miss Lou, Aberdeen Acdy Nov. 7th 1872

I believe you requested me to send you a "report" of your sisters' progress in their studies. Their work in Latin and Mathematics has been, not only as good as I could have expected or desired, but even of such a nature as to afford me real pleasure in having them as students. They have learned to think consecutively, and this is the secret of all mental greatness. I deem it useless to add anything more in this line, for truth needs no more ornament than to be spoken in simplicity and candor.

The presidential election is over, and the people seem to have relapsed again into that apathetic silence which has characterized our loved nation since they felt ours was a "lost cause."

Some noble spirits, it is true, imbued with an undying love for their country's liberty, and urged on by the glorious memory of our hallowed dead, have gathered up the scattered energies and dared in the face of 'insolent might' to speak peace and comfort to an oppressed and outraged people. Others, alas, have forfeited every principle of their once glorious manhood, sold their proud birthright of Southern honor for gold, trampled the grand inheritance of American liberty in the dust, joined in the ranks of the victorious throng, and become (for the sake of gain) the merciless oppressors of their own people. What a sad reflection this upon humanity! But I ought not, perhaps to rekindle a flame that has already caused a deluge of blood. I am no politician, but I would like to see the star of my country shine with undimmed lustre in the galaxy of nations. "Our hope," as Gen. Wise said, "is in God." Moral greatness is worth more than national greatness, and this should be the aim of our people.

Yr. sincere friend, Joseph Shackford

Dear Lou,   Nov. 18, 1872

I enclose three dollars, one to get chestnuts for Willie Garlick and Tommie and two to get some for us. I hope you can come Friday and bring some oysters which would be a great treat. Don't choke any more about us—we have plenty and not a single wry word or look at our table and I hope I am thankful enough for it. Thursday and Friday were very rainy days and we had the boys in the house all the time. They helped put down the carpets and we got along so well. Willie Garlick went in the buggy for Florence and Mr. Shackford came as usual. About ten o'clock he asked for his horse. The boys went to get him but couldn't find him, he had slipped the halter and gotten out of the stable. So he had to stay all night and he bore it with his usual resignation. Bess accused F. of having the horse turned out so she could have the pleasure of the ride with him to Aberdeen. Mary Councill said she was glad she brought Joseph and she must not send him away as she did Mr. Timberlake. Mr. C. said, "There is one thing I shall stop doing." F. thought he would say he would not let his teachers teach them anymore but he said, "I will not go to look for Joseph any more because I will know where he is." Floss blushes but takes the teasing very well. Betsy and I went to see. Peachey last week, she was very polite and her stepmother was very nice. She told B. when she first met her, she took her to be about 13 and Floss 15. Bess said, "It is because we are small." "No," she said, "it is because you look so fresh and young." P's little baby is very pretty, like her and Garnett but very dirty and unsweet. Despite that I held her and fancied I was holding my grandchild and wondered if she is ugly if I would know it. The two aunties say they will think her pretty anyway, but I think I shall *know* whether she is or not.

Peachey Ryland is confined to her room with rheumatism, barely able to walk with help—sad isn't it in so young a girl. The wood cutters are at work and we have great hopes—don't know what we would do if we did not have such a good prospect before us. We have every reason to be thankful and not the least, only five more weeks before we meet.

Yr. aff. Mother

After leaving Aberdeen Academy, Henry Timberlake, having been rejected by Florence, wrote Bessie: "The song I send has given me much pleasure. I think you will find it very beautiful if not already known to you. It will suit your and Flossie's voices exactly. Am I never to hear from you again. If not on earth, dear Bessie, may we meet in Heaven."

Dear daughter [Lou],   Tuesday morn. Dec. 2 '72

I have an astonishing piece of news!! What do you think of Mrs. Dunn's requesting me to take her back, said she is tired of living in such a fuss!! She approached me at church, I drew her to one side and she said she wanted me to send for her things as she and Hannah couldn't stand it any longer. I reminded her when she left me, I asked if she had counted the cost. "Yes," she said, "and if I hadn't been a fool I would never have gone." Seeing she was very much excited, I told her calmly I would think about it. I shall quietly wait until she renews her offer and then respectfully decline on the ground there is no more here to satisfy her than before. The girls insist I must ask you and Brother what you think of it, but I would not give a moment's uneasiness to you, my darling, and too, I feel equal to the emergency. Will says perhaps the liquor is getting low and Bess urges Mary to send Joshua over to Holly Hill to hear all about it. Did you ever hear of anyone deliberately putting back an aching tooth after having it extracted—but enough on the subject.

What intensely cold weather we have had! have you been comfortable? Bess and I intended to go visiting but we were glad to sit in our warm chamber and sew. Mr. S. hasn't turned up for a fortnight, cold and fever, too sick to teach. Bessie says she is as innocent as a "new born lamb." Indeed, I don't think she has it in her heart to give him pain even if t'was in her power. She and Florence braided the slippers. They are beautiful—blue and white—so refined and clerical looking. They say you must write them something to put in them when they present them, which they wish to do on the 14th.

I hear Dr. Steel's wife is dead—very sudden of neuralgia of the heart. He gets over the death of his wives so fast, no one has time to sympathize with him before he is out again. I feel a great deal more for her parents than for him.

Yr. aff. Mother

My dear Mother: V.M.I. Dec. 8th 1872

We have been getting our mail very irregularly owing to the horse disease and I expect our letters go just as irregularly. Everything goes on as usual here, no news whatever.

I am so sorry to hear that Wm Jewell College is getting on so badly and is having so few students. I hear there are fewer everywhere this year, than any year since the war. Money is scarcer than ever before too. I am glad we know exactly how much of the horrible security debt we will have to pay, for it has been a great worry being kept in suspense about it. I do trust I will have no difficulty in securing a situation as soon as I graduate, and I shall do all in my power to help. Those dear sisters of mine are bearing their part *nobly* and *bravely*.

What a good thing to have such sisters and you to have such daughters.

Rest assured I will never marry until I can support a wife. I certainly never loved any girl well enough to marry her and don't intend to love one until I can support her.

I'm going to write to Wilson just as soon as I can find out his P.O.

It was so kind in Miss Evelina Walker to offer to lend you some money. How came she to do it?

I am very comfortable in regard to my room this year, it being one of the warmest in barracks & not compared to the one I had last year. The advantage, you see, of being an "old Cadet" and not a "Rat."

Best love to Willie and Tommy and to Mammy and Mary and to you, dear Mother,

David

My dear Mother,   V.M.I. Jan. 1, 1873

As it is New Year's Day and we have suspension of classes, I will commence a letter to you. Mrs. Bowie invited me to dinner with them on Christmas Day. I never sat down to a better one and I enjoyed it hugely and they were so kind.

I am going to turn over a new leaf and try and study harder than ever. We have been preparing for our intermediate examinations which commence tomorrow. I feel pretty safe on all except physics and chemistry, they are so difficult but I hope to get through.

Some fellows have just come in with their banjos & guitars & want me to sing with them.

Love to all—Yours,
David

Dear Brother David,   Green Mount Jan. 10th 1873

We have been getting ice today and yesterday, it is between 8 & 10 inches thick. We haven't quite filled our house yet but there is every prospect of doing so as it is still very cold.

Mr. Lipscomb came up the other day to look at the wood which he thought suitable for cord wood. I rode over it with him and he seemed to think we have between 1500 and 2000 cords of wood and offers us $2.00 a cord delivered between Dunkirk and Ayletts, which we think we will take. If we do take it we will have a good strong wagon made and get another yoke of oxen to haul it. I will have to attend to it, so you see if we can carry out our plans, we won't have to be dependent.

Willie Garlick and Tommie send love and so do the rest.

I remain yours, aff.

J. W. Fleet

My dear David,   Sat. Jan. 11th 1873

Aren't you glad to hear of the cord wood. Cousin James is to come and write the contract next week and he said he expects Lipscombe will advance some money for us. If so we won't have to borrow except from the sisters. Florence wants to send you a hundred dollars and if we can deliver the wood she will be able to do it. You may be sure we don't forget you and will help you all we can.

Your aff. Mother

My dear child [David],   Jan. 28, 1873

A telegram arrived today from Fred saying, "We are blessed with a beautiful little girl, Mary Seddon." I read it to Milly, who remarked, "Where would she get any ugly from."

We have about 40 men in the woods now cutting wood and about the 1st of May we shall begin to haul it. I will be able to send you more after a little but at present I have to pay the men and do something about hauling. I have oxen and wagons to buy and after we get under way I hope we will be more independent. I hope we will succeed because it is our last chance 'til you all are ready to help. Don't be discouraged my boy or let trouble keep you from studying as well as possible, for the harder you work now the better you will be able to get along in the world. I got your report this evening—not so good a one as I could wish for, try again, my dear boy. Read the Parable of the Talents and determine to use what God has given you in such a way that He may receive His own and more.

Your aff. Mother

My dear Willie,   V.M.I. Feby 2, 1873

Your letter of the 23rd came safely, I can see a decided improvement in it and no telling what perfection you will reach if you continue writing.

I am thankful the Mother has made the disposition of the wood, and hope you will realize a good deal from it. I have only fifteen months to go to school and then I will be able to help.

The Institute has met with a great loss in the death of Com. Maury. He died yesterday about noon and all exercises are suspended until after his interment which will be Wednesday. His last words were—"Do I drag my anchors?" I don't know whether he will be buried in Lexington or Fredericksburg, I hear probably in the latter place. I hope I will be detailed on the special escort. I am very sorry for the young ladies, for they say they are in quite dependent circumstances, at which I am surprised. I have been singing regularly in the Episcopal choir since I came back but now I expect it will be broken up as Miss Eliza Maury was the leader and I hear they will move to Fredericksburg in the spring. Indeed I am very sorry, for I would rather have had his name on my diploma than anybody here.

I heard the other day that poor Wilson, M. A. has the consumption but hope it is not so. Don't know where he is or I would write to him.

Write soon to your affectionate brother,

David

Later: I have just paid a brief call at the Maury home. Mrs. Maury said the Commodore expressed the desire to be taken through Goshen Pass when the Rhododendron was in bloom, so he will be temporarily interred here.[55] She asked me to be a member of the Honour Guard and gave me this piece of Arbor Vitae from his coffin, perhaps Mother can root it.

My dear son [David],

I am so sorry to hear the report of Mr. Wilson's having consumption. Can't you find *where* he is by using diligent inquiry as well as *how* he is. I have a particular reason which I will tell you when I see you. I do wish you would write to him. Don't say anything about hearing he is sick but inquire why we have not heard from him for so long. Write affectionately— for if he is sick he will need it and if you hear from him let us know, but don't hint this at home.

What do you think? They are going to have an organ at Bruington, a singing machine, some of the members call it. The two Jeannettes and Lucy Garlick will perform on it and they will have to get up early in the morning to beat our two organists. Florence plays just as well as Lou.

It is time for the boys to start to school, so good bye, dear boy—

Your affectionate Mother

[55] Matthew Fontaine Maury was born in Fredericksburg in 1806. He was a midshipman in the U.S. Navy and later was superintendent of the Depot of Charts and Instruments. He resigned his commission and was appointed a commander in the Confederate navy. He was sent to England to purchase and outfit cruisers for the Confederate navy and to perfect the submarine electrical torpedo which he invented. At the end of the war, unable to return home because he was charged with treason, he went to Mexico and attempted to establish a colony of southerners, but pressure from the U.S. government forced him to abandon the project. He returned to England, where he was acclaimed for his navigation charts and decorated by major foreign governments. After securing amnesty from President Johnson, he returned home in 1868 and was appointed professor of physics at V.M.I. and superintendent of the physical survey of Virginia at an annual salary of $2,000. He died in Lexington, Feb. 1, 1873, and was interred there temporarily. Circumstances prevented the cortege's passing through the mountain pass while the rhododendron was in bloom, but his wish was carried out in the fall amid a flame of colored foliage en route to Richmond, where he was buried in Hollywood Cemetery, Oct. 1, 1873.

Edgewood

My dear Mother,   February 11, 1873

How I wish I could have a long talk with you about our mutual trials. We seem especially fitted to "bear one another's burdens," and I always derive strength and comfort from our talks. But I know it would be selfish to intrude my troubles, dearest Mother, when I would if I could, carry only sunshine to your heart. My time is nearly half over, the hardest problem I ever had to solve is whether I ought to continue for the other half. I can't manage these children to my satisfaction and if I can't make them study and behave themselves as they ought, is it not my duty to vacate the place for someone who can? I have been praying for "additional strength" as you have taught me but sometimes my trials seem insupportable.

Later—Am rejoiced that my time is half out today! And I am sure it is the worst half. Last night after prayers I had a good long talk with Cousin Browne about the management of these children, & he talked so kindly, & so comfortingly that I feel as though a thousand pounds had been lifted from my shoulders. He told me Judge Jones told him if I ruled the children it would be by love alone, and he says that is the best & most beautiful way to rule, but if it couldn't be done for love of me, it must be done for fear of him. He went to the schoolroom today, examined the children, & talked to them very plainly & kindly; & I have promised to report faithfully to him any misdemeanor & try to learn the lesson so necessary for the success of every teacher—*Discipline.* He offers to aid me in every way he can, & I know he will. If I can only learn the lessons God wishes to teach me by all my trials this year, I shall be stronger & better to bear those of all my future life. Sometimes I think of my schoolroom as my studio where I may mould immortal minds for immortality. Then again it assumes the form of a gigantic crucible in which I have been placed by the Master Chemist to be *tried*, & TRIED, & TRIED. Pray for me, dear Mother that I be not utterly consumed, & that which is left of me may be entirely pure.

Your loving Lou

My dear David,   Feb. 16, 1873

Mr. Shackford has a cousin Miss Isabelle S. from Boston, who is visiting his father this winter. Mr. S. was anxious for these girls to meet her, so we invited her, the Toombs girls (where she is staying) and the Aberdeen boys last Saturday evening—twenty-four young people in all. They did enjoy it, it would have made you feel right old to see another generation coming on so fast. Did you remember you were 22 last Monday? I had a nice supper—turkey, ham, puddings, cake, ice cream, etc. etc.—two long tables, I wished you could have been here to enjoy it too. Never mind, I will send you some money soon to get something good. The next day, Bess and Florence dined at Aberdeen with Lucy Yates and Branch. They say B. is as sweet and beautiful as when you fell in love with her years ago. Monday night the young folks went to Mrs. Toombs and had a gay time. Miss Isabelle is beautiful too and has taken a great liking for Florence, in that I rather expect follows the example of her Cousin Joe. Peachey has invited my girls to Holly Hill tomorrow night to meet Lucy Yates and Branch, but I don't know that they can go as it is snowing and the weather is horrid. Bess has a new admirer, George Berkeley, he came home with the boys Tuesday and stayed until Thursday morning. When he went away he offered to kiss little Betsy. She tried to wither him with a look and he subsided. Claggett is as constant as ever. Tom believes himself desperately in love with Gay Toombs. Willie is following the example of his brothers and flirting generally.

I must write to poor Fred, I have gotten two letters from him this week telling me how ill Belle has been. She has a little girl named Mary. I am afraid nobody is glad of it for they wanted a boy.

> Mammy and Mary send love,
> Your devoted Mother

My dear Boy [David],   Tuesday nt, Feb. 24 '73

I have just heard the Cadets are to go to Washington next week and I hasten to enclose you a little money—all I can lay hold on this morning—$3.00. If you need to borrow some don't

fear about returning it soon. I hope it is true about your going—
a trip of that sort will refresh you so much.

The sisters have had colds, even little Betsy hasn't been able
to sing for a week or two. All better now. Will has improved
so much in singing bass—and in every way.

Yr. Aff. Mother

Private V.M.I. Feb. 28 '73
My dear Mother:

I am writing you this strictly on business. A few minutes
ago the Treasurer of the V.M.I. sent for me and said Genl.
Smith told him to ask me about my deposit.[56] That they were
terribly in want of money and if I could possible pay some of
what I owed he would be much obliged. Genl. Smith sent for
me about 2 months ago and asked me the same thing, moreover
that he thought it hard there seemed to be scarcely no effort
on the part of some young people to pay for their board and
clothing and that some people preferred to avail themselves
of the bankruptcy law to paying their debts. I told him in what
circumstance we were at home, and that Brother had not been
receiving his salary, that I didn't know what I could do. I wrote
to Brother & he says it is impossible for him to help me that
he would if he could. Now I have kept this from you all, knowing
how badly off you all at home are and I hated to tell you anything
that would cause you more trouble than you have already. Now
what can we do? Is there any way in the world by which you
can help me? Genl. S. has treated me very harshly, and I hope
he will not send me away. Please let me hear from you as soon
as possible.

Yours, D. W. Fleet

[56] "The regulations of the Institute require that 'all money intended for the public
or private use of the Cadet, shall be deposited with the Superintendent; and any Cadet
whose parent or guardian shall violate this regulation, or who shall pay any account
contracted by the Cadet during his connection with the Institute, in violation of its
rules, shall be subject to immediate discharge.' Experience has shown that the most
frequent sources of idleness, extravagance, and dissipation has been a violation of
the above regulation. The Institute cannot be responsible for the conduct of the Cadet,
unless parents and guardians unite with the officers in enforcing its regulations"
(printed on reverse side of Virginia Military Institute quarterly report of Cadet, 1874,
giving David's standing).

My dear Mother,   V.M.I. March 1, 1873

I wrote you quite a hurried note being in a great deal of trouble about my deposit. I hope it didn't cause you much trouble, for you know how much it grieves me to give you trouble. I am so much obliged to you for your kind and affectionate letter. I don't know what I would do without such a Mother. The $3.00 came in very acceptably as I had to buy a book I needed. The Cadets will not make the trip to Washington.

I am so sorry to hear of Sister Belle's illness. I can't realize you are a grandmother and I an uncle. They must have named the little niece for Mrs. Seddon. I know Brother had his heart set on a boy and I used to tell him I bet his first would be a girl. Hope they will love it nonetheless. I feel so sorry for Brother that the college & other things have given him so much trouble. It is a very true saying—when a man marries his troubles begin, and I think I will profit by it.

Don't you think it would be better for me to stay here until I graduate and not come home next summer? I think it is Brother's wish that I stay and study and not get entirely out of the train of thought. It is not that I don't want to come and see you all, I hope you know, but for my own good. And the time slips by so fast you will hardly miss me. Then my expenses would be so great to go and come. Write me exactly what you think of it.

I do hope the bad weather is over for we have had the hardest winter I ever saw. I hope the horses and cattle came through it all right and you had enough provender for them.

                                        Best love to all,
                                        Your affectionate son,
                                                      David

[Before sending this letter to Lou, her mother added in pencil] I shall write him to come home by all means, we want to see him. I am sure between us we can pay his expenses. It is all a notion about its being better for him to stay away from home during vacation.

My dear David,   Tues. morn. March 2 '73
    I haven't had a letter from Fred for two weeks. Belle was getting better rapidly and little Minnie, as they call her, is considered beautiful by the ladies and he thinks her very pretty for a baby.

    Bess and Florence send love but do not have time to write. F. looks better than I ever saw her. Riding horseback agrees with her and she looks so happy in having work to do, and health and strength to do it. Bess studies very hard and carries on a flirtation with Shack at the same time. The old fellow stays all night nearly every Friday night and spends the day Saturday riding horseback with her. But my private opinion is he likes F. best. Don't say anything about it tho'. Everything is very quiet about here now—no news—no money—no parties—no anything but measles, among black and white, but a mild form, I'm thankful to say. I am hoping every day to hear of some money to borrow to send you, be assured I will send it as soon as I can.

    Mammy and Mary send much love—only three months before we see you. Come any way you like best only *come* to gladden our hearts. I am in a great hurry to get Florence and Shack off—he stayed last night.

Your aff. Mother

My dear David,   Wed. morn. March 5th '73
    Your note came yesterday and I shall go to Ayletts this week to see if I can hear of anyone who will lend me money for six months at any interest they choose to ask and if it is possible, I will send you $100. In the meantime, my dear son, go bravely to Gen. Smith and tell him very respectfully our circumstances— how I was left a widow at the end of the war with six children to support and educate, that just as I had paid all our debts only had the children to educate with your brother's help, that security debt came down upon us and it is all I can do to struggle along under the interest on that. I would gladly sell land but there is no one to buy—that we have sold all the cord wood on the place and when the money comes in we can pay our own debts and the security too. Such a thing as going into

bankruptcy or any other dishonorable way of evading our debts has never entered our heads—that we intend with God's help to pay to the utmost farthing all we owe. In the meantime, remember, my dear boy there is nothing disgraceful in our poverty. We come of an honest stock on both sides of the house and we can't help being poor—you have nothing to be ashamed of, some of the best in our land are now reduced. Don't let your troubles keep you from studying and doing your best— all the worrying in the world will do no good. It is our duty to be happy and to make everyone happy around us.

All send love, the boys are ready to go, so goodbye—

Yr. aff. Mother

[David]   March 8th, '73

Oh, my dear boy, you must come home to see the old Mother every vacation. I can't agree to let a little money stand between us and so much happiness. Among us I am sure we can get the money and you shall have the rest I know you need and as much fruit as you can eat. So don't say another word about staying away during vacation as long as you have a home and thank God you have a pleasant one, and as many loving ones to welcome you. Bye and bye when you are scattered without a common home to come to, you will look back with pleasure to the meetings you used to have. Enjoy the anticipation of seeing your family and friends in just a few months and I want you to come singing and rejoicing. I want you to sing together again.

Your aff. Mother

My dear Mother: V.M.I. March 15, 1873

If you will excuse me this time, I don't think you will ever have to lecture me again about not coming home. I have been convinced all the time that little Sister is worth coming to see, not to mention you, dear Mother, and the other noble sisters and Willie and Tommie and last but not least the fruit. I am looking forward with very much pleasure to my coming home next summer and seeing you all. I shall come laughing and singing too, and will, as you say, thank God I have a home to come to.

I wrote to Wilson about a week ago and directed my letter to his old home (Abbeville, S.C.) and hope very much he will get it, will let you know if I get an answer.

Will have to commence drill next Monday, very much to the horror of us all. The time is passing very rapidly and it won't seem any time before the 4th of July when all of us can be together.

Think I will go to Richmond by the packet, as it will cost $2. less than by rail, and they say it is much more pleasant. The packet goes through Lynchburg and some other places that I would like to take advantage of the opportunity to see. It only costs $7 or $8 to go from here to Richmond including all meals. It is true it takes a little longer but not much. I hope as the weather becomes good the mails will come regularly.

Affectionately your son,

D. W. Fleet

My dear David,   Edgewood March 19, 1873

After the wear and tear of the schoolroom duties, the remnant of the day's thoughts are not worth sending anybody.

I am so glad you have decided to come home. We did not have an idea of letting you do anything else. I think you need the recreation after the hard work, but if you really want to study, we'll let you be as quiet as you please.

You think our dear Uncle Robert didn't send Mattie and me a box by Cousin Browne with an elegant pound cake, a jar of canned peaches and a jar of dried peaches. I wish we could send you some these hungry spring days but I expect Ma will contrive some way to do it. Did she tell of the complimentary report Mr. Shackford wrote of our sisters. (D.V. you brothers will yet have reason to be proud of your little sisters and thankful for them too.)

I am very anxious to hear from Mr. Wilson and hope you will succeed in finding him.

Aff. Lou

My dear Sister [Lou],   G.M. Mar. 20th 1873
    I had intended writing another Latin exercise but will do
two tomorrow and write to you tonight. What a relief to write
a letter and just put down the words without having to think
of the mood, tense and case. Sorrowfully, I haven't a single
geranium leaf to send you, remember most of the geraniums
were in my green-house. Well, the last cold spell, I forgot to
shut down the door one night and didn't think about it till
about two o'clock the next day. When I went out everything
was frozen. I cut them all off and hope sincerely they will all
put out again. Now Sis, you mustn't be very sorry or mad either,
for you know a body can't help forgetting sometimes can she?
    I just wish you could have been with us last Friday night,
we got to Mount Elba about sun-down, where Sis F. put on
her muslin polonaise & Viola a white bodice, then we put the
finishing touches to our heads, or rather *I* did, for after seeing
my flowers so *tastefully* arranged in my hair, they wouldn't agree
that anybody else should fix theirs. When we got to Orange
Grove, we found Mr. Shackford quite uneasy about us, for he
heard we passed Bruington early in the evening. I never enjoyed
a party more in my life, Dr. Shackford and his wife are just
as agreeable and pleasant as they can be. Isabel had written
them all about us. James Smith carried me in to both suppers.
For the meat supper, they had turkey, pig, oysters, beef tongue,
etc. Then for the sweet supper—fruit cake, marble cake & coconut cake, jelly, ice cream, oranges, candy & nuts. I enjoyed
the food mightily, never ate so much at a party before. Mr.
Montague was there & I was introduced to him at last. Sis F.
concluded from the *profoundness* of the bows, we both had been
practicing for months. I like him very much & hope the liking
is mutual. We went to Cousin Betty Henley's that night (Mr.
Montague went too) and stayed till after breakfast.
                                                        [Betsy]

Dear Brother David,   Green Mount, March 25, 1873
    I have been busy lately, riding about looking for oxen. I
have bought two yokes now, they are in right low order but
it has turned quite warm and the grass is beginning to put

up and I hope they will be quite fat before the first of May when we hope to begin to haul the wood. We want to run two carts and a wagon and I reckon I will have to stop school to attend to it. I went down again yesterday evening to see Lipscomb to borrow some money on the wood but he was not at home. I hope to see him soon, we want part of the money to send you, the other to get materials for the cart & wagon. I expect to go to Richmond at Easter to get some things and Ma wants to send you another small box. Is there anything which you would like to have? You must certainly come home next summer for I heard some young ladies counting on you as one of their beaux. I have been having a right gay time lately. Mr. Shackford gave a party to his niece on the 14th. I took her in to supper then and at another party. She is sweet sixteen, pretty and quite accomplished. I told her she must wait for me but she didn't say she would or she wouldn't, I inferred she would, as "silence gives consent." I expect I will have to stay at home and take care of the mother and sisters, but I want to try to get an education so if I am thrown on my own resources, I can make a living. Ma will fill up the sheet. Write soon to

> Your aff. brother
> J. W. Fleet

Next Sunday Mr. Garlick is to preach for us. I shall pledge to the church, five dollars apiece for you, Will, Bess, & myself and ten dollars apiece for the two sisters, making $40 for the family. Next summer, you and Will must work for yours. Bess wants to add a line.

Dear Bro David,

Si Florence, Sister and I came by Orange Grove to take leave of Isabel. Mrs. Toombs seems to be very fond of me says she loves to hear me talk, but *she* does the talking, I make a good listener and then she thinks how much she has enjoyed my conversation—like Cousin Lelia you know.

> Your aff. little sis, Betsy

My dear David,   April 6, '73
    We are determined to try to have a boarding school next year and have the promise of three boarders already—Sallie Browne Fleet, Nettie Gwathmey, and Mattie F. Bird. We will charge $100 board, $30 tuition, $35 music with use of a piano, washing, etc. $10, making $175 for a full time boarder. We hope for a good school, for the terms are certainly low—and I will do my best for them. The boys will have to go as boys and girls can't get along together because they seem to learn the peculiar art of love-making quicker than anything else in the world. We have prospects of the greatest quantity of fruit which we will put up in various ways for the boarders.
    Lou spent a delightful Easter holiday with me and is looking better than either of her sisters. We had a quantity of company, forty or fifty persons came to see her and she did not do like Fred, but received them all so kindly and affectionately.
                                    God bless my dear boy,
                                        Your aff. Mother

                                William Jewell College
My dear D.   Apr. 23 '73
    Your report came in Sister's letter yesterday. I congratulate you with all my heart. You are doing splendidly! Better than I ever thought you could. You are bound to succeed if you continue as you have begun. I sent the report and the note. You sign it and hand it to Gen. Smith. Has Mother written about Mr. Douglas' efforts to make Ella Fauntleroy take land in payment for the debt? Before anything can be done about it, we have to pay nearly $1000 due McConky of Baltimore by Dr. Fauntleroy's estate. I wrote Mr. Douglas I would give my note with your name & Mother's to it bearing interest from date & you & I would pay it off in the next one to five years at the rate $200 to $300 a year. Thus I may not be able to advance you more than $100, and the Institute can take our note for the balance, $300 a year, $900 in all, you can arrange to pay this off first when you go to work and leave me for the last. I am happy to help my brother make a man of himself. I feel very well satisfied about you now, and I am sure if you

can come from the Institute unscathed, you can stand the storms of life.

I rec'd a letter from Maynard Fleet from St. Louis, where he is with Jacky Ryland & several other friends. He wants a place on a farm & I wrote telling him to come & I will send him out to a farmer a mile or two in the country who wants a young man to help feed his stock this winter. He said it was impossible to get anything to do in St. Louis. He wants to farm on his own hook next spring. He may like that sort of work but I'm sure I shouldn't & I *know* you wouldn't.

All send love, Fred

My dear David,   Tues. morn, Apr. 29th 1873

I wrote you a long letter last Friday telling you I would send some money by Wednesday's mail. Mr. Shackford stayed all night with us and this morning heard me ask Willie about going to see Lipscombe about getting some money to send you. I remarked I never knew money to be so scarce. I had tried for six months to borrow some at 12% to send you. He asked me how much I wanted? I told him $100. He handed it to me and wrote the bond at 6%, wasn't that kind? So I wrote Gen. Smith and enclosed it all and shall register the letter at Ayletts today. If I can get $200 from Lipscombe must I send $100 to Gen. Smith or $80 to him and $20 to you? I know none of my children spends money foolishly and thank God I can trust you. Its only one more year before you can go to work and help yourself and us—so work to qualify yourself while you have an opportunity. Remember the better qualified you are the better your position and pay will be.

Only eight more weeks before little Sis comes home and in a few more you will be here too. If you come down in the canal boat when will you start and when will you be in Richmond? The 4th of July is Friday, if you could be in Richmond by Sat. eve. you could come home that night, tell me all your plans. The Aberdeen boys are going to give a party the last Friday in June—wish you could be at home then. Each will put in a dollar and as there are about thirty, they can have a very nice supper.

There is a great prospect for fruit this spring. The cold weather doesn't seem to have injured it. Miss Susan is here making Willie a nice suit of clothes. Goodbye, my dear boy,

Yr. aff. Mother

My dearest Mother,   Edgewood May 10, 1873

I had a right bad cold all the week, & am too hoarse to sing a note, but I was so anxious to have that Saturday work done that I taught yesterday and have thoroughly earned my right to reach you one day sooner. I had dreaded my Saturday's work; but when all my day scholars came with their hands full of wild flowers for "Miss Lou" & and still better with the money for the books I ordered for them I commenced my labors with a light heart, feeling that duty performed does surely bring its reward. I was very tired when the day was over, but I hope in spite of my hoarseness & weakness, I planted some seed that will blossom in eternity.

I have only six more Saturdays to be here, and my time is so fully occupied that it flies rapidly.

Yo. devoted Lou

My dear David,   Sat. morn May 10th 1873

I got this letter from Gen. Smith and send it to you. Now tell me what advantage would it be to be a state student? would you have to teach after you leave instead of engineering? What does he mean by "closing up our indebtedness"?—paying all we owe or giving our bond?

Mrs. Toombs has promised Florence $100 soon and she wants to send it to you. Must she send it to Gen. Smith or to you to get the things you require and to give the balance to Gen. S.? Tell me all about your affairs and let us help you all we can.

I heard the saddest thing the other day. My friend, Mrs. Newton, who lives near Dabney's ferry is deranged and has been sent to an asylum in Staunton.[57] Her poor little girls have gone

[57] Mrs. Mary Mann Page Newton was the widow of William Brockenborough Newton, who was killed at Raccoon Ford in the fall of 1863. Their home, Summer Hill in Hanover County on the road to Richmond, was devastated by repeated enemy raids.

to their grandfather's to live. They say the care of her large
estate, debt and other troubles were the cause. I feel I can't
be thankful enough for my health and reason.

We have had a very rainy month but everything looks so
green and beautiful. Did I tell you we set out 100 pear trees
in the clover lot last fall, they are nearly all living and look
so pretty. Sam Wilson is to put the lot in tobacco to cultivate
the trees and after a few years, I hope the pears will sell.

Write soon and answer all my questions & tell me how you
are.

Yr. aff. Mother

My dear David,   Edgewood May 10th 1873

I intended writing but was confined to my bed with the worst
headache. I received a long letter from home so full of happy
hopes & plans for the future that it would have charmed away
the pain if anything could.

Can you realize it will be only six weeks before I go home—
never to be separated from my dear Mother, I trust, so long
as we both shall live.

I am glad you received your box safely. You must be almost
starved for something good to eat. I wish you could have some
of the nice oysters we have been feasting on. Is your fare the
same monotonous round of beef & potatoes, potatoes & beef?
Try to bear your burdens bravely, you know the Bible says
"It is good for a man to bear the yoke in his youth;" & He
makes things even & those who have borne the yoke in youth
are especially blessed afterwards.

I enclose another dollar & wish it were ten but I want to
send Bessie all I can to buy our summer clothes when she
goes to Richmond.

I got some beautiful songs last week and anticipate great
pleasure in hearing you sing them with B. Are you glad to
get my letters in spite of their being sermons? If so write soon
to

Your aff. Sister [Lou]

My dearest boy [David],   May 29th '73
  I am so thankful you are employing the talent God has given
you in his service. You know man is judged by what he has
and not by what he has not, and all we can do is to use with
thankfulness what we have and God will increase our usefulness.
Then too, we have great cause for gratitude in Gen. Smith's
offer. See the Providence in my being able to send him the
money and write to him myself. You know we never thought
of applying for the place but it is too good not to accept. Florence will send you $100 as soon as she can. Lou no doubt
can spare another $100 and you can sign a bond and send it
to Fred and he to me as securities. You can tell the General
you will be glad to get the place on those terms—$250 will
be a great help.
  The sisters have determined not to go to Richmond next
year. Bess is getting on so well with her Latin, it seems a pity
to stop till she will be able to teach. We plan to have a school
for Sis at home and hope to have enough scholars to keep
Florence too. Bess can practice under Sis and study Latin under
Shack another year. Then when you are able to "paddle your
own canoe", we will be better able to do something for the
girls.
  We have at last commenced hauling wood in earnest—a
wagon with the mules & two ox carts. Willie seems very anxious
to help and does as well as a man. He keeps up his math with
the girls.

                                              Your aff.
                                              Mother

My dear Sister [Lou],   V.M.I. May 30, 1873
  Your very kind and cheerful letter came safely. Thank you
for it and especially for what it contained. I have only 5 weeks
to stay here before I have the pleasure of seeing you all at
home, & only 4 before you can have quiet and rest with them.
Am very glad to hear of the plans for next year, so you can
be with the loved ones.
  We will soon stop recitations now and go to work to prepare
for our examinations. That together with the hard drill which

we are having every evening and cleaning up our guns & plates, will give us just as much as we can do. But when I think what a pleasant time I anticipate when I get home, I feel very much encouraged, and still more encouraged when I think I have only one more year to be so dependent. I hope affairs will be better next year as Genl Smith has told me he would see if he could get me the position as State Cadet & I will, by that means, save from $200 to $250. I expect to leave here on the morning of the 5th, get to Richmond that evening & start home Monday if the Mother can arrange to send for me. I will write to her several times before then.

I am always *very* glad to get your letters even though they be sermons, for I do love you very much.

Aff'y yours, David

My dearest Mother,   Edgewood June 8th 1873

Cousin Browne Evans renewed his offer to me to teach his children and in addition I would have the tuition of all the other scholars and music pupils I can get and he will board them for $10 a month. I told him of our hopes for a school at home. He said, "Doubtless your mother will carry it through; from what I have heard of her I am confident there are few such women in the world." He asked that I write you and ascertain the progress of the plans. His father told me last night that he met Browne in the road and he stopped to tell him his troubles, not the least of which he was afraid Cousin Lou wouldn't return.

Your loving
Lou

Fred, who was to assume the presidency of the Baptist Female College in Lexington, Missouri, in September 1873, sent his mother a brochure of the college which described it as an "institution which offers to young ladies the highest education both solid and ornamental." She requested him to enroll Florence and Betsy.

Wm. Jewell College
My dear Mother,   Aug. 28th 1873

Send both the girls and Caroline and Lorelle [58] too. Tell
David to buy their tickets via the Balt. & Ohio; Ohio Misr &
St. Louis, Kansas City & Northern R.R. from Baltimore to Lexington. Take a sleeping car from Baltimore through to St. Louis
so they will not have to change cars. If there is no one to
meet them in East St. Louis, let them step in an omnibus &
have the driver take them to Mrs. Davis' (card enclosed) she
has a nice quiet boarding house, as they will have to remain
in St. Louis some 6 or 8 hours. She will send them to the
RR depot, where they can purchase a berth and sleep comfortably all night & I will meet them in Lexington.

Tell the girls to spend as much time as they can with the
servants so they won't get homesick.

Love to all, Fred

Sept. 12th 1873
My precious darlings [Florence and Betsy],

I did not realize your absence till two or three days ago and
have been feeling so lonely and desolate, but your dear letters
cheered me so much. In the last 30 years, I have had but one
object in life, my children's highest good, and if I can attain
that, I can live content altho separated so widely. Willie Shackford invited my Will to go to Orange Grove to shoot sora and
Monday morning Joe S. came by ostensibly to ride down with
him but really to hear from you, judging by the questions he
asked and the interest he evinced. They went in the marsh
with two dogs and they killed 60-odd the first day and 30-odd
the second. Tell Fred I shall value a note from him as he has
so many of my treasures in his keeping. What do you think
of your music teachers and the people and the West generally?
Every little item will interest us away off in the backwoods.
Mr. John Ryland says I am founding a colony in Missouri, sending out black and white, he has no doubt I will go myself and
carry Mammy and all the rest.

[58] Caroline and Lorelle were Mary Gaines's daughters; Caroline was to be the maid,
and Lorelle the nurse, for Minnie.

Mary and Mammy send much love and say—"Tell Aunt Peggy they thank her for looking after Caroline and hope she will be a mother to her and Lorelle. If they get homesick not to send word here, but keep it there and talk it over with you all." I know you will comfort them. May the good Lord watch over you is the prayer of

Your affectionate,
Mother

II
"Virginians will educate their children if they possibly can even if they have money for little else."
1873–1888

In the summer 1873 the following modest circular had been circulated.

GREEN MOUNT HOME SCHOOL FOR YOUNG LADIES
KING & QUEEN COUNTY, VA.

My daughter, Miss M. L. Fleet proposes to open a Select School for Young Ladies at my residence, Green Mount, in King & Queen County.

The location is quiet, retired, and proverbial for healthfulness; the society refined and intelligent, and churches of the different denominations are convenient. I desire to have six or eight boarders, who will be regarded as members of my family, and in every respect treated as my own daughters. My effort will be to secure to them the enjoyments and comforts of home.

The usual English branches, Mathematics, Latin, French and Music, will be taught systematically and thoroughly.

The Session will commence the 18th of September next, and terminate the 15th June following.

TERMS:
Board, including Washing, Fuel, Lights and every
necessary, per session. $130.00
Tuition 30.00
Music, with use of piano 40.00
One-half payable at the time of entrance, the
remainder on 1st February, 1874

For further information, address the undersigned at St. Stephen's Church, Va.

Mrs. M. L. Fleet

On September 18, 1873, the Green Mount Home School for Young Ladies was opened with seven boarders: Page Acree, Sallie Browne Fleet, Mattie Bird, Ida Ryland, Lelia Dew, Hannah Bagby, and Nellie Jones. The day scholars were Ella Fauntleroy, Sallie Brooke, and Lelia Smith. In addition, Lou gave music lessons to Page, Sallie Brooke, Ella, Mattie, Lelia, Mary Brooke Councill, and Claybrooke Fauntleroy. Ma wrote David: "A brother of Lelia Fauntleroy wants to come to Lou for music lessons. He is said to be very weak in mathematics but very talented in music. He is fourteen, awkward, and ugly so I hope he won't demoralize my girls but isn't it a nice way of gaining access to my school? I wouldn't be surprised if she had more boys wanting to take music before long."

Soon after the opening of the school, Page Acree and Mattie Bird originated and planned the Evergreen Society. At the end of classes the girls assembled in the classroom and elected officers for the year. Wednesday was selected as the day to meet as it was in the middle of the week and would "relieve the monotony of daily duties." The meetings were always opened by reading a familiar chapter in *La Bible Sainte*. Later when German was added to the curriculum, an alternate chapter in *Die Bibel* was read. Miss Lou suggested they combine pleasure with good works; so they decided to take up a collection which they voted to give to foreign missions.

After the Bible reading, they "repaired" to the parlor during the first years; but when the second piano was acquired, to the music room. The music pupils always played or sang or both. Miss Lou usually had a verse for them to commit to memory. Some of her favorites were:

> Work is the weapon of honor; he who lacks the
> weapon will never triumph.

> I would be busy too
>   For Satan finds some mischief still
> For idle hands to do.

and

> The world, dear child, is as you take it
>   And life be sure is what you make it.

She always managed to see and point a moral in the selections the girls read. After Miss Florence and Miss Bessie came home to teach in the school, they usually played and sang, sometimes together, and the Society minutes express great admiration for their music.

When the weather was inclement, Mrs. Fleet had the girls take turns serving tea so they would be "at ease in polite society." But when the weather was fine, it was the custom for the girls to take daily walks as a group with one of their teachers. The favorite walk was down a lane leading toward the lower farms, past the graveyard, and down a hill to the ice pond. This pond was large and clear, fed by innumerable springs and surrounded by virgin pines and oaks. A good stream of water, lined on both sides with mountain laurel the height of small trees, fell over the pond's spillway and dodged around huge trees in a gradual descent through the unbroken forest. Along the edge of the pond grew cattails, spiderwort, pickerelweed, spatterdock, and blue flags, a delight to the eye, but they had to be cleared away without a trace before the winter when it was hoped a hard freeze would furnish good clean ice for storage in the icehouse. But every spring the plants reappeared. In the fall, butterfly weed, blue and lavender asters, and goldenrod grew along the wide path. When they disappeared, the running cedar and crowfoots seemed to emerge and the deciduous trees were etched against the dark green of the cedars, cypresses, and hollies with their bright red berries. In the spring, bluets, the moccasin flower or lady's slippers, yellow partridge peas, and blue lupine lined the path, and everybody's favorite for its fragile beauty and delicate aroma—the trailing arbutus— was tucked under the banks.

In the hush of the deep woods, the gentle ripple of the stream swelled to a roar when suddenly, without warning, it dropped about a hundred feet. The falls formed a deep ravine, called the "cellars," which the stream cut to a depth of about two hundred feet as it flowed toward the river. It was said that during the Civil War, the cellars were used as an underground railroad where slaves from the surrounding countryside hid while waiting to board the ships which came up the Mattaponi River and make their escape.

Lexington, Mo.
Sept. 14th, 1873

My dearest Mother,

You may like to hear our program of studies—after chapel, I have a Latin class, then French and German. After lunch, I have an English literature class, then I either practice or study my lessons for the next day.

Caroline and Lorelle are both well and seem to be happy tho' the other night Caroline said, "I like very well but I think I rather live in Va." Aunt Peggy is an excellent cook and we have very good meals. There are twenty-six boarders, all are friendly, good-natured girls, not quite like Virginia girls, I can hardly tell you where the difference lies, except some of them are not so refined, break the third commandment much of the time and none of them talks grammatically. But you know we have seen nothing of the world except the backwoods, and this may not be different from other parts of it. For my part, when I get back to the backwoods, I feel I will be thankful and more than willing to stay there.

Caroline says tell her mother—"My girls have given me some ribbons and made me some collars to set me off when I goes out."

Write me about the school and give my love to all my friends,

Most aff. yours,
Bessie

Dear Brother [Fred],

I think of you very often and wonder if you have to work much harder than I do. I teach eight hours a day, and have to study very hard for my advanced classes. You know I only studied Latin, French and mathematics for two years.

It gave me great pleasure to send you the first money I made when I taught at Waterview to repay you for the money you lent me to take music lessons in Richmond. Now I am sending you the first money we have collected to pay you for my precious sisters' tuition and board. Ma and I can get along for the next year or two at home with almost nothing new to wear, in that way we will be able to send the money. We are thankful they can be in your school, close to you and Belle and the precious baby.

We will bend our united efforts not only to "pull through" ourselves, but to help you through too. We are firmly bound together for life as only misfortunes can bind us. I believe God will give us strength to rise superior to all these ills and make us all the more useful for having had them.

Your devoted sister,
Lou

Green Mount Oct. 1st 1873

My little darlings [Florence and Betsy],

The girls are sweet, pleasant and good and take the place of my absent ones as much as possible. They all prefer coming here to going elsewhere to school and I daresay will spend a happy and profitable year. What a happy situation it is for us to be working together and how thankful the mother is that she can do her part. I shall teach English grammar, composition and literature and endeavor at the same time to build the girls' *characters,* without that an education is a very empty thing indeed.

Tommie has been very disgruntled at having to become a boarder at Aberdeen. You know how strongly I feel that when boys and girls are together, they become so engrossed in each other, they neglect their studies. Willie is in our former overseer's house, managing the farms in addition to attending Aberdeen; and Nancy, in the house nearby, fixes his little meals. He expressed gratitude at being old enough to help "the dear Mother" but Tommie declared himself "much put out by being dispossessed by the girls." Were they here they would unite in sending love, as I do,

Your aff. Mother

Tues. morn Oct. 10, 1873

My darling children [Florence and Betsy],

Your letter found me in bed with a horrible headache and you can imagine how glad I was to get it. It was the first time I have been sick since you left. The girls were so kind and considerate and Lou and Milly made as good a dessert as I could have done.

Betsy has never told me whether she wants to take private singing and guitar lessons next session. I am anxious that you may teach them with Sis next year and you know, you may never have another opportunity. It's not a question of whether Mrs. Doll sings well but whether she can teach *you.* I never knew how well my children sing till I hear Sis trying to teach these girls and you always thought I was a very prejudiced Mother, didn't you. If I can't sing myself, I know what good singing is. I found out David's voice before anyone else and see what Mr. Crane said about his tenor. When I tell Bess she has a voice worth cultivating, I know what I am talking about, no prejudice about it.

Sunday, Mr. James Latané preached an excellent sermon for us.[1] We expected company but no one came except all the girls, Owen Gwathmey, Lucian Acree, and Claggett.

Love to all,
Your aff. Mother

My precious Mother,   Thursday Oct. 15th 1873

I am afraid Brother made you very uneasy last week about Caroline. Don't know what he said but expect it was something disparaging. The truth is Caroline didn't get well in the first instance before she commenced to work again & every day or two, she would have a slight chill which made her feel very badly & of course, she was slower than ever. So last Thursday after having a worse chill than usual, Mrs. Seddon decided she should go to bed, take more pills & try to get rid of them entirely. So she stayed in bed till Monday, missed the chills & is as well as ever & able to do her work with some heart. Sister Belle got her some red flannel & after 5 o'clock I cut out & made her a shirt & made her put it on. Don't think she will be sick again & I will make her take great care of herself hereafter. Mrs. Seddon says you must have another motto for Green Mount—"In making others happy we gladden our own hearts."

Love to all,
Florence

My dear Mother: V.M.I., Oct. 17, 1873

Your very kind letter together with the sisters' came today. I think you really ought to be proud of your children, all except me for all the others are real exceptions to most children.

---

[1] James Latané, afterwards bishop of the Reformed Episcopal Church, lived at Bewdley, a pre-Revolutionary house on the Mattaponi River.

I am feeling quite low-spirited tonight about my being so dependent, and a great many other things too numerous to mention. I hardly feel that I will be able to stay here this session. I am so tired of the Institute and everything connected with it and my time here isn't half over. I feel if I could go off somewhere by myself and have a good cry, I think it would do me good. But I ought not to be writing such a letter to you for fear it may make you sad.

Miss Agnes Lee, youngest daughter of Gen. Lee died two or three days ago with cholera morbus.

I received this letter from Miss Ely this morning which I send. Please return it in your next. The mutiny which she refers to, was nothing more than "Rat bucking," about which I wrote you in my last.

I am truly thankful to hear of Brother's prospects and cheerfulness, & of what a help those dear little sisters are to him. He certainly has a model of a wife. I am almost inclined to think if I could do so well, I might get married some of these days. Has Shack renewed his suit to Betsy? If he does, let me know all about it.

Will write again shortly,

Yours aff'y, David

[Written in pencil across the letter] I can't think what is the matter with my poor boy. I shall not send Willie there and only wish Dave were safely away. I send this to make mine worth three cents. Love to Belle and Mrs. Seddon and Fred.

Good night, dear children,
Your affectionate Mother

Monday evening Oct. 26th '73

My darling children [Florence and Betsy],

We went to Beulah Wed. Tommie drove the wagon with Lou and all the girls and Willie took me in the buggy. It was a bright beautiful day and the girls seemed to enjoy everything— the holiday—the ride with Tom—as only young girls can enjoy. Only think Ida Ryland had never been out of this county before!! And she will be 19 next spring. As for me it was so unlike the old Dover Association used to be when I was young and I missed the old familiar faces so much it was no pleasure—

not a single Richmond preacher but Dr. Wilson. "Uncle Broaddus" preached a very dry and uninteresting sermon. He looks as well as usual but is very infirm. Dr. Gwathmey and Owen sent their love to you both, they told me that Lewis Gwathmey had gone to Germany to spend two years. The congregation was not nearly so large as at St. Stephens or Bruington. I came home feeling decidedly weary and old, that I was outliving my old friends and only fifty one.

Yesterday Lou, Will and I went to Shepherd's. Shack preached and as Peachy had promised to dine with us, and I had a very nice dinner, I invited him and Willie Shackford. They all come with Tommy, C. Fauntleroy (Sis's boy music scholar) and another little one from Aberdeen—quite a company. Only Peachey and her family left, the others stayed all night. This morning Mr. S. left after breakfast but as it was still raining the boys spent the day. Poor Tommie says he is *so* lonesome and is more affectionate than ever. All left when Jimmie Acree brought Page, except little Shack who stayed all night and is very poorly—lying on my bed all day. He sends his love to you both.

Do you take singing lessons? I want Bess at least to take private lessons from Madame Doll. I want your voice cultivated as I think it will be of great advantage to you some day. As a case in point—Col. Aylett's sister, Rosalie, married a Mr. Samson of N.Y. Well, in the great trouble [2] he failed completely and instead of trying to retrieve his fortunes, he left his wife and five children, leaving a note saying she would never see or hear of him again unless he could recover himself and she and the children are at Col. Aylett's dependent on his charity. Now if she could teach or do anything for her own support, how much better off she would be & you know music is better paid than almost anything else. I am trying very hard to build up a good school at home so you can all three live at home if you don't fall in love with the "great west", and in the division of labor, none of us would have so much to do. Do you like the idea?

I hear poor Mr. Timberlake has lost more money by having it in some of the banks in Richmond, am so sorry for him,

[2] The financial panic of 1873 developed into a five-year depression.

wish he had lent me $500 or $1000 and it would be safe. Did Fred lose anything in the banks or was he like this old lady, none in that or any other.

Kiss my little darling, I was so glad of her photograph. Be sure to say all you can about Caroline and Lorelle. Millie and Mary turn away after hearing your letters with such a look of disappointment if you don't mention them. It makes me feel so sorry as they are so polite and do everything for us so well, I want to give them all the pleasure I can.

God bless my children,

Your affectionate Mother

My dear Florence,   Tuesday night Nov. 18th 1873

Tomorrow is your birthday (do you feel freer because you are of age?) When I was told I had another daughter I was suffering such intense pain, I didn't care if either of us lived or died. You have lived to be a blessing for 21 years and I thank God for sparing my darling child and enabling her to pay me so well for all that terrible agony. My quiet, gentle, loving, lovely child! If you ever marry (but who is good enough for you) and have children of your own, I hope they may be all to you that you have been to me—that will be enough.

Tommy came by Sunday from home, he is carrying on with Page and Ella, but tells Will it is very hard to flirt with two girls at once when they are confidantes but he tries it. Will doesn't flirt but he teases the girls unmercifully.

We expect to have a little "soirée" Dec. 5th and repay those in the neighborhood who have entertained my girls and of course we will have the Aberdeen boys. The girls are very full of it. Won't you and Bess wish for wings, never mind, next summer I expect your friends to come. I have the ice pond stopped, it is quite full and we hope to have ice for you.

Good night, dear children,

Your aff. Mother

My dear boy [David],   Friday night, Nov. 20th 1873

I received your letter yesterday and was very sorry to see you in such poor spirits, but hope you feel better today. My dear child, do try to stand it until the end of the session. Of course, I don't know every trial you have to bear, but hope God will give you strength for your day and task. I am nearly alone tonight—the girls all gone, only Willie and Tommy are with me.

Last Sunday we went to Shepherd's to hear Shack preach. Peachey had carried Mattie and Ella home with her Friday and brought them back and dined with us Sunday. We had one of our old big companies—Capt. Fauntleroy and Peachey, Tommy and two other Aberdeen boys, old Shack and Willie. As it rained, all but Capt. F. and Peachey had to stay all night. The next day it was still raining so the boys stayed all day. The next day Viola and Gay Toombs came and stayed till this evening. As you see "men may come and men may go" but I stay at home, and enjoy being quiet sometimes.

You ask if Shack has renewed his suit. He writes to Bess and she answers—letters of friendship, you know. I don't know what will come of it but he seems as much in love as anyone I ever saw—comes here very often. Tom says he is flirting with my girls. My girls seem very happy and altho' little Sis has so much to do, she says she is resting on beds of roses compared with what she had to do last year.

Now I have a sad piece of news. Poor Bunny Gresham died the very day she was to have been married. People say, "How shocking!" yet the feeling seems to be that perhaps she was taken from evil to come. Lewis Tyler was very dissipated and what chance has a girl married to that kind of man. You see, we all have our troubles, let us try to bear our crosses and not be impatient under them. Tell me when you are obliged to have some money and I will try to send it. I believe you children have first claim on me, and shall pay your way before I do anything else. Tommy and Willie are going to a political meeting today. Be sure to vote for Gen. Kemper, a brave soldier and honest man.[3]

God bless you, dear child,
Yr. aff. Mother

---

[3] Gen. James Lawson Kemper of Madison County had been severely wounded leading his brigade at the battle of Gettysburg. A Conservative, he supported fiscal integrity and legal, but not social, equality for blacks. He was elected governor in 1873.

My dear David,   Dec. 2nd '73

Can't you see Genl Smith and politely offer your bond with
me or Fred or both, till we can have a little more time. The
pressure in the money market is felt even here, but as soon
as I can get some I will send it to you to have your teeth fixed
and pay what you owe as far as it will go—try to do all you
can to get *time,* that is all we ask and don't feel too depressed.
You have all inherited honesty and integrity of purpose and
if God gives you health, you will be independent soon.

Willie will go to Aberdeen next session, then there will be
a vacancy in this district for the University and Fred and I will
try to secure it for him—and as he is the last, I hope to see
you all educated and able to take care of yourselves.

I wish they could ship the ring leaders in that disgraceful
affair, and think the faculty ought to make an example of them,
regardless of consequences. If they had treated you so your
first year, I should have taken you away if I had known it.

What do you think of the sisters' coming back? I have thought
of little else since their last letters—it takes all the spring out
of my life to think of not having them at home in vacation. I
know our poverty strikes Fred very forcibly but money is not
everything.

Uncle Robert came up last Friday and spent the night. He
looks well and cheerful. Brought us apples, brandy peaches,
chines, sausages, fresh beef, Irish potatoes, and a nice ham
for my "party." We are to have some boys and girls next Friday
night and they call it a party and anticipate a great time. It
would be a party if we could have you too!!

Your aff. Mother

My dear child [David],

I went to Erin this evening, Dr. William Fleet has not returned
from N.Y. The girls looked even more care worn and sad. William Christopher's wife is dead leaving seven little children—
poor dear lady—she had a hard time in this life. Worked too
hard for her frail body and the rest of Heaven will be very
sweet to her. The poor little children will just be scattered.

Think how different would have been the lives of my children if I had died when Willie was a baby, when I was so ill.

Look out for your box before Christmas, I am beginning to pack it now.

God bless my dear boy,
Your affectionate Mother

My dear boy [David],   Tuesday night Dec. 16th 1873

I have just received your letter, poor fellow, I know you have suffered and worried and all to no purpose. Cheer up, dear child, Mr. Lipscomb sent me word he would pay us all he owes us up to this time. Will will go to see him tomorrow and I will send you a check for $200 as soon as I get it. I would be much more sorry for you, if I did not think it was working for your good in some way. Providence has always provided for us heretofore and we can trust the Lord for our future. The fathers of two of my girls wrote they would pay us the 1st of Jan. so you see the school is coming to our rescue. You can't think how thankful we are that we have that to fall back on. We are so blessed in having such good, sweet girls, everything is moving along smoothly and harmoniously—not a single discordant note. Oh! my child pecuniary troubles are the very easiest to bear, because if people are honest and truthful and industrious, they can work out of them.

I have packed your box and a nice one it is. Mr. Longest will take it to Richmond tomorrow so watch out for it and write of its arrival.

God bless you, dear boy, good night.
Your aff. Mother

Lexington, Mo.

My dear Mother & Sister,   Dec. 18 1873

We received your long most interesting letters, I am so glad you told us all about "the party," I was with you in spirit. I am surprised at the way Claggett behaves what makes him do so.

Minnie gets sweeter and smarter and prettier every day, I

wish you could see her. Lorelle told me this morning with the most evident pleasure, her mouth stretched to its utmost capacity that Mr. Fred and Miss Belle said if next Saturday was a good day they were going to take her down and have her picture taken with Minnie in her lap. She (L.) has never seemed the least bit homesick, but is always bright and cheerful. The girls think she is the smartest, funniest thing they ever saw, and by laughing at everything she says and does makes her a little more saucy than she would be otherwise. She and Minnie have camp meetings as Mrs. Seddon calls them, with Lorelle singing at the top of her great big voice and Minnie doing her best with her little one. Mrs. Seddon's practice is very much like yours, she sends her love and wants to know if there is anything *special* you want her to do for us.

Brother knows about my correspondence, and isn't much in favor of my keeping it up. I can't see any harm in it though, and don't see how evil can come from anything that gives so much pleasure on both sides. I don't know how it will end, but in no bad way I am sure.

With much love to everybody,
Bess

[David]   [Dec. 31, 1873]

I know of no better way of employing some of the last hours of the old year than writing to my dear child. I hope your last year at the Institute will be your most pleasant. Was your Christmas box in nice order when you received it? Have you written to Fred about looking out for a situation for you? Take pains whenever you write to him and spell correctly, you know he is so particular.

Now, my darling boy, wishing you a very happy and useful New Year, I remain your most affectionate

Mother

My dear David,   Jan. 2, 1874

I have just received your letter and I know how hard it must be to a man of your sensitive feelings to feel so very dependent but thank God it will not be much longer.

With the money from the wood, I have just paid the taxes on this place and the interest on the security debt, $131.10, so we haven't a cent left. I will send you some by Wednesday's mail to get the pants, if I can possibly borrow it. I will not wait for the calf—a beautiful little creature, which will be ready for market in 3 or 4 weeks if I can get it there.

God bless my boy, Your aff. Mother

Dear little Bess,   Jan 2, 1874
How do you really feel about Mr. S[hackford]. Do you think it would be better not to see him next summer? I am at a loss to know what to advise you but we know we are in our Father's hands and he will dispose of us according to His Will. To His kind care I commit you, my precious darlings.

Will worked hard all week on the farm but Tommie came Friday evening and they hitched his horse to a buggy & went to a party at Mr. James Latané's. It is a very nice place to visit but it made me feel right old to see Willie and Tommie, my youngest ones off to a party. Of course we questioned them closely but could get very little satisfaction from them.

Love to all from us all,
Your aff. Mother

My dear boy [David],   Sat. night, Jan 3, 1874
Enclosed you will find a check for eighty dollars, get it cashed, take what you want and hand Gen. Smith the balance. Tell him I will continue to send it as I get it till I send $200. Had Mr. Lipscomb been at home yesterday, I daresay I would have had the whole amount to send. Will try again tomorrow. Don't give yourself any uneasiness, just study with all your might, and the next six months will pass away.

The girls say Fred thinks it would be "sinful" in our reduced circumstances to waste $175, which it would take to bring them home this summer and carry them back again. I will try to submit and bear the cross as best I may. Florence wrote a long letter to Milly from Caroline. Bess writes in the bravest way, she enclosed a letter to Mr. Shackford which she asked me to read. Fred is so much opposed to the correspondence that she proposes to him to stop and they try to forget each other. I don't know what he will say to it, will let you hear. Poor fellow, he has been sick all the holiday with dreadful sore throat.

Lou told her girls they must all be back the 1st of January and they all came but Ida Ryland and she will come on Monday. Hannah Bagby is here. I told you we offered her board and tuition this session for her father's sake.[4] She seems very grateful and is a fine girl. We have a very sweet set of girls. I am more and more thankful that we have a school at home for it not only keeps Lou here but is a great comfort to me to have these young girls with me keeping my heart fresh and full of sympathy. They are very affectionate to Lou and me as well as to each other.

The weather is beautiful and as mild as spring, have had only one "cold snap" when we got forty loads of ice, one to two inches thick.

Your aff. Mother

Dear Sister Fleet,   Milton, Jan. 3rd 1874

It is with feelings of peculiar pleasure and gratitude, I commit my darling Hannah to your care, and Miss Lou's instruction.

I consider it a great honor to have her live under your influence, and hope you will never hesitate to tell her whenever she may do anything unbecoming a Christian, or a young girl.

I shall always esteem it a privilege to have you or any of your family to visit us.

May the Friend of the fatherless, and the widow, ever be with and comfort you and yours is the prayer of your affectionate friend,

A. E. Bagby

---

[4] Richard Hugh Bagby (1820–1870) was educated at Richmond and Columbian colleges, married Anne E. Motley, and was pastor of Bruington Baptist Church for twenty-seven years.

Green Mount, Jan. 6 '74

My darling children [Florence and Betsy]—

Willie went to John Fleet's to a large party. He said many young people were there and they had a very nice supper—elegant Middlesex oysters. They saw the old year well out and that was the end of the frolicking. Next day as we had ice on the ponds, I set to work and housed it all, only 40 loads though.

Soon after breakfast Dr. Bagby brought his sister Hannah. In a little while Uncle brought Sallie Browne, then Mr. Bird and Mattie, and Peel Dillard brought Ella Fauntleroy. Page got here that evening and Mr. Joe Ryland brought Ida on Sunday, so all six are ready "to get straight to work."

Tom came Saturday night and Sunday he drove the carriage and Willie the wagon and we went to church, and all of us—ten in number came back to dinner. The sun bade fair to set splendidly so all but me walked down to Butler's to enjoy the view. I lay down and thought of my dear absent ones.

About dark, they all came in and someone announced that George Councill, Claybrook Fauntleroy and his brother Maxwell had arrived. I felt considerable curiosity to see Max. Mattie talks a good deal about him and he is considered quite a catch in her neighborhood. How thankful I felt for my boys! a more awkward, ugly, simple, countrified, blink-eyed chap, I never saw. Dressed in such fine clothes too, I really felt sorry for his father and mother. Poor Claybrook can scarcely talk at all, he stammers so terribly and it would be well if Max could be silent too for he can hardly speak a correct sentence. Girls, money is well enough but it can't compensate for everything. Fortunately they left about 9 o'clock for yesterday was a very close rainy day and it would have been a terrible bore for us to entertain them. Tom stayed all night and I asked him to ride to Aberdeen to see if there was any school and bring our mail. He returned saying Max was there and spoke of coming to see the girls but he told him they were constantly in the schoolroom and had no time to see company, so he didn't come. Tom couldn't get away because of the rain so you can imagine how happy he is, how noisy and full of life—the same old Tom Boy.

Peel Dillard dined the day he brought Ella, sang a great deal but I didn't concur in thinking no one can sing as well as he. He is fuller of conceit than he was when he was at Aberdeen, for he is larger and can hold more. He's the only person I ever saw who can strut sitting down.

You know our circumstances but you know money is by no means the first consideration. When I look around me I'm convinced pecuniary troubles are the easiest to bear if we can work and retain our health.

Your affectionate Mother

My dear boy [David],   Feb. 10th 1874

This is your birthday. Did you think of it? I have been making good wishes for you all day. Altho you are twenty-three years old you will always be a child to me. Well, when you are a mother you will understand it and how well mothers in general love their boys and your mother in particular.

I have been wishing I could get some money to send you but Lipscomb has disappointed me again and again—as well as everyone I promised to pay when he pays me. I have a draft for $40 from Mr. Roderick Dew but I owe Caldwell $33 for blacksmith's work which he passed on to one of his men who threatened to sue me, so I must pay that to save the expense of a warrant.

We have seven girls now and that's as many as we care for this session but next fall we shall prepare for and expect a full house. I think we give satisfaction to all but I didn't think we could be so impartial, I really can't tell which is my favorite. Little Sis and I are going to establish a school next year that will enable us to keep one, or both the sisters at home. When I look back and see how merciful God has been to us heretofore, my faith grows strong that He will open a way for our support in the future.

The young people got up a party at Mr. John Temple's last Friday night. It snowed so hard only Willie went from here. He said it was a very pleasant company, they must have enjoyed it for they sat up all night.

Your aff. Mother

My darling children [Florence and Betsy],   Feb. 23, 1874

We have had nearly all of our winter this week but have plenty of good wood and are able to keep the girls comfortable.

How do you like German in comparison with Latin and French? When little Sis has a large school and you two assist her you must decide what you want to teach. We are aiming to have enough scholars to enable all of you to teach at home.

Our half session ended last Friday and Sunday evening we were very much surprised to see Mr. Roderick Dew drive up with Lelia. She is a sweet, quiet, pretty girl—poor child she was so homesick and disturbed at leaving home and coming among so many strangers that it made her right sick. As soon as her father left I had to doctor and nurse her and tonight she's much improved in health and spirits. We have seven girls now and when Nellie Jones comes we will be as full as we care to be this year. You have no idea what a pleasant, cheerful parcel they are.

I tell our girls, a lady never apologizes. If she does something inadvertently, everyone knows she is a lady and no offense was meant. If she stoops to an ignoble or mean act intentionally, then no amount of apologies will do any good. And don't make excuses—because most excuses are but lies. I tell the girls too, there are some people in this world who can go along well enough over a smooth road but there are very few who can make rough roads smooth. May I say, my darlings, you both have that faculty.

Yr. aff.
Mother

My dear David,   March 25th '74

It is *very* cold now and I fear for the fruit as most of the trees are in full bloom. I asked Willie to ride to Lipscomb's and try to get the check to send you. Just as he was coming out of the Aberdeen gate his horse slipped on ice and fell with him and hurt his ankle so badly, it was with difficulty he could ride home. Lipscomb usually comes in the woods on Friday (tomorrow) to oversee the cutting and I will go down and do all I can to send you the check as soon as possible. You have no idea how very hard it is to get any money. Sometimes I don't have a dollar for a fortnight, so we live in hope and that will do very well at home—but I feel for you at college. I thank God though, our troubles are only money troubles.

Dear little Willie is studying with his foot propped up, it wasn't broken but a bad sprain.

Have you talked with anyone about your next fall's work, let me know what you hear.

God bless you, dear child,

Yr. aff.

Mother

My dear Mother: V.M.I. Apr. 1, 1874

The 1st class has been excused from academic duty today for the purpose of preparing for an examination on Rhetoric tomorrow. As I am tired of studying I will drop you a few lines, as I will not have time to write Saturday. Your letter came safely on the 27th (Little Sister's birthday) with Fannie's picture and the $6.00 from Sis. Thank her for it. Don't think Fannie's picture does her justice. She is a much prettier girl from what I recollect of her. I send you one of my pictures which is a little flattering. The class picture will contain one exactly like it.

I wrote to Cousin Tom Harwood in Texas and hope he can do something for me, also to one of my college mates in Missouri.

I am going to send Miss Gillie Daniel one of my photographs for one of hers. She has gone to Charlottesville and Richmond to stay two or three months. I will miss her very much as I used to see a good deal of her. I expect to go to church with Miss Lizzie Letcher next Sunday night. She is an intelligent, refined and accomplished lady.

I promise I will not run the block again to see any girl as I am determined to graduate and as to your admonition not to carry on any more flirtations, I assure you they are very light ones.

Have never been so busy in my life and will be until I graduate. Thank you for your cheerful letter and the check,

I remain your devoted son,

D. W. Fleet

My dears [Florence and Betsy],   April 15th 1874

You know I never have a dollar which I can call my own as I am always paying off back debts which will accumulate in spite of all I can do—but if I had it you may know I would prefer to send it to bring you home to doing anything else I know. You know too that Lou has been hard at work for the last three years—not to speak of the years she taught you all at home—and it has all been spent for the benefit of her family. I think if she chooses to borrow money to bring you home, she ought to be allowed to do it and be helped by Fred and me too, in every way we can. When you girls are married, I can't expect to see you every summer, but until you are, I think you ought to spend the vacations at home. Let me hear where to meet you and Oh! the happy time when we shall meet again. Lou wants to add a line but I have time only to add dearest love to you all,

Your affectionate
Mother

The Garnetts spent the day with us on Sunday and were just as kind and sweet as ever. I think they understand better than any girls I ever saw that—

> "Politeness is to do and say
> The kindest things in the kindest way."

[David]   April 25th '74

Well, my darling, here is the check at last, let me hear when you get it. Last night Mr. Shackford spent the night so I have only a few minutes to write this morning. I enclose a letter from Fred, I am so glad he is going to lend you a helping hand and I am sure you will do all you can to help yourself.

All the girls went to Judge Jones yesterday, only Sis, Will and I at home.

We got your card yesterday and are so glad you are well through all this gloomy, rainy weather—have only planted corn one day—too cold and wet. Am so glad we have something else to depend on beside the farm for a support.

Your aff. Mother

My dear boy [David], Tues. morn.

I have only time to enclose this check for one hundred dollars and tell you to take out what you need to pay your way home and hand Gen. Smith the balance. Let me know how you stand to give him your bond with me or Fred, or both as security. Tell him we will pay as soon as we can. Don't buy the ring till you can do it with your own money and we will pay what you owe to the Institute. Be sure to get the class picture. I am so much obliged to all your friends for their kindness.

Write at once if you get the check—and believe me as ever

Your devoted Mother

My dear boy [David], June 30th '74

I believe it was Samuel Johnson who said, "Gratitude is a fruit of great cultivation, you do not find it among gross people," so thank all your friends for their kindness to you and invite them to visit you this summer and we will do all we can to repay them. You know we will have an abundance of fruit—strawberries, cherries, apples, peaches, plums, raspberries, gooseberries, chickens, ducks, lambs and hams. If we can't repay them, I pray the Lord will and He is the surest security. The thought of seeing my darling children is so cheering. I am counting the days until I hear your sweet voices and see your bright faces at home again. There are few families who love each other as we do. No matter how far you go you must always love and cling to each other.

Your aff. Mother

Sept. 20th 1874

My darling children in Missouri [Florence and Betsy],

Sunday, Alfred Gwathmey brought Rosalie, as she was the only one that night I took her to sleep with me in the big bed and almost fancied I had one of my dear daughters again.

The next morning we put up two new bedsteads and sheeted all the beds. Before we were quite ready, Mr. George Leigh came bringing his oldest daughter. Then Uncle and Martha brought Browne and Jimmie Jones, Maria Louisa and Nellie.

I think his mother had been lecturing him about staying because he wouldn't even come in. Then Mr. Acree and Page arrived. We sat down to dinner the first day with the same number we ended with last session—seven girls. They are so sweet and pretty, all but Nellie who is more subdued than ever. I hope you have settled in as happily.

Your aff. Mother

After graduating from VMI and spending the summer at Green Mount, David had left before the school opened and had gone to Missouri to visit Fred and his family and thence to Texas.

Sherman, Texas

My dear Mother,   Oct. 6, 1874

Yours and Sister's letters with Willie's photo came this morning, just think in only six days! I really don't feel much farther from home than I did in Mo. Willie's picture is right good but doesn't do him justice. I have been intending to write for some time but before I got something to do I didn't feel I could write very interestingly or cheerfully.

Since I have been in the office of the hotel I have been quite busy fixing up the accounts & getting things to rights generally.

My week in Mo. was as pleasant as any I ever spent and it was with a little reluctance that I left. Miss Boykin is one of the finest singers I ever heard, & I fell completely in love with her voice. Miss Fannie is very pretty and sweet; saw right much of her and think I made a *little* impression on her, but didn't get up my courage to ask her to wait for me. Little Minnie is the prettiest little thing I ever saw. Mrs. Seddon is such a dear lady. When I left she put up for me the finest and most beautiful lunch which lasted for several days.

I started off that Monday morning quite blue but tried to hide it. Had to lay over in Sedalia that night, & next morning at sunrise took the M. K. & T. for Texas. The southwestern part of Mo. was literally burned up. Corn was very small and so dry that some of it caught fire from the train and burned up. Near the Mo. & Kansas line I began to see grasshoppers

& their effects. Every tree had been stripped of its leaves, even
the weeds were eaten. At Oswego, we stopped to take on water,
I got off the train & took about five steps from the tracks,
without exaggeration I suppose as many as a bushel got up
from under & around my feet. At Vinita in Indian Territory,
or the Nation as the people down here call it, I saw my first
Indian. The Creeks, Cherokees, Choctaws & other tribes
through whose country I came are very friendly & civilized,
but those tribes in the Western part of the Nation are terrible,
such as the Kiowas, Commanches & Apaches. There is not a
day that we don't hear of some raiding party & of their terrible
outrages or murders upon settlers in the frontier.

The Nation is the prettiest country I ever saw, rolling prairie
& pretty well timbered. The land is rich as can be with hills
or ridges upon which one can see for miles around. The country
is not inhabited along the railroad at all. I don't think I saw
50 people from Vinita to Red River, the boundary between
the Nation and Texas. My attention was attracted to a mound
between Muskogee & Oketaha about half mile from the railroad.
In the center was an image of a woman, cut out of stone, with
her hands & arms extending towards heaven & her head inclined
downward. Along the route, I saw several herdsmen on horseback watching over droves of cattle, thousands of heads. The
poor fellows looked so lonesome & sunburnt. They say it is a
money making business, but terribly confining, out in all kinds
of weather & ruffing it generally.

You have doubtless received my postal telling you I have a
position which pays my expenses. It's clerk in a hotel. I am
given my board & washing & the privilege of leaving whenever
I can find something more profitable.

There are a good many pretty young ladies in town, but
not very wealthy, they say. Southern Texas is the place to find
rich girls, this part has so recently been settled that the people
haven't had time to make money. The climate is delightful but
the majority of the people outside of town are ruff and
uneducated.

Am expecting letters from parties on the frontier telling me
whether they can do anything for me in the surveying or engineering line. A friend knows the Chief Engineer of the Texas

& Pacific R.R. and spoke to him about me. He said work was very dull at present but if I was willing to run the risks, he would employ me as an axman, $30 pr. mo. but he would advise against it, for there were a great many worthy young men who had been doing the same thing for several years & they must be promoted before anybody else. Besides the young men were constantly being killed by the Indians. I think I will remain here longer & watch my chances as several men of influence in town are looking out for me. So direct your letters to this place until you hear differently.

Affectionately,
D. W. Fleet

My dear Sister [Lou],   Oct. 10th
    You know you & Ma very kindly offered to send me some money if I needed any. I expect I will have to go farther south to try & make more & when I do I will need a little money. Therefore I am asking if you can please send me $25.00 by check as soon as you can. Do hope it won't be long before I have it in my power to help you all.
    I heard from a young man whom I wrote to two weeks ago, who is a surveyor on the frontier. He said nothing was doing in his line at all. The Indians were very bad & had stopped all emigration. Am almost inclined to go & work on a farm. I am blessed in that my health is very good. Times are getting harder & harder I believe, but I don't intend to despair.

Best love to all,
D. W. Fleet

    David found a place to teach in a small school in Cleburne but he had difficulty in collecting money from his patrons. His Mother wrote, "It may seem a mysterious Providence, my son, that anyone so anxious to make a living should find it so hard to do but do not give in to discouragement as that is the devil's sharpest tool."

My dear Sisters [Florence and Betsy],   Dec. 30, '74

I want to express my gratitude to you for the beautiful, unexpected and most acceptable present. I hope you did not inconvenience yourselves while working the slippers, as I know time is very precious, and I appreciate all the more the loving affection which prompted every stitch. I miss you both very much—although we have a houseful of girls there are none to take *your* places. Miss Bettie Bird came to see us and said she didn't think there was anything serious the matter with Nannie. If Christmas could last all the time, she didn't think she would need any medicine. Seems she would have learned before this, life is not a series of Christmases.

Write sometime to your most affectionate brother,

J. W. Fleet

P.S. I read my letter to Ma and she said when we get out of debt, she will give us a *large* party.

Dear Sister Bessie,   Summer House Dec. 31st 1874

Mr. Councill broke up school on last Friday week—he intended breaking up the following Tuesday, but the boys broke it up for him. I went straight to Green Mount. Pa sent for me the next morning. On arriving home, I found arrangements had been made for me to take Aunt Lizzie to Richmond, she wants to have her grinders remodeled.

I had a serious notion of going from Richmond to New York this Christmas to have my broken nose mended but decided to wait til summer as Willie told me there would be several parties in the neighborhood and we took them all in.

I got the best report the last time that I've gotten since I have been going to Aberdeen—first in all my classes.

Miss Alice sends her love to you and Si Florence. The old year is about pegged out, I wish you both a happy new one.

Write soon to your affectionate bro.

Tommie [Haynes]

My darling children [Florence and Betsy],   Jan. 5th 1875

Will you believe it eleven girls have come and not one cent have they brought, so we can only live on credit for awhile longer. Yesterday Col. Pollard rode by and asked if I could receive the hundred dollars which he got for our lots in West Point. He told me he would send it by Judge Jones from Court. That will have to go to pay on one of the Fauntleroy claims for $335. I hear they will leave Glenwood, it makes no difference with me where they go but I shall be glad when they go where I can't see or hear of them—I can't do justice to the subject so will change it.

I haven't heard from David and can't help but be anxious about him. Tell Fred if he has heard and if he needs money, please send it to him and I will see that he is paid, as David may hesitate to ask me for it.

I am so glad you are taking tapestry lessons, Florence, do you know it is the favorite work of queens and ladies of their court—at least it used to be. Mary, Queen of Scotland did a great deal of it during her imprisonment and the nuns in the convents amuse themselves with it too. I don't wonder at it, do you? It is so fascinating. Please express my gratitude to your teacher for taking such pains to teach my little girls, was she born in France?

We are very much exercised about what Will should do next year, whether to send him to Richmond College or the University. I prefer the latter if we can manage it.

Love to all and a kiss for the darling little "comfort" [Minnie]—bless her and you too, my precious children.

Yr. aff. Mother

Dear D.   Jan. 16, 1875

Only time for a word. Yr. postal came promptly telling of your arrival at Cleburne. Write soon & *very* fully. Sit up an hour or two longer and tell me all about yr.self. I sent you a budget of home letters last week & will always keep you posted by sending all that come.

Here is my advice. Write to Maj. Douglas to try to get you a place in the Marines & if he fails you won't be hurt. If he gets it, you can go in for a few years, make enough money to get square with the world & save enough to start in whatever you wish. If you like the profession, stick to it. If not, you can resign at any time. You will have a great deal of time, & if you would study engineering & other things, you might make it very profitable.

If that fails & you are not in a position wh. will pay you better than a small school near Gonzales, you might go there. Tom Harwood is a kind fellow & will do what he can to help you. If your work pays you where you are, stick to it.

We get on pretty well. Some new students coming & some going out. Have just finished examinations and begin a new term Monday. Am driven very hard with work, hence no more now.

Yours aff'y
A. F. Fleet

February 14, 1875

My darling little sisters [Florence and Betsy],

Last Sunday it snowed all day and Mon., Tues., and Wed. were the coldest days I ever felt. Fortunately we had plenty of wood, but I never saw it so hard to keep warm even with blazing fires. Wed. evening, we had a nice time skating and sliding each other in kitchen chairs at the icepond.

I promised Nellie to let all the girls go home with her Friday and although the roads were bad, Claggett came up and took them down in the wagon. All the Aberdeen boys were there and of course they enjoyed themselves hugely. Claggett and George Councill brought the girls back Sunday evening and stayed until after eleven. We sang a good many of the sweet old songs we used to sing together. Claggett grew quite sentimental in his recollections of "bygone days." Willie and I concluded the old fire is not quite extinguished. Do you think it will ever be rekindled, little Bess? [5]

Your loving sister, Lou

[5] Claggett was always in love with Betsy. Even after he became engaged to Julia Latané he wrote a letter to Betsy begging her to marry him. . .

Lexington, Mo. Sunday, Mar. 7th
My dear Mother & Sister,

Mr. Tom Seddon, who was looking for a letter from his lady love & hasn't as many scruples as Brother, went to the P. O. this morning and brought us your dear letters. We are charmed to hear of the organ; hope it may prove as great a pleasure and comfort as we have anticipated and such a bargain too.

The long expected concert came off last Friday. The house was crowded & the whole thing a complete success everyone says. Sis Bess was as much scared as I was when I came out & says she got as far down in her seat as she could for fear I would fail. But after I finished she felt very proud of me, thought she had never heard me play so well. On getting home I found a beautiful little gold cross set in pearls from Prof. Gimbel. I send you the card that came with it. Maggie Norton acquitted herself finely and he gave her a little heart charm.

About living at home next year—it is the thing above all others I would rather do. You must never think of our not being .satisfied to live in the country again. We both prefer it to town, and will be so glad to work together at home.

Love to all,
Florence

Aylett, Va.
Dear David,   March 17th '75

I received your letter on yesterday. In reply I must say whilst it would afford me much pleasure to serve you in the way you request, I do not feel I can give you any encouragement. There are very few such appointments made from civil life & those that are have to be distributed among the several states so the appointment of your young friend so recently will make against you. But if you wish to press the matter, get all the testimonials you can—particularly from the Va. Mil: Inst: & send them to me in December when I shall take my seat in Congress. I will present them in person to the Sec. of War & do what I can for you.

Yr. very truly
B. B. Douglas

My dear children,   April 4th '75
   Andrew Montague [6] has been extremely ill at the University,
so ill his Father could not see him for several days—overwork—
he was rather better and there is some hope of his recovery
when we last heard from him.
   We put the organ in the dining room where the bookcase
was. Now with that and the two pianos the house is filled with
music when the girls are practising. Priscilla spent last night
and said she never saw such a hearty, healthy set of girls in
her life and several mothers have expressed themselves as delighted with their daughters' improvement which is very gratifying to us. Yesterday all of us went to St. Stephens to church.
Jeannette Ryland asked me to let Willie go home with them.
I told her he drove the wagon and as Tom was not there—
he worships at Bruington these days, Page, you know—I
couldn't spare Will. "Oh," she said, "pick up another boy I'm
sure he would be more than willing." So I asked Beale and
Booker, both came. I asked little Shack too, but he declined,
said he was afraid of so many girls. Lucian Acree came too
and Claggett to even up the boys and girls. I had an elegant
quarter of lamb and chicken pie, etc. Then gooseberry tarts
and sponge cake. We can't well help having company on Sun-
days as the boys have to bring their sisters and altho some of
them left we had as many more for supper, and you know we
have been accustomed to it all our lives. You have not been
forgotten for they all sent love, as I do.
                                                Your aff. Mother
P. S. Wouldn't it be well to take organ lessons too. It would
enable you to play for Sunday School or church and perhaps
teach others to do so. Remember, daughters, I am not trying
to "shape your destiny"—I leave that to a higher power—only
giving you a choice.

Dear Mrs. Fleet,   Apl 23 1875
   I am more than glad to have it in my power to say that the
Court, at its term this week fully and finally ratified and con-
firmed the compromise agreement, and discharged Dr. Fleet's

   [6] Andrew Jackson Montague (1862–1937) was governor of Virginia, 1902–6, and a
member of the U.S. House of Representatives, 1913–37.

estate from all liability except that assumed by the agreement itself.

Now bear in mind my *promises* in your behalf, about payments to Capt. Smith, McConky & Parr and Mrs. Fauntleroy. Let nothing but an *impossibility* prevent their fulfilment.

Very truly yours,

J. H. C. Jones

[This letter was sent to Fred with the following penciled note] Of course we will pay all these things Mr. Jones promised. Mrs. Fauntleroy, $500, McC & P $350; Ella about $800 minus two years board and tuition. I hope she will come back next year and we can pay more in that way, the organ will prove an attraction. We owe Maj. Douglas for legal work, but hope to have his little daughter. We will manage it all with the help of the Lord.

My dearest David, G. M. June 14 '75

We were rejoiced to have your postal telling us of your improved health. I trust you will have strength to hold out to the end, and can collect your money and come home to us. Mother sends her love, she is busy pickling and preserving cherries and says she can do it with ten times the pleasure because she thinks you will have some. You need the rest and home will be the best place to take it.

How would you like to help me with my school next fall? We are determined to send Will to the University in the fall and you have no idea how we dread being left alone. If you help me, of course we will share the profits equally and I will teach you to play on the organ. I can assure you of $200.00 free of all expense and will let you go as soon as you have a more advantageous offer.

Be sure to write us when and where to meet you, with best love from all,

Your devoted sister, Lou

My darling Fred & David, July 23rd '75

I send this to Fred and he will send it on to David and save me one letter, you both know I don't like to write. I received your letter and thank you for letting me hear from the dear

sick children. I hope most earnestly they are entirely well now.
I put out some kindness a week or so ago and have faith to
believe the Lord will repay it to my children. One evening Mrs.
Sterling brought over a young man named Clopton, a cousin
of hers from Richmond—Susie's brother, David, whom they
fear has consumption (both his mother and sister died of it
recently) and they have sent him to the country for fresh air.
I have sent him ice, fruit and Mary's good loaf bread several
times. All the time having a presentiment that some of my
children were sick and it would be returned to them. When
he came over and thanked me, I told him he was most welcome
I had so many children entirely out of my reach, it was a real
pleasure to show a little kindness to somebody's child close
by.

We are all well and much cheered by the fair prospects before
us. The whole country seems completely revived by the most
delightful season we have had since the war. We have not suffered a single day for rain and everything looks green and beautiful. Then too, it is so favorable to our school for you know
Virginians will educate their children if they possibly can even
if they have money for little else, so altogether we are very
hopeful.

I have been collecting and paying off some debts which does
us honest people a world of good. We owed a debt of $200
at Cardozo's which has annoyed us for nearly two years and
have just paid it all. Major Douglas only charges thirty dollars
for what he did in the Fauntleroy business. It was so much
more moderate than we expected, I got Willie to hand it to
him this week. Report has it he will marry Miss Fanny Lockhart
at last. She cannot resist the temptation of being a Congress-
man's wife.

All send love to all of you,
Your aff. Mother

With Maria Louisa Fleet it was touch and go for her children. As
soon as she got one through college, she started another off. Florence
and Bessie completed the junior and senior classes of the Baptist
Female College. Bess remained in Missouri and joined the faculty

of the college of which Fred was president, teaching Latin and German. Florence returned to Green Mount with glowing recommendations from her teachers. Professor Charles Gimbel wrote, "It gave me great pleasure to have Miss Florence Fleet in my classes as she is an excellent scholar and musician, successfully mastering the most difficult classical works on the organ as well as on the piano." The girls also studied ornamental and fancy work under a French woman who wrote: "Miss Florence Fleet has executed a beautiful piece of tapestry depicting the story of St. Pierre's *Paul and Virginia. . . .* We regret to part with the picture but much more with so refined, lovely and gentle a friend."

Florence added German to the school's curriculum as well as organ and vocal music and relieved Lou of the mathematics classes. The school year ran from September 20, 1875, to June 22, 1876. The expanded brochure of the Green Mount Home School for Young Ladies explained how each day was to be spent.

The Bible will be studied systematically each day by all the pupils of the School during the whole course. The government of the School is designed to be accomplished by three rules: First, Obedience to teachers; this must be prompt, cheerful, faithful. Second, God's Golden Rule—"As ye would that men should do to you, do ye even so to them." Third, A place for everything and everything in its place. Daily exercise in the open air will be required. After walking, in the evening comes the "charming hour" of the day. Then all the girls, with work of some kind, gather in one room while the best readers read aloud some pleasant and improving book. During the winter evenings, a lovelier picture can rarely be found than these bright, busy, happy girls. Every effort will be made to cultivate the good morals and gentle manners with which we would have each one of our scholars adorned.

Will entered Richmond College with his friend Tom Haynes, who wrote Bessie, "Visiting the girls in Richmond is like doing penance after being with you." David found a teaching position in a Texas college.

Mansfield, Texas

Dear Brother [Fred],   Sept. 6th 1875

I arrived here last Saturday after having travelled all night. Today the students were matriculated and the classes arranged. We opened with 61 & Prof. Collier says that is about a fifth of the number he expects.

Prof. Collier is a preacher of the Presbyterian faith, & a graduate of Yale. He has been teaching for about 15 years in Texas, & has gained quite a name as an educator.

I am to have the departments of Latin & Mathematics, such as Trigonometry, Surveying, Analytical Geometry & Calculus. We have some grown young men who seem to be in earnest & determined to succeed. I will have no class in Latin this session higher than Horace.

We have sons & daughters of some of the most prominent men in Texas. The College is not quite completed; but sufficiently to go in next week. It is three stories, frame with a large room for a chapel on the first floor & on the second, four rooms for the professors. Mine has not been assigned yet but will be in a few days. I expect I will have my hands pretty full with a good deal of work to do but I am perfectly willing if I get paid for it. He is to give me $75 per month with a prospect of more. I made about $30 from my school in Cleburne and collected it all but one bill, sufficient to pay expenses during vacation. I hope I will be able to collect some from Alvarado shortly.

My health and spirits are good and I am prepared to go right to work. Let me hear from you & tell me how your school commenced. I will send you a circular, I must close & go to work.

Aff'y, D. W. Fleet

According to the circular, "Mansfield College is situated on the east side of Cross Timbers twenty miles from Dallas, seventeen from Fort Worth, twenty from Cleburne and twenty from Waxahachie. Society, best grade."

Mansfield, Texas

My dear little Betsy,   Sept. 24, 1875

I was very thankful to hear you arrived safety in Lexington, Mo. and know you met with a warm reception.

I am very much better for the work this session than I was last, for you know, I did not have any rest during the summer. My health is very good and I have as much as I can do. We commence at half past eight, from that time I have a class in English Grammar, University Arithmetic, University Algebra, Surveying, French Composition & Rhetoric; each lasting half an hour. Then I eat dinner and commence again at 1:30 with beginning Latin, Virgil and a class in Caesar, which has read nearly through the course in Latin but doesn't know much about it & am reviewing them and teaching them to parse; Horace, and from 3:30 to 4:00, German. Have six young men in German and they all like it very much, they are beginners. When I get through I am pretty tired you must know.

The other day a young man came while we were at dinner and asked to make an announcement. He said he was going to preach that night and wanted everyone to hear him, that he was a prophet and said the devil was in Texas—that I didn't dispute but we found the poor fellow was deprived of his reason.

Your devoted brother,

David

My dear Will,   Sept. 28th 1875

I received a dear letter from Alexander yesterday from Kentucky enclosing this check, and we think it best to send it to you that you may lose no time in insuring the house and furniture for at least $5,000. Write me the amount you paid and keep the papers until you come home as I don't trust the mails. With what is left over if you want the clothes now, get them; if not at once, pay Starke on our account as far as you can. I enclose their account so you can see how we stand. Then when you get the $76 from Mr. Jones, you must pay the college and your board. Aren't you thankful we love to pay our debts and that it is getting easier to do.

Alexander wrote so cheerfully, said "I sincerely hope you

are prospering in your enterprises. These are very trying times from a pecuniary point of view, perhaps the climax of hard times. But as surely as you live there is a good time ahead of us and you will live to see it." Dear boy, I hope he will live to have a better home. I don't think you can compute the worth of a cheerful spirit in dollars. Lou says mine has been worth millions to us, for if I had been despairing like Mr. Fauntleroy and Capt. Smith, I would never have borrowed the money and pushed the education of all you children. There is no computing the amount of happiness in the world to ourselves, and others we may influence by cultivating a cheerful, happy, hopeful disposition. Besides being a religious *duty,* it is good policy always to look on the bright side. I acknowledge it is a gift from God and am thankful for I believe I should have been in my grave years ago—or only dragged out a miserable existence without it.

Your aff. Mother

[Minutes of the Evergreen Society]

Sept. 29, 1875. Today we reorganized our Evergreen Society having elected as President, Page Acree; Regulator, Hannah Bagby; Secretary, Manie Leigh; and Treasurer, Mary Washington. We regret that five of our members did not return but we welcome three new members and hope they will prove useful to our Society. Our teachers played "Meditation," Miss Florence at the organ and Miss Lou at the piano. Lottie played the banjo and it sounded like a fish on a hot griddle. Nellie played "Angel Voices Ever Near" which gave consolation to us who are away from home for the first time. Then Miss Lou said, "We will now hear the Great Centennial March of General Washington by his kinswoman, Miss Mary Washington," who played it remarkably well and all of us congratulated her on her rapid progress in music. Kate, like Macaulay, entertained us with brilliant flashes of silence.

Dear Child [Betsy]   Oct. 8, 1875

Today is your birthday! You have never been anything but a blessing and pleasure to your loved ones and I trust God will lend you to earth for many a year to make it better and brighter by your presence.

Do not let your musical talent be buried under the rubbish of neglect.

I went down for a visit at Goshen and Uncle James remarked on how wonderfully we had gotten along and I told him it was by working together and helping each other. Everything there was so quiet, I could only feel thankful for the house full of life I have around me to keep me young.

Your aff. Mother

Richmond College

Dear Si Bessie,   Oct. 24th 1875

I am glad to do your errand, as to inconveniencing me, if it does, it doesn't matter.

Jackson's statue [7] is to be unveiled next Tuesday and I reckon Dr. Hoge [8] will "split a horn," as he's the orator. The Cadets are here from the Institute. They, with the companies, will form a procession and march about town a bit, and then to the Capitol Square. The faculty and students of this college are assigned a place in the procession, which we will accept as 'twill be our only hope of hearing the speakers, as the procession has to go into the Capitol Square before they will let anyone else enter. They have erected the base of the statue and lots of arches and fixtures about town. We will have Tuesday, Wednesday and Thursday holiday, so I reckon we will have only a day or two at Christmas. I witnessed the procession which marched with Gen. Pickett's remains today—the Cadets formed a part of it.

It was good of Will to write you I was studying hard but I am more and more convinced that I don't know what *study* is.

---

[7] Thomas Jonathan (Stonewall) Jackson's statue in Capitol Square, presented by an English admirer, was sculpted by J. H. Foley, R. A.

[8] Dr. Moses Hoge (1818–1899) was minister of the Second Presbyterian Church in Richmond for fifty-four years.

If you want me to come up to your expectations, lower them enough for me to reach them. I am surprised Miss Cam Pollard is so taken with my photograph, I don't feel complimented as you supposed for the photograph is what I was; what I am, alas! too well I know.

My love to Si Florence and yourself,
Tommie

My darling David,   Nov. 4th '75
I forgot I am writing to a grave professor and only think of *my* precious boy. I often wonder if you are as much of a boy as you used to be or if you are a dignified gentleman all the time now.

I sent you a paper giving an account of the unveiling of Gen. Jackson's statue in Richmond. The first thing I thought of when I heard the Cadets were there was—if only they had had something of the kind while my boy was there, wouldn't he have enjoyed it. Will went and saw the old Stonewall Brigade and Mrs. Jackson and her daughters. He heard Dr. Hoge is courting Mrs. Jackson.

You did perfectly right to apply to us, instead of Fred for help. Never mind about the bond, when the sisters and I need, you pay us then, if only in kindness and love. Remember love is worth more than "untold gold" for where love is nearly every other blessing will be there. "Love is Heaven and Heaven is love."

God bless and keep you always,
Yr. aff. Mother

My darling boy [Will],   Sat. morn.
Thank you for your dear long letter. Mr. Jones sent me $30 by Nellie, I thought of paying Mr. Councill but concluded to pay the hands and to send you $15 to pay your next month's board so you will feel comfortable when you come to the table.

Monday Walter, Tom, Joshua and Adam dug the sweet potatoes. Harry hauled them up in the wagon and Lorelle, Amanda and I sorted and packed them away, about 15 bushels.

You must not trouble about home affairs while I am as strong and well as I am now; I can get along and why not believe the Lord will supply all our need in the future as He has in the days past. Mr. Jones told me he thinks he can get $4 an acre for the 80 acres this side of Dunkirk—$320 at once, what a help it will be! Take a good occasion and thank Prof. Harris for waiting with us. Tell him you are the last of six to be educated, we all pull together and hope to pull through after awhile. My dear boy, it is a good thing to have all the privileges you now enjoy but it is better to be able to appreciate and improve them. I know you will do your best—haven't you been doing that all your dear life? Who knows that better than your Mother and she will always pray for you and encourage you and trust and *love* you, and do all she can to help you make a man of yourself. You have patience and keep pegging away. Don't expect too much of yourself the first year, but take things quietly.

I have concluded not to send the wagon load of sheep this fall, the mules will be tired when they are done plowing and I have readily sold two or three quarters of the two I have killed and this I can continue to do, and then have the wool too.

When you write again tell us something about the election and state of the country. You know we very seldom see any gentlemen to tell us anything and we don't subscribe to the magazines and papers we used to. Never since the war could we have gotten along without you and it is such a comfort to have you in Richmond.

Your aff. Mother

Mansfield College
My dear Mother,   Nov. 15th 1875

Your long and interesting letter was received, I intended to answer it last Saturday but I went down to Alvaredo and my friends seemed very glad to see me. I succeeded in collecting only about $25.00. I don't know how I will come out collecting this session but think there is no doubt about getting all my salary, even if I do not collect all. In teaching, one has the consolation of knowing he is doing a great deal to help his fellow man as you wrote me, but such hard work and no pay doesn't help me for I have to work out of debt, you know.

When I came to Mansfield, Mrs. Halsell sent me word by a student to come to see her because she was a Virginian too. She was born in Norfolk and came here when she was about twelve. She is about 40 now. She is very kind and hospitable and plays splendidly on the piano. Last night I went to see her and her mother, Mrs. Harris. Mrs. Harris asked me to sing the *Ninety and Nine* for her. I did and before I got through the old lady got as happy as could be. Shouted and blessed the Lord & didn't get over it all evening. She gave each of us a hug that nearly crushed me. I thought if my singing had such an effect, I had better go & join Moody & Sankey.[9] I really don't believe the old lady could help it for she had always been very gentle and quiet and sensible.

Thank Page and Mamie for sending their love. (Entre nous, who is Mamie? but don't tell her).

With my love to my little sister and my big sister Floss and to you, dear Mother,

Aff'y D. W. Fleet

Mansfield College, Mansfield, Texas
Nov. 21, 1875

Maj. B. B. Douglas
Dear Sir:

I received your kind letter, offering to do what you could towards getting me a commission in the U.S. Marines when you took your seat in Congress last spring. I know the chances are quite doubtful and such appointments are very rarely made from civil life, but if I could be so fortunate as to get such a position, I shall be very thankful, and at the same time under many obligations to you, for even making the effort for me.

I have a pretty good position at present as instructor in Latin and Applied Math; but I fear my salary is not altogether certain. I am very anxious to get out of debt and help my Mother and our estate. A commission in the marines, or in any other branch

---

[9] Dwight Lyman Moody (1837–1899) and Ira David Sankey (1840–1902) were American evangelists; Sankey wrote "Ninety and Nine," a hymn based on Matt. 18:12–13.

of the service, would enable me to do this much sooner than my present position.

My kindest regards for you and your family.

Very respectfully,
Your obedient servant,
D. W. Fleet

My dear child [Will]   Dec. 2

This snow reminds me to ask you to go to Putney & Watts and try to get me a pair of shoes, you know what sort—size 2 or 2½. When the snow is gone I want to send Walter over with some apples for you. I put in some pretty ones to give away, but you stick to the winter cheese and try to take care of some to last until I can send more.

The girls will send you and Tom some wedding cake "to dream on"—I have no doubt you will eat it. Florence wrote Bess an account of the wedding but says she will tell you about it when you come Christmas. This unexpected weather found us with plenty of wood. James William bought Smithfield for $5.00 an acre.

You and Tom take care of each other—
Your aff. Mother

Mansfield, Texas

My dear Sis Bess,   Dec. 31, 1875

I have spent a very pleasant Christmas—hunting, visiting a little and eating. It has been a glorious rest and recreation. Have been out nearly every day and have killed 40 prairie hens, a good many partridges, hares and squirrels.

Tomorrow, the beginning of a new year, we begin our work in the college. The season closes the last Friday in Jan'y until which time I will remain here and after which I am determined to leave. I have lost my place in Alvarado not being able to get off here in time. How I would like to come to Lexington to see you & Brother and his family and to hear Miss Boykin sing. Perhaps I may go out "west" about 200 miles where the Indians are & try my fortune among the ruffians of the west.

I don't think I could stand another spring term with the work I have to do and the close confinement.

There is a great deal of excitement down here about war & I wouldn't be surprised if there is one. If so I will be in the first volunteer regiment to leave Texas to see that Tilden is inaugurated.[10] That may sound a little rash but nevertheless, it is true unless things change materially from what they are at present.

Write soon to your affectionate

D. W. Fleet

My darling child [David],   Jan. 2nd '76

Friday, Will happened to meet Maj. Douglas in Ayletts, he said he filed an application for the Marine Corps for you. There are only two ahead of you—both recommended by the President. The man expressed himself as pleased at getting an application from Texas as they wished to scatter the appointments all over the country. My first thought was I shall see my precious child and you will, I hope, have more congenial employment. The pay of $1,000 or $1,200 will be certain and will enable you to pay your debts.

We have had a delightful holiday, I stayed quietly at home but the "children" frolicked considerably. Lou and Will dined at Mr. John Ryland's on Christmas day. Jacky is coming home after five years of failures and disappointments—sad isn't it? But you know he would neither take an education nor stay with his father on the farm. Now he is glad to get back and go to work at home. I struggled under so many difficulties, as you well know and insisted on giving you all the best education I could and now this beautiful year opens very encouragingly. Back to Christmas week—Tues. they dined at Mr. Fauntleroy's, then Will went to a large party at Wm Haynes'. Wed. Will carried Floss to a party at Mr. James Latané's—there they enjoyed themselves very much all night long, did not get back until after sunrise. The night was very dark and rainy so

---

[10] In 1876 the disputed election of Samuel J. Tilden, Democrat, and Rutherford B. Hayes, Republican, was decided in favor of Hayes.

no attempt was made to break up until day break. They rested
Thursday and Friday night all went to a large party at Judge
Jones, got back at four, enjoyed it very much—so you see old
King and Queen is alive and lively.

We have made all arrangements about help. Mary and her
family stay of course, Walter and his, Tom and Amanda, and
then we have plenty of labor for the farm. We are blessed in
respect to servants. Mammy sends her love and says she "will
dive down in the bottom of her *chist* and get her nice clothes
to wait on you even if you don't bring your bride with you,"
she wants to see you so much.

Your aff. Mother

My dear Fred,   Monday night, Jan. 3rd
    I can't let Lou's letter go without saying a word. She always
says so much and says it so much better than I do. She told
you of the lively times the young folks had this holiday, I have
stayed very quietly at home and enjoyed my rest exceedingly.
I think the holidays at Christmas and Easter are very cardinal
to health, mental and physical. I always have the house cleaned
and aired. I don't think one can really enjoy *rest* unless they
have a school and see the last boarder leave and enjoy the
luxury of just milk toast or any little thing one may fancy and
feel *free*. Do you ever feel free, my son? and dear little Belle,
how does she stand it. If you all succeed in raising an endow-
ment for Wm Jewel, will you go back there?

Did you see by the Va. papers what a sensation the earthquake
produced all over the state? Did you hear or feel anything of
it? It waked up some people in this neighborhood and two of
the girls who were sleeping over the parlour, were roused and
ran over this room, thinking somone was in the house. Other
than that we were not at all disturbed. Lou remarked that we
were so accustomed to earthquakes overhead that we did not
regard this one as anything unusual.

Give our most affectionate love to Belle and Mrs. Seddon.

God bless you all,
Yr. aff. Mother

My dear Children [Fred and Belle],   Jan. 25, '76

We received your dear letters & you can hardly imagine how delighted we were to get them. Dear little Belle, if you only knew how much better than anyone else, you can write about "our darlings." I can never be thankful enough for your affection and good council. I agree with you in thinking it best to remain in the college at Lexington for a few more years altho' it would be easier for you for Fred to fill a chair in a University. But you have the satisfaction of knowing you are helping in this position and, dear child, when you are very tired, think how gladly so many people in dear old Virginia would work if they only had the work to do. Fred is a very fortunate man and should be a very happy one.

From our twelve boarders, we have only received thirty-five dollars at the second term. 'Tis true the merchants, Mr. Acree and George Leigh give me credit, and the farm supplies a good many wants, and matters might be much worse, but I had calculated on paying some pressing claims and was so disappointed as one after another came without bringing any money. It is all good and we shall not lose a dollar, I hope, but corn is low, only fifty cents a bus. and no one wants to sell if they can help it. When our sky seems overcast with clouds, it is so comforting to look towards the *West* where my dear ones are, often there is a beautiful sunset and I take comfort and courage from it.

Now, my son, can't you think of some plan to come home next summer? Couldn't you bring dear Mrs. Seddon and the babies [11] and leave them with me while you and Belle go to Philadelphia. It would be a great pleasure to the children to spend the summer in the country, to say nothing of the delight it would give the aunties and me. We will try not to spoil them.

Your aff. Mother

[11] Alexander Frederick Fleet, Jr., was born in Lexington, Mo., Oct. 13, 1875; he died June 18, 1876.

Ingleside
My dear Friends,   March 3rd 1876
Accept my most sincere thanks for your great kindness and attention to Emilie during her recent sickness at G. M. I was not surprised at it since I knew in whose care I had entrusted the keeping of my child; therefore was prepared for the angelic ministrations she received at your hands. Let me say also that I am endebted to you for saving a doctor's bill which we would have had to pay had Emilie remained at home.

With sincerest affection
Your friend, Henrietta Gwathmey

House of Representatives
Washington, D.C.
Dear David,   March 23rd 1876
Your letter was received a few days ago. After giving me great encouragement, old Robeson has done nothing and I do not believe he has the least intention of doing anything for you. My advice is to discard all thought of the appointment and turn your attention to something else. In the meantime I will not wholly give up and if unexpected success should reward my perseverance, I will promptly apprise you of the fact.

Yrs. very truly,
B. B. Douglas

[Minutes of the Evergreen Society]

April 25th 1876—It is my sad duty as secretary to write of the death of our darling little Mary [Washington]. She was right sick before Easter, but when her father sent for her, she seemed a great deal better and talked cheerfully. After she arrived at home she gradually became worse and on Tuesday April 18, she died. I cannot begin to say how much all of us miss her for we loved her dearly. Our President read the ninth chapter of Matthew and we went in the parlor today and sang "Asleep in Jesus," Miss Bessie sang "Beyond the Smiling and the Weeping" and Miss Lou sang "Remembered." We adjourned without having the regular program.

My precious child [Will]   Sept. 16, 1876

Mr. Councill has seven boarders and eight day scholars. Now
I must tell you about Dido and the little ones. The other day
she took them all out in the sunshine. I was upstairs looking
over bed linen when Mary called me down to see all five of
them standing on their hind legs taking refreshment from the
maternal fount. Said she would have called Miss Lou out of
the school room but was afraid and she was bound to show
someone such a pretty sight. We all feed Dido very well for
your sake.

Rosalie Latané's grandfather wants to bring her here for music lessons but her father seems to be afraid to spend too much
money on her, for fear he will not have enough for the still
increasing tribe of younger ones.

My devoted love to you and Tommie

Your aff. Mother

My dear Willie,   Oct. 2, '76

Tell Tom with my love, I saw his father and he was looking
better than usual.

How are you getting on? Does your work seem hard? Do
you ever feel sorry you are at college, or are you as thankful
as you ought to be.

You just ought to see the little dogs, they love me almost
as much as they do their mother. We don't allow them to come
in the house or down the cellar and they look so pretty sitting
at the door of their house waiting to be fed. I suppose it is
my love for you that makes me pet your dogs so much. You
would be amused to see me walking about the yard with the
puppies nipping at my ankles.

I am already looking forward to Christmas because I will
see you then. Bless you, my boy,

Your aff. Mother

My dear child [Will],   Oct. 27th '76

I was delighted to get the shoes, they fit as well as any I
ever had and came in so well for this rainy damp weather. I
will try to send Walter with the vinegar next Tuesday and you

take what ever it sells for and get anything you may want. Another lighter of wood went off this morning. I hear the tea I sent for to New York was sent by Alexander Bagby, please inquire for it and send it over by Walter. Isn't it good to get those things again.

Next week, I will get Elijah to stop the icepond, I hadn't thought of it and am so glad you mentioned it. The little dogs are beauties, just as fat as pigs. The one we sent Alfred Gwathmey was hailed with great delight by his little children. Little Bessie held out her arms to it saying, "Kiss your little Sis."

A note from Bess said little Min goes to Church with her father and they sing out of the same hymn book. Did you ever expect to hear of Fred's taking a daughter to church to sit by him?

Love to my boys from,
Yr. aff. Mother

Bewdley

My dear Bessie,   Dec. 22nd 1876

I had a glorious time this summer, especially while I was in Staunton, which you know is my old home and of course I have a great many friends there. Maggie and I made up our minds to enjoy ourselves from morning till night (midnight I should say).

Among other things we took a lively interest in the politics of the day, and inspired the youth of our acquaintance, by precept and animated exhortations, with a laudable amount of party zeal. Two of the beaux, knowing our proclivity, came up one night and asked us to go with them to the Town Hall to hear a political speech! That was branching out in a new line for Staunton females, but finding that a few other ladies would go if we did, of course we were charmed to introduce the fashion.

The hall is a new one and is said to be the largest in the State. It was crowded with men of all sorts and conditions, but way up in a little corner by the stage, we found the ladies about twenty in number! They looked like a pitiful little band amid their rough surroundings, but nothing daunted we pushed through the crowd and got seats. The speaker at last was introduced, Major John Daniel, the "Lame Lion of Lynchburg." He is considered one of the finest orators in the State and his speech on this occasion did him credit, if I can be considered a judge. Such deafening applause I never imagined! and such elegant music from the band. I was never so excited in my life. During one burst of applause I surprised myself and amused my neighbors by shouting "Hurrah for Tilden!" at the top of my voice.

Since getting home about the middle of November I have been as quiet as a mouse, haven't been anywhere, seen anybody or done anything. The beaux of King & Queen have, with few exceptions, gone away and those who remain have gotten married. Mr. & Mrs. James Ryland took tea with us last night. The bride and groom looked smiling but theirs seems to be a "quiet happiness" as they had little or nothing to say other than they were "very well."

Most of our flowers are a little injured owing to a crack in the pit doors, but my "Bessie" is in the parlor window and looks beautiful.

Sincerely your friend,
Julia Latané [12]

Lexington, Mo.
Feb'y 18, 1877

My dear Mother;

As you know I have been suffering from a cough since before Christmas but I have had a very severe attack, worse than any I can remember. The night I arrived I was taken with such an acute pain in my right side that I slept none at all. The doctor pronounced it neuralgia caused by coming from so much warmer climate to this. We hadn't had any fire for a week before I left Texas & I nearly froze on the train coming up although there was a good fire all the time. When I met Brother he did not know me I looked so badly and asked my name. He doesn't look a day older nor is he nearly as gray as I am. He realizes that I have seen a pretty rough time & tells me he

---

[12] Julia Latané, the daughter of Bishop James Latané, married Claggett B. Jones, who became judge of the Thirteenth Judicial Circuit of Virginia.

wants me to remain here perfectly contented and build up, that I can read & study & help him until next fall, when he & I both think I will go to the University of Virginia and study medicine.

Little Betsy was with me every moment she wasn't otherwise employed and rendered me untold assistance. Bless her little heart, I can never forget nor repay her for it. Brother was just as kind and sympathetic as he could be. Mrs. Seddon was so good and kind that I concluded no place on earth was good enough for her.

David in Lexington, Mo.

Yesterday I sat up nearly all day and today I am feeling so much better I went down to dinner and am writing to you.

I received the express package from Willie yesterday with three prs socks & four silk handkerchiefs. I gave Brother his two, for which he sends many thanks and says they are the first he has had since the war. For mine & the socks you have my warmest thanks, dear Mother, & to Willie for his trouble. I hope he has come out successfully with his examinations.

Bro' is very blue over the political condition of the country, in fact, so is everybody else. Minnie is very sweet and smart.

Love to all,
Aff'y, D. W. Fleet

My dear little Bess,   Feb. 17, 1877

I am so glad you could be a comfort and help to our dear David, we are willing to forego the pleasure of your letters.

I took a most unusual holiday Monday & went with Ma to see Kate Taliaferro, who is staying at Marlboro with her three little girls. Last Sunday while she and the Dr. were at church, their house took fire and in less than an hour was entirely consumed. All his books, medicines, instruments—in fact everything they had was burned. They had dined at Newtown, when they were nearly home they met a negro boy who asked them where they were going. When they told him "home," he replied "You ain't got no home, 'tis all burnt up, children and everything." Imagine their feelings!! They found Dr. T's father and the children's nurse had gotten the children out but could save little for looking after them. We carried her a white counterpane, blankets, sheets, pillows and cases, soap, towels, writing paper, canned & preserved fruit and ten dollars with our needlepoint motto, "The Lord will Provide." She thanked us as the tears streamed. Her father wrote Ma, "My daughter, Kate has given me such an account of your kindness to her in this her hour of darkness, that I must write you how sincerely grateful I feel to you. You have not only consoled her with the promise that the Lord will provide—but have furnished her a present and pleasing evidence that He does provide. I do hope that her poor broken spirit will be revived by these balms of consolation which you and other loving, noble friends are pouring into it, and that God may reward you a hundred fold for your generous sympathy. Yours affectionately, R. Ryland." [13] I am more grateful than ever that we could help them, since it has gained for us the gratitude and prayers of this good man. Truly, "it is more blessed to give than to receive."

Love to all the dear ones,
Your devoted sister Lou

When Manie Leigh, one of the schoolgirls, was summoned home because of the death of her mother, Mrs. Fleet wrote her, "God gives but does not take away, he only safely keeps above for us, the treasures that we love." Her aunt replied from West View: "Manie is distressed at the time she is losing from her studies and constantly looks forward to the time when she can return to them. Dear child, I fear her school days are over as much as we would like to prolong them. We are thankful for what she has had and will always love all of you a double portion for your kindness to her. She writes cheerfully and seems to enjoy keeping house though part of the time she has no cook. She quoted you in her last letter as saying, 'Sunny hopes for the future, brighten many dark days of the present.' "

My dear child [Will]   Feb. 19th '77
    Did you really get this beautiful bonnet your *own self?* I always thought you were a man of taste and now I know it. I don't think I was ever so pleased with a new bonnet before, and best of all, nobody in all my travels can say, "She had better pay her debts instead of buying a new bonnet" for I have paid all we owe around us. Can't you study better because of it?
    Now, I want your advice about our harness. You know the carriage and buggy harness are very much the worse for wear and I must do one of two things—get harness leather and Mr. Self from Bowling Green (an excellent harness maker) to take the old ones and make new or let you inquire the price of new sets and what you could get for the old, if anything. I

---

[13] Robert Ryland (1805–1899), a clergyman, was in charge of the Virginia Baptist Seminary, 1832–40, when it was chartered as Richmond College. He was its president from 1840 to 1866.

would greatly prefer the latter if it doesn't cost too much. You see about it, dear, at your earliest convenience. We want it *good,* but of course, not showy. Walter and Lawrence commenced plowing with two double plows today.

Good night, my son,
Yr. aff. Mother

My dear Will,   Sunday March 11th '77

We received the seed and oris root and the organ spring safely, thank you so much for all. How shall we get along without you in Richmond when you go to the University. We are well and doing well except money is "awful" scarce. I've stopped all my secular papers, and if anybody says election to me, I want to fight.[14] Ignorance is bliss now.

I too, am very sorry you have no holiday this spring for we want to see you—what word shall I use to convey to your mind how much? but that is one of our trials now, which I hope will work for your good, and if your, then ours, for thank God, we all have one aim, one purpose—each other's good. I have tried to instill that in your minds all your lives and trust you will remember it always.

My son, some Saturday when you have time, get some advice about how to advertise this property. You see I will make a man of business of you yet and the best way I can pay you is to let you study law, if you wish and not bring you down to teach at home. Dear child, I trust some day you will be paid for all the loving care you have given the mother and sisters. We will finish the sowing of spring oats tomorrow (D. V.). You and Tommie take care of yourselves, this month of March is so changeable.

All send love, God bless you both,
Your loving Mother

My dear little Bess,   March 23, 1877

Last week the Aberdeen boys invited the girls to Mrs. Berkeley's old place to see them play baseball. Of course I would not hear of their going. So Lou invited the boys to come here

---

[14] Rutherford B. Hayes was inaugurated March 4, 1877.

William F. Bagby, James William Fleet, John Muscoe Garnett, Jr., and Llewellyn Bentley, classmates at Richmond College about 1877

and play. They came yesterday evening and played in the field just opposite our yard gate. After the game, they escorted the girls back and I had cake and lemonade for them. They enjoyed themselves talking and eating awhile and went home before tea. They were all very polite to the girls and we were glad to be able to give them the pleasure.

Belle Nason is such a fine type of our "Northern sisters," loves horses and driving and wants to drive the carriage if I would let her. We have such a sweet parcel of girls this year it's a real pleasure to have them.

I can't help but be disappointed at David's not coming home but I reckon it is well enough for the sake of the girls that he does not come—their expectations and hopes were very high.

We want to invite the Aberdeen boys to a croquet party sometime after Easter and the girls are anticipating great pleasure. Playing croquet is such an easy way to entertain them and make them enjoy themselves. Mammy calls it "courtinkay."

My love to each one of my Mo. family,

Your aff. Mother

[In pencil] I think Ma intends to make some linen sheets for the cradle tomorrow. You would be amused and touched to see how our every thought centers in those precious children [15] in anticipation.

Your loving sister Lou

When the daily routine bore down upon the girls too heavily there were always some who could think of ways to break it. Returning from church one Sunday, Charlotte Baylor remarked to the other girls: "Every other woman I saw was wearing a Mother Hubbard. If I dressed up in one, people would think I was in a 'delicate condition.'" "I dare you," Lizzie Latané said. Charlotte had no difficulty in borrowing a dress which she wore under her coat until she got to the church door, removing the coat just as Miss Lou struck up the first hymn. Lottie started up the aisle, and her progress was marked by gasps and giggles.

[15] Belle Seddon Fleet was born Dec. 30, 1876.

Lexington, Mo.
My dear Mother;   Mar. 24, 1877
   Veni, vidi, vici!—My little Fannie loves me, and we are engaged!!! Your dear long letter came last Saturday and I am
so thankful to you for it, and for your consent. I think I ought
to say to you as Brother did, you ought to be very thankful
and pleased to give your "boy" to such a noble, pure, and
sweet girl as Fannie. I have seen a good deal of her since I
have been here, and am convinced she is all the above and
more and that we were intended for each other. I have talked
with her father and mother. Mrs. Waddel said she couldn't
give away her Fannie but she supposed I would have to *take*
her. Mr. W. said he could not give up his dearest Jewel but
would have to abide by his wife's decision. I don't know when
they will give her up but not sooner than a year I suppose. I
don't wish to marry sooner, as I want to be established and
see my way clear before I do.

Mary Seddon (Minnie) Fleet

Am very well & happy, so much so that I can't write any
more and Betsy will have to finish this.

Love to all,
Aff'y, David

Monday morning—Brother D. is as crazy as a man can be, and
it's as well he doesn't write any more, for I am sure it would
be incomprehensible. He seems to be desperately in love and
acts just like all others in the same state.

Last Friday was a rainy day and Good Friday too, so the
girls all begged so hard for a holiday that Brother had to give
it to us to the great delight of the teachers and pupils. Our
new library books arrived that day and all of us selected a book
& enjoyed reading & resting.

Affectionately, Betsy

Lexington, Missouri

My dearest-Homes-ones: March 25, 1877
Weren't you surprised that "our Dave" has at last fallen in
love and submitted his fate to a lady? I was never more astonished when he told me, for I had not suspected it although I
was here with him.

In many respects Fannie is a most estimable girl, and would,
I know, make a devoted wife. She is not equal to Sister Belle,
but you know Bro. David and Brother are very different, and
what one would like, the other would find entirely uncongenial.
In the opinion of the world he would do a fine thing to marry
such a girl. All these things though are directed by a Higher
Power and it is very consoling to feel and know that they are.

I showed Brother your letters, and he seemed very much
astonished that I had an idea of being anywhere else than right
here next year, and said he hadn't the least idea of letting
me go. Now we all know I had infinitely rather be with you
dear ones than anywhere else in the wide world, and I am
sure you all want me as much as you say you do, but if Bro.
wants me very much and Bro. David is here too, what must I
do? Do you think it would be best for us to be separated one
more year & then join partnership never to be dissolved? [16] I

[16] Betsy joined the Green Mount School in the fall of 1878.

know from a pecuniary point of view it would be better for us all, but the rest and quiet of my dear sweet home is exceedingly tempting. Brother says if he could see and talk with you he is sure he could persuade you, but he is afraid his is a selfish view and we must decide the question. As I wrote you I have stood the work remarkably well and am willing to try it again if we altogether think it will be best. Where ever I may be next year, little Sis, I do want to take guitar lessons just for you.

Weren't you delighted to hear from Brother's last letter that there is a prospect of our having Sister Belle and the darling little children during the summer. I know it will be right hard not to have any rest after our school is out, but it is so necessary that the baby should be in the country and it will be so charming for Minnie, and so restful to the dear little mother to be with us all, that we will be delighted to have them and rest together.

Brother, Sister Belle and I had a talk last night about coming home. I expect we will come through Baltimore, down the York, and to Fish Haul. Will you be able to send for us all? How are the horses? I am sorry the school will not be out, but I will help Sister and Sis F. with their examination papers. Bro. seemed shocked when I told him how much company we had last summer and said it almost scared him away for he wants a good quiet time when he comes. So don't give very hearty invitations and I hope we won't be overrun as we were last summer.

Lovingly, Betsy

My dear Will,   Sunday, Apr. 8th '77

I send you Mrs. Nason's check for $25 which was very acceptable. You can pay a month's board I hate for you not to be prompt and then can make the other go as far as possible for our wants, I enclose a memorandum. We shall want you to get right many things to make us ready to receive Fred and his family but I shall try not to overwork. We have plenty of servants, ice and, I hope, fruit. Altho' I shall live in quite a bustle, it is so much better than too much quiet—which would amount to stagnation. I want you all to feel as welcome at your old home as if you had never left and found another. Bear that in mind as long as you live and I have a home. Pick out a good book and send me, I want something to read while I am knitting. When you go down town to perform my commissions be sure to get yourself some ice cream and I will feel better about asking you.

Henry told me the lot I had had put in oats and grass was the neatest piece of work he most ever saw, which pleased me very much.

Bless you my dear child,

Your aff. Mother

My darling Bess,   Sunday morning

We were so glad to have the good news about Belle's bringing the little darlings instead of sending them and I hope this place will do them as much good as it did Ida. When Mr. Westwood first saw her he exclaimed, "I wonder if Mrs. Fleet would take a million for Green Mount." When I think of having such a healthy place for the children and grandchildren to come to every summer, I value it as I never did before. Tell Fred he has heard the expression, "Give me this now, and leave me less when you die," a very homely saying but some truth in it. Let us enjoy in the summer some of our hard worked for money. He will come too, won't he? and dear David? and rest and sleep and wake up refreshed for the next session. It was very unselfish and sweet in you to offer to stay in Mrs. Seddon's place and it showed you felt and appreciated her kindness to you. It was just what I would have had you do, but I hope nothing will require you to make the sacrifice but that you can come and enjoy your home and your friends. Last week I had the pianos moved—the parlour one in the dining room and the little one upstairs. Now I hope we can collect enough money to send for the new one.

Mattie Bird came on Friday from Lloyd's where she had been staying with Lucy Spencer ever since her marriage. She seems to be enjoying herself going around visiting her friends. I sometimes wish you girls could have a little leisure but then I think of those who are so much worse off and try to be satisfied. I have great comfort in knowing my girls love their home so well. I am having the ice house covered and will take all the care of it I can for your sakes—but ice or no ice, you will all have the best welcome our hearts can give. Time & paper are both out.

God bless you all,

Your aff. Mother

In the fall of 1877 Sallie Lee Blount, whose father, a Methodist minister, died when she was a baby and whose mother died when she was thirteen, was sent to Green Mount School for Young Ladies by her guardians. Her account of her experience there appears in *Sallie Lee Mahood, 1864-1933, Autobiography,* published in 1965 by her son, Alexander Blount Mahood, quoted here by permission of Julia Mahood.

Four of us Richmond girls set out together. We had to go by a heavy old stagecoach, which left Richmond at six o'clock in the morning and after lumbering over corduroy roads, changing horses at Old Church in Hanover County, crossing two ferries, we reached our destination at dusk. We had traveled thirty-five miles.

Green Mount was a charming old place, set in a large lawn with lots of locust trees. . . . The back yard opened into the sweetest old garden, laid off in large squares, bordered with gooseberry or current bushes. There were tall grape arbors over some of the walks. Old fashioned roses and shrubs were in abundance, and many fruit trees. . . .

I'll never forget the excitement of arriving, seeing lots of girls playing croquet on the lawn. Miss Lou welcomed us, showed us to our room and introduced us to her sister, dear Miss Florence, and to the other girls. There were fifteen of us my first year. I was the youngest, only thirteen, and the oldest was twenty. It was a very select school and many fine families were represented among the students.

Our schedule was planned so systematically that we got in a lot of work, and two hours daily practice on the piano, without feeling tired or worked to death. The rising bell rang at six A.M. and we were in bed and lights out at 9:30 P.M. We studied or practiced an hour before breakfast. After breakfast we had to walk or run up to the road gate, a quarter of a mile and touch it. We went into school at nine and got out at three. We had a recess of fifteen minutes, and a half-hour for dinner. We were required to walk in the afternoon, but to be back for the reading hour, just before supper. After supper we studied two hours from seven to nine, with a teacher present to help when necessary.

Miss Florence was my favorite of all my teachers. She was medium height, and quite plump. Her arms tapered to slender wrists, and her hands were beautiful, with very tapering fingers. She was fair with deep blue eyes, and golden hair which curled around her forehead and temples in soft light curls. She taught me music and French. I felt while practicing that if my mother could know, she would be more pleased by this than by anything else I could do. At night if I ever got lonesome or nervous, I would creep down stairs and get in bed with Miss Florence. She would hug me in her soft arms and I'd go to sleep at once. Miss Lou was fine and kind, but I never felt the same freedom. Miss Bessie was witty and bright. Most of the girls loved her best. I was a little afraid of her wit and sarcasm. Mrs. Fleet was the prettiest old lady I ever saw. Her hair was white and it waved beautifully. Her eyes were deep blue and her lips pink.

Our weekly excitement was to go to church. I cannot give the preacher credit for the intense interest we felt in going to the small Baptist Church called St. Stephens, situated in a grove of oak trees. It was here that we first saw and met the Aberdeen boys. Col. Council had a select school of boys, from fifteen or sixteen to the early twenties, at his home called Aberdeen.

These young men would meet our vehicles in the grove a short distance from the church, and we would pair off walking to the church door. There we had to separate as men and women sat on opposite sides of the church. After services they walked us back and helped us into our vehicles. These short walks gave food for conversation for a whole week.

Another great excitement was the frequent serenades by the Aberdeen boys. During the last of our study hour we could hear the distant tuning of fiddles, guitars and banjos down in the woods by the Aberdeen Swamp, so named because it was their way of approach. Suddenly beneath our windows, the sweetest music would peal forth to our eager ears. The music was sometimes instrumental, sometimes vocal, generally choruses in which our names would be adroitly introduced. We would peep through the blinds and throw flowers. We were prepared with flowers because a young colored man from Aberdeen would come over to visit a colored girl on the place and bring word the serenaders were coming. Once I tied the bouquets to strings, so when we threw them, they stopped above the heads of those who rushed to catch them. The boys said, "Miss Sallie Blount thought of that so Bob Willis could get all the flowers."

When I first arrived at that school, I was a tall, pale, thin girl, weighing seventy-two pounds. When I returned to Richmond at Christmas, I weighed ninety-five pounds and had a brilliant color.

Wentworth Military Academy

My dear Mother,   Lexington, Mo.—Sunday

I am getting along splendidly with my school. When I speak they obey like soldiers and respect me as if I were 50 or 60 years of age.

I took Betsy to tea at the hotel yesterday. She is looking well, is a dear little girl and a great comfort to me. I don't know what I would do without her. I haven't been up to the college much this year as I didn't want to come in contact with a boa constrictor! [17] I leave you to judge what I mean.

Betsy read me your letter, give my love to Mammy and Mary, how is their health. Has Joshua recovered from his attack? Give my love to Mary Eliza and Walter. Has their little one who fell in the well grown any? They were so sure it would frighten him out of "seven years' growth."

[17] Probably Mrs. Waddell; David's engagement to Fanny had been broken.

Sis, I am amused at your "new manner of teaching"—Can't you write me a few lectures that I may catch the spirit too?

Sallie Brooke must be in her element, has she ever been out of King and Queen and Essex before?

How I would love to gather you all up in my arms—I love you.

Yours,
David

My dearest little Betsy,   Green Mount Oct. 9, 1877

Just think, my darling, how much the old Mother was pulled about yesterday to forget your birthday until four o'clock this morning when I waked up as usual and had time to think. God bless you, this day and every day & give you many happy returns of your birthday.

I have written to Mabel Brown's mother, in answer to a letter she wrote me when she sent her darling to our care. I have put off answering it until now. But it is done and *well* done, tho' I say it myself. She has two or three other daughters and I am recruiting for you, little one, next year. I really think I could do almost as well as Fred if I could only travel like he does.

I got a long letter from Fred yesterday in which he says of you, "I want to tell you how well Bessie is looking and how manfully she comes up to her work. She has shown herself fully equal to the emergencies and responsibilities of the position. I think she will make an excellent teacher and she is certainly a popular one, the girls all love and obey her." I was delighted! I knew you would do your very best but didn't know whether you could give entire satisfaction. That is a good deal for him to say.

Your devoted Mother

My dear children,   Mon. morn. Oct. 29th '77

We were very glad to get David's letter, dear boy, I have been intending to write but have been attending to the girls, the farm, company, everything, my hands are very full but I am well and thankful. Today is bright, beautiful and so warm

I am sitting on the front porch writing and waiting for Dr. Bagby to come and draw a tooth for Lou. The poor little girl has been suffering with toothache and last night couldn't sleep so I sent for him.

I suppose, little Betsy, Dr. Gatewood's letter prepared you for his visit. He came up Friday evening brought Nannie Evans and stayed till yesterday. He said he enjoyed his visit so much he should be up again before Christmas. No doubt he, like Cousin Landon, will find the way much shorter next time. He seemed very much delighted with the improvement he thinks his little girl has made and if compliments could turn our heads—they would be spinning, we've had many lately.

Saturday evening, Mr. Brown, Mable's father, came from Richmond and spent the night with us. He is a "self made man" as the saying is. I suppose has never been much educated himself, but is very anxious his children should be. He told me he could not feel too thankful he sent Mabel here after seeing us and getting my letter to his wife. I have no fears about the success of our school if the Lord blesses us with health and strength, the people are appreciating my children and "success is so successful." All this is between ourselves and I don't say it in a spirit of bragging but just with humble thankfulness that the Lord has blessed our feeble efforts in this our time of need. It is not often that women and children succeed as well as we have done.

Mr. Bird got me a stove in Baltimore which cost $50 and when it comes will send a man to put it up, wrote "it will make times hot at Green Mount." If we like it we shall have another next year—we will have a good many comforts which will be fully appreciated because we worked for them ourselves.

Dr. Bagby has been and drawn Lou's tooth and she is in the classroom teaching but looking and feeling very badly. The girls are very considerate and kind. I never saw a set who gave as little unnecessary trouble and altho Lou and Florence work very hard, they don't have any worry.

Irene expects to be married to a Mr. Gregory, a brother of the Judge—older than her father, but 'tis to be hoped he will know how to take care of the child.

I hope in making your arrangements, David, for next summer, you will include a trip to see the Mother and sisters if practicable. Excuse this random letter, I have changed the subject almost as often as the dictionary.

Give my most affectionate love to all my children,

Your devoted Mother

[Minutes of the Evergreen Society]

Jan. 23, 1878—Lottie played Fleetwood March like she had never touched a piano before. Miss Lou read a piece by Bishop Whittle on the round dance. Emma read "Sweet are my dreams," it was very lovesick and suited B. T. to a T.

The fire, I suppose, should be recorded too. We were in the schoolroom Monday night, when accidently both lamps were upset & we had quite a little scene. The girls rushed out of the room not even offering to assist our President to her feet, our dear teacher's fright, our heroine (Ida's) composure as she threw a rug on one lamp and carried the other from the room which prevented the fire from being worse. We all escaped and even the schoolroom was spared.

The natural desire of the Green Mount girls and the Aberdeen boys to see each other was not disregarded, and occasionally the boys were invited to supper. Afterwards they gathered in the parlor and one of their teachers read their characters and fortunes. Each wrote the date of his or her birthday, and the teacher would ask, for example, "What is your character, Gentlemen?" Then she would select a date and read the corresponding message from her book. If their schoolmates did not already know to whom the birth dates belonged, the blushing confusion of the subjects would betray them. Some of the character descriptions are given here:

What is your character, Gentlemen?

"You would shake hands with the king on his throne,
  And think it kindness to his majesty."   Halleck

"You speak an infinite deal of nothing."   Shakespeare

"Who can play off your smiles and courtesies,
  To everybody of her lap-dog tired
  Who wants a plaything."   Southey

"A man thou seemest of cheerful yesterdays
And confident to-morrows."   Wordsworth

What is your character, Lady?

"The world has won thee, lady, and thy joys
are placed in trifles, follies, toys."   Crabbe

"You are a riddle
which he who solved the sphinx would
Die guessing."   John Tobin

"You have turned up your nose at the short,
And cast down your eyes at the tall,
But then you just did it in sport,
And now you've no lover at all."   S. P. Morris

"Uncertain, coy, and hard to please."   Scott

"None knew thee, but to love thee,
None named thee but to praise."   Halleck

"Your only labor is to kill time."   Thomson

"You have a natural wise sincerity
A simple truthfulness."

What gratifies your taste?

"There's little that you care for now,
except a simple wedding ring."   T. Miller

"Dogs of grave demeanor
All meekness, of gentleness, though large of limb."

"The dance,
Pleasant with graceful flatteries."   Miss Landon

" 'Tis heaven to lounge upon a couch,' said Gray,
'And read new novels through a rainy day.' "

"Sleep, soft closer of our eyes,
Low murmur of tender lullabies."   Keats

"A noble horse,
With flowing back, firm chest,
And fetlocks clean."   Leigh Hunt

"Give all things else their honor due,
But goose-berry pie is best."   Southey

For what have you a distaste?

"Conversation, when reduced to say
The hundredth time what you have said before."   Mrs.
Sigourny

"Hence, you long-legged spiders, hence!"   Shakespeare

"To have old and remnants of wit broken on you."
Shakespeare

"To tax a bad voice to slander music, had he been a dog
that should have howled thus, they would have hanged
him."

"To hear the French talk French around you
And wonder how they understand each other."   Byron

"You are weary of the endless theme of Cupid's smiles
and sighs."   Charlton

What season of the year do you like? What hour do you like? What
flower do you like? Going through all these questions must have
consumed many evenings by a large open fire, while roasting chestnuts
and popping popcorn. The personal questions were the most popular:

What is the appearance of your Lady Love?

"Not fairer grows the lily of the vale."

"Half the smiles that deck her face
Arise from powder, shreds and lace."   Goldsmith

"Excellently done if God did all."   Shakespeare

"In face an angel, but in soul a cat."   Dr. Wolcott

" 'Tis not her eye or lip we beauty call,
But the joint force and full result of all."   Pope

"If to her share some errors fall,
Look in her face, and you'll forget them all."   Hayley

What is the appearance of him who loves you?

"A goodly person and can manage well
    His stubborn steed."   Spencer

"The tartness of his face sours ripe grapes."   Shakespeare

"He hath but little beard, but time will send more and
    the man will be thankful."

"A phantom, fashionably thin,
    With limb of lathe and bearded chin."   Scott

"He is fat and scant of breath."

"A short, active soldier-looking stripling."   Byron

"He is handsome, valiant, young,
    And looks as he were laid for nature's best
    To catch weak woman's eye."   Dryden

What is the character of your Lady Love?

"A perfect woman, nobly planned
    To warn, to comfort, and command."   Wordsworth

"I would my horse had the speed of her tongue."

"She speaks but says nothing."   Shakespeare

"You are as rich in having such a jewel
    As twenty seas if all their sands were pearls."

"She loves—but 'tis not you she loves."   C. F. Hoffman

"Though on pleasure she is bent
    She has a frugal mind."   Cowper

"She will turn a love breathing seraph away,
    If he come not in purple and gold."   Mrs. Osgood

What is the character of him who loves you?

"He's too costly for every day,
    You'd want another for working days."   Shakespeare

"Strange that his nobly-fashioned mold
    In which a very god might dwell,
    Should only live to dig for gold,
    And perish in its narrow cell."   Browning

"He will prattle shrewdly with such witty folly
As almost betters reason."   Payne

"Oh, he is as tedious
As a tired horse or a railing wife,
Worse than a smoky house."   Shakespeare

"A little, upright, pert, tart, tripping wight
That holds his precious self his dear delight."   Burns

"He draweth out the staple of his verbosity
Finer than the staple of his argument."   Shakespeare

Where will be your residence?

"Child of the town and bustling street,
What woes and snares await thy feet."

"Beside a public way,
Thick strewn with summer dust and a great stream
Of people, hurrying to and fro."   Shelley

"All day within your dreary house
The door upon their hinges will creak."   Tennyson

"That dear old home,
Something of old ancestral pride it keeps,
Though fallen from its early power and vastness?"   Fannie Kemble

"You'll think yourself superbly off
Though rather cramped in bed
If the garret keep the winter rain
From dropping on your head."   Pike

What is your Destiny?

"In the narrow sphere,
The little circle of domestic love,
You will be known and loved; the world
Beyond is not for you."   Southey

"Single as a stray glove."   Fannie Kemble

"Through many a clime 'tis yours to go
With many a retrospection cursed,
And all your solace know
Whate'er betide you've known the worst."   Byron

The Aberdeen boys were well aware of the Green Mount girls' daily schedule, and they arranged theirs accordingly. They would bolt their two o'clock dinner, saddle their horses, ride over, and pin little billets-doux on the trees along the path the girls usually took. Then they would dash back for the remainder of their classes. When the girls would start out for their walk, Miss Lou would be in front pointing out the wild flowers and reciting:

> Be good, sweet maid, let those who will be clever
> Do noble things, not dream them all day long—
> And so make life, death and that vast forever
> One grand sweet song.

Some of the girls would lag behind, pick up the notes, and sort them out to their delighted owners. The girls were prepared for any eventuality. When the weather was inclement and they had to stay inside, they would bundle up Martha Ann (Mary's daughter, who waited on the table and was pleased to be Cupid's assistant) and send her down to pick up the notes and bring them back to their eager recipients. After those days the records of the Evergreen Society show the collection for foreign missions to be very small indeed. Somehow these operations leaked out, and the following exchange of letters took place.

Young Gentlemen:

I wish to make the polite request that you will not come on our place or near it without Mr. Councill's permission or mine. I am quite sure I now address gentlemen, who will understand my motives if they will only stop and think. Not one of you would have a sister of yours meet a young man clandestinely, nor would you consider any man a gentleman who would do it. If you come on or near our place you might be very apt to meet some of my girls by chance, and there would be plenty of people who would believe it was done purposely, I wish my girls not only to avoid every evil but every appearance of evil. I am sure not one of you would wilfully injure one of my scholars in any way, then let me beg of you not to do it thoughtlessly.

Believe me ever your friend truly,
M. Lou Fleet

Enclosed you will find a copy of the request which I asked Mr. Thomas to show to all the young gentlemen of your school.

I suppose he had good reasons for not doing so. Will you be so kind as to read it and place the signature of each one of you, young gentlemen, showing you have read my request and are willing to grant it. If you will it will confer a great favor on

Your friend truly
M. Lou Fleet

The following abject apology arrived—and on Valentine's Day too.

Miss Lou: Aberdeen, Feb. 14, '78

On this miserable piece of paper I am going to ask you for pardon. Miss Lou, I acknowledge that I am in fault. When you gave me that note you asked me to show it to all of them. I only let the ones see it that go to Green Mount, and they said that we would burn it up so I did it. I have since told them about it. I own that I have done wrong and I ask for forgiveness. Will you grant it? I have acted very ungentlemanly and it makes me feel very badly to think I have treated a lady in the manner I have.

Forgive O! forgive me.

My guilty conscience cannot be at ease until I have told you the whole story. I have been to the ice pond and to the swamp, but I will give you my word and honor I will never do it again. I know you think very hard of what I have done and I hope you will forgive me. Please don't show this to anyone or tell anyone of its contents for I feel so badly about it, by so doing you will greatly oblige your devoted friend,

W. Linithicum Thomas

P. S. I feel as I was asking a great deal of you but I trust you will grant my request.

[Written in pencil at the bottom of the letter, which was evidently copied and sent to Linithicum]

Dear Sir;

I confess I was very much surprised when I found you had failed to show my note to the boys as I requested you to do. I would be the last person in the world to refuse my forgiveness to one who is determined to try earnestly to do what is right. Hoping this experience will teach you never again to commit an act which your conscience condemns as "ungentlemanly."

Believe me, sincerely your friend,

M. Lou Fleet

My little darling, [Betsy]   Sunday evening, Feb. 17, '78

You say you are open to proposals and I propose that you shall come home if you wish and share with the sisters the troubles and pleasure and pay of our school. We don't know how many we shall have but this I know, it is not so vitally important that we should get a large school next year as it has been. We are so much nearer out of debt that we can afford the luxury of having you at home, precious child, if you prefer it. Mr. Jones told Florence when she told him about the summer houses which Sis is having built, he was glad to hear it, he thought we ought to have whatever we wanted, we had been so self-sacrificing, so hard working, and we have concluded to want *you above everything else* if you want to come.

How would Dave suit Fred as a teacher? Couldn't he help very much to travel around and recruit students? Or does he still want to study medicine? I am so glad he can help you, tell the dear boy whatever he does for you, he does for me. Nothing gives me more pleasure than for my children to be together and help each other whenever they can.

I have been making comforts of the bed quilts I made two years ago, filling them with carded wool and I hope to have enough boarders to use them all.

Your aff. Mother

My darling Betsy,   G. M. Sunday Feb. 24th '78

It seemed as if I wanted that letter more than any I expected the whole session because I so longed to know what you had decided on, and very thankful I was to see you agree with us in seeing where your duty lies. Tell Fred he must not be hurt with any of us about it.

Today I am all alone. Lou took Sallie Blount (our little Methodist) and little Ellen to Shepherd's in the buggy. Florence and all the others are gone to St. David's [18] where some of the Aberdeen boys will be baptized. I stayed at home—glad of the rest.

Our dear Sadie leaves us (D. V.) next Friday. We shall miss her so much for we love her dearly, but we have the satisfaction of knowing she is perfectly restored to health and strength. Her mother is so grateful she makes as much fuss about it as I would. She has fattened nineteen pounds and I hope she will gain another by Thursday night. Florence or Lou drives her to the postoffice every morning. Yesterday Mr. Evans rode along with them. F. says he was riding a little black horse exactly like Charley, said he got him from Mr. Shackford and is a delightful ladies' riding horse. He spoke of wanting to sell it as he wants to get a larger one. She asked him to give us the refusal of it. So you see we are looking out for you. Tell Minnie she will be large enough to learn to ride next summer and Grandma wants her to be as fine a horse woman as you are, my darling,

                                                    Your aff. Mother

My darling [Bess],   Sat. Morn.

Lou as usual has expressed my feelings and wishes better than I could, but I must add my heartfelt congratulations that it is "well with the Mother and well with the child." [19] Would you believe it we were thinking and dreaming about Belle and Fred all that evening and night. The first thought after hearing Ellen's announcement of a "grand baby"—after the thankfulness, was I wonder if they won't let us have little Belle, till they can come for her next year—for I trust they will bring all the little ones to spend the summer "at home." What do you say, dear father and mother? It will save the child two most fatiguing trips and you know how we will love to have her. She will need a nurse more than the baby and the healthy country air. I await your decision knowing you will do what is best.

[18] St. David's Episcopal Church in Aylett.
[19] John Seddon Fleet was born May 11, 1878.

You did not tell me a word about the baby—Beautiful I know it is. "Where could it get any ugly from?" but what type, like father or mother? What is his name? Tell little Belle she is not as good as her father was, because he slept all night before he was a year old and I used to get up to see if he were alive. I shall never get over my delight at the arrival of a baby in the family. My girls are calling for attention but I must ask one more question. We expect to give the girls and boys, who have been so attentive to them, a croquet party. Would you prefer we have it the 7th of June or wait till the 14th when we hope you will be at home. The school closes on the 20th and we want to do what you would like best. Will wants to know if you would like to go to Richmond to his commencement.

Love and a kiss to David, Belle, Fred, and Mrs. Seddon and to you, my precious.

Yr. aff. Mother

My dear Bess,

How glad we will be to get you safely back home once more but how we will miss all the others. The only thing which reconciles me is that we are not prepared to give them such a happy time as we had last summer. So little ice or fruit and everything so parched by the drought. They must all live on the memory of last summer and the hope of the next. Mr. Garlick, his wife and little girls spent Saturday and Sunday with us, and went to Mr. Councill's on Monday. He seemed in very good spirits about his school (much better than I am about ours). He was very full of the railroad from Gloucester Point, on by Richmond to *California.* Mr. G. said he talked with an acquaintance who had paid $10,000 the day before for land which is being surveyed in Gloucester. It is a Boston company and he said they had already spent several millions in Virginia. To me it is like our *Ivy root,* just enough hope to keep us up 'til something else turns up.[20]

Love to all,
Your devoted Mother

[20] Ivy root: a resinous exudate from the stems and roots of ivy used in medicine as a stimulant and emmenagogue. The railroad never materialized.

My dearest little Bess,   Green Mount May 17, 1878

Monday morning Harry brought such an imploring message
from the Aberdeen boys to let my girls go to a lecture at Bruington, I decided to do it. All of us went except Mattie Kate, who
said "School boys are the biggest geese in the world," and
two of the girls who wanted to stay with her. She met some
University boys last summer and they quite altered her ideas.
Mr. Dunaway's lecture was on "Women" and was very good.
Judge Jones, dear good man as he is, eased my conscience
about giving holiday by saying my girls had learned more than
I could have taught them in a day. The girls wrote him a note
of thanks to be sent by Nellie this evening.

We have been having the long season, "blackberry winter"
as Mammy calls it and it is so cold one of the girls suggested
Mrs. Fleet might fill her ice house. We have enjoyed good fires
in all the rooms. I was very glad our nice piano was not on
the way in all the dampness this week. I wrote Mr. Weber to
have it tuned to concert pitch so it will be in accord with the
organ. I hope it will be safely here by the time you arrive.

We have the prospects of just as many good girls as we want
to teach right here in our home, where we can live together
and help each other, and if we are not contented and happy—
why we don't deserve to be.

Your devoted sister,
Lou

[Minutes of the Evergreen Society]

June 24, 1878—Our last meeting—Millie Belle played "Goodbye," some of the girls cried and all of them looked sad. Then
Miss Florence and Ida Westwood played "Consolation" splendidly. We are thankful to record we have full attendance this
evening and especially thankful because we are to have ice
cream.

Goodbye one and all

Baptist Female College
Lexington, Mo.
Dec. 24, 1878

My very dear Bessie,

I am afraid my letters are like angels' visits, few and far between. Your brother summoned the faculty to make the announcement that he had been unanimously elected to the Chair of Greek in the University of Missouri & he had resigned his position at this college to accept it. Of course, we all feel that no man & his family can be found to fill the place as they have done. He says he shall recommend his faculty to his successor, whomever he may be & hopes we will all return. I have no idea what I shall do but have committed it to the guidance of One who never errs. The opposition to his leaving is understandable.

David is, if possible, handsomer & more elegant that I ever saw him, with the look of a Cavalier, a real "prince of the blood." His deep devotion to Maggie [21] seems to have settled him somewhat, which is all the better for him. I trust his patience, perseverance & love will bring him his reward. All this is a profound secret, & if David had not confided in me as he said he had in you, I would not have alluded to it. God bless the dear children for they are both so kind and affectionate to me.

Just a year ago today, what a time we had getting you off to Platte City, where you spent the Christmas holidays so delightfully with "darling Margaret." Maggie is the same sweet thing, though it still looks strange to see her without you. You seemed to be made to be together & something tells me you may enjoy each other more & that too in "nearer, dearer, tenderer ties." God grant that it may be so.

I suppose David has written you of the deep snow which has been on the ground for ten days. It is thirty inches deep and drifted in some places five and six feet deep. We are constantly hearing the merry jingle of sleigh bells, as 'tis next to impossible to travel in any other vehicle. Wagons, carriages and buggies have been requisitioned and placed on sleds.

I wish I had a handsome Christmas present for each of you

---

[21] Margaret Norton was the daughter of Judge John Norton of Platte City, Mo.

at Green Mount, but, alas, Poverty! Give a hug and kiss to your sweet mother and sisters, and to my Garlick cousins and to my King and Queen friends—haven't space to mention them.

Affectionately,
Evelyn Hill [22]

P. S. Dec. 25th—David has quite overwhelmed us with beautiful gifts. A handsome chair apiece for Mrs. Seddon, Mrs. Temple and myself besides an elegant silver butter dish for his brother and sister and a beautiful Backgammon Board for Miss Thompson. Bless his generous heart!!!

My dear Mother,   Lexington, Mo. 2/24/79

I am sorry you find money so scarce, for the first time in five years, I have paid off everything and am ahead and I assure you I feel very comfortable about it. I can lend you $200 at 6% if you want it to help you with your spring work provided you can save that amount of interest in purchasing what you need for cash.

Mrs. Seddon will come to Va. next summer with us of course and will spend part of the summer at Green Mount and the rest at Snowden. She is going to stay here and teach next year. She wants to help Willie [23] through college and she thinks she can do it best that way. So we have given our consent to leave her behind for awhile.

No, I will not have to hunt up students for the University, and I presume there will be no objection to my spending my summers in Va.

Yes, there are some girls in the University, I wish there were none and I think the time will come when they will be left out.

Your aff. Fred

[22] Evelyn Hill, a friend and neighbor from Woodruff in King William County and sister-in-law of Dr. John Staige Davis, was teaching at the Baptist Female College.

[23] William Little Seddon became vice-president and chief engineer of the Seaboard Airline Railway.

Fred wrote he and Belle were planning to spend several weeks at the end of the school in Philadelphia and New York to enjoy the cultural advantages and wanted Bessie to meet them in Baltimore and take the children to Green Mount. His mother replied:

March 27th 1879

My dear son,

Lorelle begged to have the privilege of going up with Walter to Hanover Court House and take the baby and help Bessie all she can with the two little girls. I feel so complimented at your and Belle's being willing to trust the precious little ones to our care—so gratified and so thankful for the home to gather in the children and more than all for the love which induces you to send them. Tell Minnie, Aunt Lou is going to fix up the summer houses beautifully and she shall have one and Belle the other and play "come to see" one another. Let the little girls enjoy the anticipation. If you make children happy now you will make them happy twenty years hence by the memory of it.

I agree with you and Belle about raising the price of tuition next year but I do not agree with you about not giving aid to some of the girls. We helped Sallie Browne Fleet and her father and mother were as thankful as can be. Mamie Davies—I shall never regret helping—the daughter of the lady who was so good to my darling when you were wounded in her brother's home and they are all as grateful and affectionate as possible. Hannah Bagby, who is here now is lending a helping hand in every department. Lou sent for two hanging baskets for her. When they came she was greatly pleased and showed them to me. I said, "You see, Hannah, Lou will never let anyone work for her for nothing." She replied, "As I told her, if I were to work for you all the rest of my life, it would not be for nothing." Ellen Garlick, we gave tuition and board this year and she brought us three of the finest scholars we have here and interested other Richmond girls in the school and we expect to have more in the future. That is our experience and we are much better satisfied to see the good we do than to give money to be sent out of sight and hearing.

Dr. Garlick came to pay a long-promised visit and brought

Lillian Waite Fleet

Attie who will stay with Ellen until after Easter. He preached a good sermon yesterday to a church almost full, though the day was cloudy. Mr. Temple Gwathmey and family and school and escorts, twenty-five in all came from Tappahannock, among them the young scamp who pretended to kill himself over Nettie Gwathmey. Pity he didn't do it. If all "they" say about him is true, it would have been the *best* thing he ever did.[24]

We expect to put up a long new porch in front when Willie comes home to help us. Then in October, the best month in the year for painting, we hope to have the house painted. I will be so thankful when he comes. I used to say he and I together were equal to one man and how I have missed my right hand. I am only a woman and cannot carry on farming and building and painting, and a school and all a woman's work too at the same time without William's help. And you must remember too, I can't go to a bank every time I want a sum of money, but have to wait patiently, till somebody pays us. Perhaps it's as well I can't, as I'm inclined to be extravagent and need some check.

Now I must stop, it's bedtime and I need rest.

Love to all from your devoted
Mother

My dear Brother [Fred],   May 17th 1879

Ma had been very low-spirited all morning, burdened with the care of feeding four workmen in addition to our family of eighteen, these scarce spring days and grieving because she has no money to pay them when they have finished. I had tried to comfort her with the thought the school would soon be out and then we would certainly get some money. Yet this afternoon when we had a meeting of the Evergreen Society, she spoke to the girls and said, "Girls, if you do not learn but one thing at Green Mount, I want you always to remember to put the best foot forward and look on the bright side—and if there is no bright side then *polish up the dark one.*" She

---

[24] Robert Temple Gwathmey conducted Vaucluse Female Seminary in Tappahannock. Antoinette (Nettie), his daughter, did not marry "the scamp" but the eminently respectable John Ryland of Farmington.

said to me later, "I am sorry I was so downcast this morning. I can't do otherwise than take my own advice, can I?"

Your aff. sister Lou

My deal Will,   G. M. May 17th 1879

Of course you were right to write us the good news. Ma had been very low-spirited all day and I don't think *anything* could have lifted the cloud so completely as your winning the declamation contest. After reading the letter to her, she said "that boy will be a judge some day, I shall not live to see it, but he will, or if he is not, he will deserve to be and that is even better." [25]

I am going to place over the new ice house—"Keep Cool" and I put "Rest" over one summer house and "Peace" over the other. Can you think of a more appropriate motto for the ice house? Actually it is a good one to take with us wherever we go. We have it whitewashed and I will plant some vines across the front.

Your devoted sister Lou

David was appointed U.S. government engineer in the summer of 1879 and operated out of Independence, Missouri, sectionalizing and surveying Nevada and the Wyoming and Arizona territories.

                                                 Lexington, Mo.
My dear Bessie,   Oct. 10, 1879

I am so much obliged to you, for making such a long quotation from David's letter. I am delighted to hear of his well-being and well-doing. Mrs. Temple wrote me he was not reappointed to the place in the Wentworth Military Academy. I was not surprised for he told me he did not expect it. Political and church reasons, I suppose, for all acknowledged he filled the place admirably well. I can't say I regret the result at all & trust & believe it is all for the best. Do write me of his plans

---

[25] James William Fleet was appointed judge of the King and Queen County Court by Gov. J. Hoge Tyler on Feb. 18, 1901, about a year after his mother's death.

as they unfold. He came to see me the day you left & told me of his arrangement with the surveying party. Give my love to him when you write & tell him I am glad he is getting along so well among the buffaloes, & other wild things of Wyoming, & hope he will not stay too long, or I shall be uneasy about his scalp.

Love to all at Green Mount from
Your friend,
Evelyn Hill

My dear David,   G. M. Dec. 9, 1879

We can't help feeling very gloomy when we think of Va's future in the hands of such men whom we will have for the next few years. Who do you think are in Richmond now trying to get Judge Jones' place! Mr. Tyler, Mr. J. D. Foster & Mr. Wm. Gresham, who never studied law in his life. There is nothing to expect from that legislature but that the meanest men will be the ones to succeed. This will drive all our best citizens away—who can get away. It is sorrowful! Sorrowful! Perhaps Virginia had too much state pride. Surely we are to be humbled now, but I hope we are not all dross, surely there is some pure gold in the old state yet.

The family have just had a good laugh at me because I said I could look around in my greenhouse and point out something to show for every visit I made last summer. You know my friends, knowing my love for flowers, give me slips from their flowers and you have no idea how many have taken root and are flourishing.

About the Brunswick stew, you know Ma & Mary always make everything by their "eye and tongue" with what they have on hand and Mary says nobody but the good Lord knows what that will be.

How we wish you could be one of the family circle at Christmas.

Your loving sister Lou

[Minutes of the Evergreen Society]

Jan. 28, 1880—We regret not being able to have our meeting, but as Cousin David came home from Missouri, we didn't meet.

David returned home for a vacation when the heavy snow prevented outside work. He told the girls of having been out for a week with a surveying party in north central Arizona. While riding in to the nearest outpost with a friend, they noticed a man who came in from an oblique trail, who rode some distance behind them. They called to him and invited him to join them. The stranger seemed loathe to talk so David proposed that they sing. He and his friend sang hymns until they reached the trading post where there was a hotel, a church and several saloons. David and his companion went to the hotel and the stranger went to a bar. The next day to their surprise they saw him in the little church. After the service he joined them and they went to the hotel and had dinner together. The stranger said, "When I rode up on you fellows last night, I was planning to rob you and take your horses, but after I heard you singing those hymns I just couldn't do it." The outlaw settled down at the trading post and lived an exemplary life. He was so public-spirited and did so much for the growing town, it was named Williams in his honor.

March 3rd 1880—It is raining this evening and nearly all of us have the blues. [In a different hand] It is not my turn to keep the record of the meeting, yet Miss Lou has imposed the disagreeable task upon me and all for talking so much. Lucie played "The Last Smile," she put into practice what Miss Lou is always quoting to us, viz: "Whatsoever thy hands find to do, do it with thy might." Sallie Blount played "Adelaida" beautifully. I think her talent for music is almost as great as her talent for drawing. We had tea in the parlor and Lou poured. P. S. Mr. and Mrs. Fleet have another son born Feb. 24, 1880.[26] [Note appended to minutes] Virginia was telling the girls how they ought to write when I very gently suggested that she should

[26] The baby was named Henry Wise Fleet but when General Wise's son, John, became a Republican, Fred changed the child's name to Henry Wyatt, an ancestor. Although his son, Sir Thomas Wyatt, poet, diplomat and lover of Anne Boyeyn, had a son, Sir Thomas Wyatt, who was beheaded on Tower Hill for leading a rebellion to prevent the Spanish marriage of Queen Mary, those sons were preferable to a son who had become a Readjuster and a Republican.

do it. There is a valuable lesson to be learned, viz: Put yourself in the place of anyone whose work you wish to criticize and you will find it much easier to say how a thing ought to be done than to do it.

March 29, '80—After reading a Psalm in German we adjourned to the music room. Lou read with much confusion "Some Advice to Young Ladies," not at all suitable to the occasion, as it told only what "turned out young ladies" should do & did not refer to school children in the least. Julia read quite an instructive piece, "Laughter as a Medicine," but I don't think it could possibly make some of us laugh more as we are constantly giggling to Mrs. Fleet's discomfort.

April 14, '80—The Treasurer's accounts being a little mixed up, a few minutes were spent in getting them straight. Sallie read "The Celestial Visitor" which we hope to see soon in the shape of a brilliant comet. Then followed an animated discussion of comets. After getting the account straight we find we have $1.50 which we decided to send to foreign missions. Mattie Kate played Gen. Beauregard's Grand March—grand in name only. Miss Bessie sang to our great delight. Then Miss Lou said she wanted to leave this verse with us:

> "Honor and shame from no condition rise,
> Act well your part, there all the honor lies."

June 1st 1880—We have been interrupted very much of late by our examinations and were obliged to give up our meetings for two weeks but we determined we would meet again before we part, perhaps some of us forever. Lou played a sonatina that had more instruction in it than beauty. Mattie Kate played Il Trovatore. Miss Lou wished me to record that two of her girls have been married, Miss Ella Fauntleroy to Dr. Webb, April 21st and Miss Minnie Belle Crump to Mr. Dew, May 11, 1880. Miss Bessie sang to our great delight. It has been a pleasant session. I hope if we never meet again on earth that we will meet in that home above.

M. L. Henley

Sept. 15, 1880—Green Mount—We reorganized the Evergreen Society. Sally Blount was elected President, Mattie Kate Fauntleroy, Vice-president and Lucy Fleet, Treasurer. We decided the duties of Secretary should be equally divided among us all. Mattie Kate introduced and we passed unanimously the resolutions: "We will try not to use any slang; we will strive together for the improvement and happiness of each other, both in and out of school."

Mattie Kate played Gimbel's variations on "Old Black Joe." Sallie read a piece called "The Mountains of the Moon," which was followed by an animated discussion of what is really there, and the expressed hope that we may have the opportunity to see it for ourselves one of these days.

Miss Florence played "Music of the Sea" & then we adjourned to hunt sloes in the Mount woods.

Oct. 21, 1880—Lulie played "Bohemian Girl" very well considering she didn't know it—or said she didn't. Misses Florence and Bessie were not present, having gone to the marriage of Dr. Henley and Miss Dora Walker. I am glad he has at last married the object of his choice, for I hear he has been in love with her ever since he was in *dresses*. I think it is a good lesson in perseverance to the end. I would write more but Miss Lou is marching us out to walk.

Dec. 1, 1880—Mattie recited a piece called "Gentle Words and Loving Smiles." I wish our tongues would roll off some of these oftener as "Sister Blount" said the other day her head was about to roll off & I think we had better roll out some gentle words than she should lose her pretty head, then Mr. R. [Browne Ryland] . . . wouldn't have anything to smile at. Lou played "Silvery Waves" but the breakers overtook her before she was halfway through. Mrs. Fleet came in to bring some dates and stayed to hear Nannie read from Mrs. Browning— "Let us be content in work to do the thing we can. . . ." We adjourned to enjoy skating on the ice which has formed rapidly during the past unusually cold days and I must go before the others get all the kitchen chairs.

Dear Fred,   Dec. 8, 1880
I went to Goshen a few days ago, I declare it's perfectly appalling to think of the children Christopher and Jimmy Fleet have to be supported and educated and no apparent means of doing it.

I came back by Aberdeen to see Cousin Mary and Col. Council. Gertrude and Garland [27] were talking a great deal about Christmas and wondering what Santa Claus would bring them. Cousin Mary told them they mustn't expect much this Christmas because they were so poor now. Gertrude replied, "That's the very reason Santa Claus ought to bring us more, 'cause the Bible says you ought to give to the poor."

An old article by Commodore Maury, which I just read says, "The latitude of Virginia is the same as that of the Holy Land"— which surprised me as I thought it was much warmer. He implies that Va. is in the same category.

Yesterday Dr. Broaddus was returning from Richmond and turned in at our gate to pay us a little visit, you know how fond he was of your father. He remarked on how happy we all looked. I replied, "Yes, we *are* happy. I am not going to let the want of a little filthy lucre stand between me and happiness, I have too many things that money can't buy."

Love to all from your aff. Mother

My dear Fred,   Jan. 3, 1881

Your letters were the most joyous part of our holiday. Now about the trip home next summer. I never cease to thank Belle for bringing you all to see us and think it is evidence of her good sense to prefer it to the springs or seaside. So come one, come all, and never doubt the welcome. Someone said the three elements of happiness are—something to do, something to love and something to hope for and the anticipation of your coming gives me all three.

What do you think of Willie's taking Mr. Waddell's offer? You know he is honest, sober, intelligent and industrious—all the qualities Mr. W. requires. We have been talking it over in the last week and we see no way to work out of debt. Old Hall in the best of seasons cannot produce more than enough to pay the hands and the interest on the debt. I can see no future except in his going away too. He will do the best he

[27] Garland Councill married Cornelius Sullavan, an Aberdeen student. Their daughter, Margaret, was a stage and motion picture actress from 1927 until her death in 1960.

can with the two farms and his profession [28] but nobody can pay much for legal work, we'll decide with your advice.

Your aff. Mother

Green Mount
Dear Brother [Fred], Jan. 10, 1881
You have doubtless gotten Mother's letter and answered it ere this but I will answer yours. I had about given up the idea of getting so many law books at this time and will await developments before getting any more.

You know I have always said, and I believe it to be my duty, that I would take care of Mother and the sisters, but the question arises, how can I best carry out my wishes. Why of course I must conclude to go where I can make the most money and where there is a prospect of doing something in my profession. It will be very hard to give up my home influences, comforts and the thought of some day owning Old Hall and farming and working among my own people, but I can't see my way clear to do that, so I will be willing to seek other fields for work. I don't think I can possibly leave until you all go back this summer and I have completed my arrangements this year and make all I can towards paying you the interest on Old Hall. Then you buy my interest in that farm and either sell or rent it. I will take in part payment all the bonds held by yourself and Bro. David against any of the home ones, for it is my fixed determination to get them on a cash basis and out of debt just as soon as possible. Of course, this will give me a small amount of capital to invest, but I would rather depend on saving a part of my salary each year than to leave Mother and the sisters at all embarrassed financially. When you come next summer let us discuss the matter calmly and dispassionately. I believe I am getting more from my study of law than I would at school, then too I want to put through some extra work I have planned to do on the farm.

The dear little Mother acts as nobly and unselfishly as is

[28] Will had read law under Maj. B. B. Douglas and Judge J. H. C. Jones, then had attended a session of the University of Virginia Law School.

her custom when she believes the good of her children is concerned. Let us take time and canvass the matter fully before deciding the questions about the farms, etc. If I decide to go I never expect to settle in this part of Virginia again. I have not quite completed my arrangements about servants yet, the weather has been too bad to move them or for work,

Write again to your affectionate brother,

J. W. Fleet

[Minutes of the Evergreen Society]

Mar. 23rd 1881—I have the pleasure of announcing the presence of one of our old schoolmates, Aileen Sinton. Although she is a turned out young lady, it is a pleasure to meet her as it brings to memory the days of yore.

Sallie Blount read about our "New Administration" and Lou about the "New Cabinet." Mattie Kate ended the otherwise pleasant evening by butchering unmercifully "The Sweet Bye and Bye." Sounded more like the other place to my uncultivated ears. I almost forgot to say our new President [29] began his administration by a most beautiful example of filial and marital affection. He astonished all beholders by kissing his wife and mother on the spot. I should have pulled him behind the door to receive the smack. The old people admired it in him and the young ladies glanced at their beaux exclaiming "How lovely!"

I want to put this in the record. After nearly a week of cloudy, wet weather, yesterday was sunny and warm and we could take our walk again. More than anything we wanted to find trailing arbutus. We searched all the spots where we had found it before but it had either disappeared or hadn't come out. We stayed longer than usual and begged to go on but Miss Lou said it was our duty not to upset the schedule of others. So reluctantly we started back on a little used path—a short cut. There on a bank at the top of a hill was the most beautiful bed of arbutus you ever say. Miss Lou stood by it and quoted from Tennyson's

---

[29] James A. Garfield, Republican, was inaugurated March 4, 1881; he died as the result of an assassin's bullet, Sept. 19, 1881.

Ode, "Not once or twice in our rough-island story—The path of duty was the way to glory." I am not sure it will lead us to glory, but we will never forget the path of duty that led to the trailing arbutus.

                                                              Marialva
My darling Miss Lou,   Sept. 2, 1881
    How I wish I were back at Green Mount. I don't think I ever appreciated my happy home there until this summer. I know I will never find a more pleasant home filled with love and harmony or meet with kinder friends than those I made at Green Mount. I hope all the new girls may prove pleasant additions to the household and give as little trouble as possible.
    Papa speaks of starting Brooke and myself off the Tuesday

David in 1881

after Court, though he hasn't decided what college we're to stop at. He told me today if he carried me to Canada we would spend one day at Niagara.

Your loving Mattie Kate

[Minutes of the Evergreen Society]

Sept. 14, 1881—Today we reorganized the Evergreen Society, Mattie Westwood was chosen President, Janey Steel, Treasurer and we will take turns writing the minutes. Our President made a motion that if anyone spoke or was inattentive during the reading of the Bible, she should be fined two cents and everybody agreed to it. Loulie played Gen. Lee's Grand March but she did not play it as well as she does when she wakes me up every morning practicing. After the meeting, Dr. Henley vaccinated the whole crowd.

December 19, 1881—Kate Chidchester played "A Maiden's Prayer" accompanied by giggles. Nannie played "Corinne Waltz" in honor of a new scholar by that name who came recently. Janey played "Bobolink Polka." Mattie sang "Thou has learned to Remember, Thou must learn to Forget." The pleasant exercises were ended by a song from Miss Bessie, "The Day is Done" which was enjoyed by all present. I forgot Corinne read some "Advice to Young Ladies on choosing a Husband," a piece no doubt selected because of the coming wedding of Mr. Sinton and Mollie Garlick. Miss Lou played the Wedding March in preparation for the event.

My darling [Florence],   March 9, 1882

I enclose the letter describing the children's jubilation over receiving the good things in the box we sent Fred.

I am very much better from a fever which lasted seven days and left me very weak indeed. However, I put the best foot foremost and Saturday Bessie drove me to Old Hall to fix up Willie a little. He moved the first of March and this was my first visit. It was a beautiful day and he had two double plows running and he and another boy were burning brush. I felt more thankful than ever that he did not go away with David and is running the farms. He is very well fixed and Nancy cooks his little meals but he comes up every night to supper and seems to enjoy it. Don't you hope he will succeed, its such a comfort to have him. Mr. Reynolds came last week and used up a barrel of lime, doing brick work and plastering and he will put the house in good repair—good enough for Will to bring a wife to live in, till she can have a house built to suit herself, that is if she will only bring the money to build it.

God bless you,
Your devoted Mother

[Minutes of the Evergreen Society]

Mar. 18, 1882—After the Bible was read by Miss Lou—in French this time, Corinne read a "Letter from John Ruskin to Girls"; a piece which would have disgraced the society had it not been a religious piece. She alternately giggled and blushed while she read and Miss Lou made her read it over again and it sounded like an entirely different piece. Lou played "Home, Sweet Home" very well for a beginner, but she seemed to think the more she jumbled up the notes and the faster she played the better it sounded. As Julia did not have to read she sat in the corner looking as sour as if she had eaten up all Mrs. Fleet's pickle.

M. T. W.

After Fred went to the University of Missouri, his summers were free from having to recruit students for the colleges which he headed, and he brought Belle, Mrs. Seddon, and their four children to spend the vacations at Green Mount. In May 1882 Belle wrote Bessie, "Tell Mother I don't believe Mr. Fleet could be paid to stay away, so she needn't waste breath in persuading him."

Soon after they arrived Fred would invite Meredith to come and spend the day with him. Three days after reaching the age of eighteen, Fred had joined the Confederate army and Meredith Diggs, brother of Mammy (Milly), had gone along "to look after him." On those occasions, Meredith arrived early, and they would sit in the summer house in the yard and reminisce about the war—the withdrawal from Gloucester Point, picket duty on Chaffin's Bluff, the Seven Days' battles around Richmond, the Williamsburg Campaign, the defense of Charleston, and the Battle of the Crater. Then, after "biling the cutlery and dishes from the camp chist," Mary served them a large dinner. Afterwards the old army blankets were brought out; they stretched out on them and napped peacefully.

Baptist Female College

Lexington, Mo.

My dear Bessie, Oct. 17, 1882

First of all I know you want to hear about David.[30] I hope and believe Mr. Sellers & himself are making an admirable success of the Wentworth Military Academy. They have 71 pupils and they make almost as fine looking body of Cadets, as those from our own VMI. Everywhere you go on the street, you see a squad of little soldiers, after school is out and drill is over. With their handsome commander at the head, they make a fine show. The uniform is splendidly becoming to David and he is looking better and handsomer than I ever saw him. He comes to see me occasionally and is very sweet and affectionate.

Mrs. Austin says I must tell you with her love that she took the girls walking this evening up Main Street and had a fine view of David drilling his Cadets—a beautiful and interesting sight. Of course, the girls were charmed, and desire to walk that way every evening though heretofore, that part of Main Street was their abomination. Mrs. Austin was very sick a few weeks ago and says she missed Mrs. Seddon's soothing words and tender touch. I replied "Who would not miss it, if they have once been favored with the "angel of her presence" under such circumstances.

All are well at my own dear home. Bro. Staige, not long ago was so broken down, Dr. Cabell ordered him away for a long rest. After staying ten days with his sister in Campbell County he returned to the University, well and greatly re-

---

[30] David returned to Missouri and the Wentworth Military Academy hoping Margaret Norton would marry him.

freshed. God grant his valuable life may be spared. John Staige
is not as well as he might be for he will study too hard. I
wish he could not see a Latin or Greek book or anything on
Mathematics for years. He had better not be so learned and
have more physical strength.

May good angels guard you and yours,

Affectionately,

M. E. Hill

Wentworth Military Academy

Lexington, Mo.

My dear Betsy,   Oct. 29th 1882

Your very welcome letter was received several days ago, many
thanks for it and Mother's, and to sister for the flowers, which
bring such sweet tokens of her. I am very busy, having 74 boys
in our school, 25 of whom are boarders. Still I took the time
last Saturday to run up to Platte City to see Miss Margaret
and found to my sorrow and disappointment (entre nous) she
was going to be married this fall. We talked about you and
she said she wanted you to come and spend the winter with
her.

You are as welcome as can be for the stove, it was said to
be the latest design and I hope, will make you more comfortable.
I am thankful to hear you are all doing so well and are so
happy at home. I will surely come next summer.

Best love to all,

Aff'y, David

Platte City, Mo.

My dear Bess,   Nov. 10, 1882

I can't tell you how much I appreciate your invitation to
spend the winter with you. Please give my love and thanks to
your dear Mother and sisters for their invitation. I have many
pleasant memories of my visit to Green Mount & never expect
to have a happier visit anywhere—nor do I intend it to be my
last.

I would give anything to see you, I need you to talk to. I

have about made up my mind to marry Mr. Woodson, whom I met last May on my return from Florida. He is a lawyer, about thirty, five feet eleven tall, black hair and dark blue eyes— a Christian gentleman and I believe we will be happy together.

You were in my mind constantly in my decision regarding "Bro David" & I truly believe you would have decided as I did. Do not censure me if he feels badly. I could not have been the truly devoted wife that he needs, nor do I think I could have retained his love. I am glad he has given up business in the West, he must have been exposed to all kinds of danger.

I don't deserve half the love and tenderness I have received from your family and it is a source of painful regret that I may have caused even momentary disappointment to any one of you.

I feel both sad & joyful this evening. Please pray that I may be a true, faithful wife.

With much love, I remain

> Your ever attached friend
> Margaret [Norton]

> Wentworth Military Academy
> Lexington, Mo.

My dear Betsy,   March 31st 1883

Many thanks for your letter, you're one of the *bestest* girls I ever saw. And it was I who owed the letter? Well I kind of thought so but I have been so busy and my mind so distracted with the discipline of these horrid boys, I couldn't think of anything else. I have determined to give up teaching and the terrible worry connected therewith and go and live in Dakota among the Indians. I hear glowing accounts of the country— cheap lands—homes and so forth, and there is a tremendous tide of emigration thither. Therefore, I am going when the weather is warm and this school session is over and establish myself as a civil engineer & surveyor and when the cold weather comes next winter and I can't do outdoor work, will run over to Virginia and see you all a month or two. Don't you and Mother and Sister and Florence and Will think that will be a capital idea? I believe there are opportunities in that country for a young man with my attainments and I have only to go out and find them.

I received a long letter from Brother written in the most jubilant spirit just before his two lectures. Do you suppose they really were worth listening to?

Do you think with my fair prospects I dare fan the old flame with Miss Fannie Waddell? She has never looked very happy to me since our engagement was broken off. Miss Evelyn can't bear to see me go with any girl except Miss Fanny but I am going to take one of the prettiest girls in America to *The Bohemian* Girl.

Kiss everybody for me, Ma a million times—all including Mammy and Mary.

Lovingly your Brother David

My dear Sister [Lou],   University April 7, 1883

I am always glad to get your letters, for various reasons, among which may be mentioned that my heart always turns to Green Mount and its inmates as my loved home folks. Another is I so seldom get a letter which is worth reading.

I can scarcely tell you the extent of strain imposed upon an unfortunate applicant for the B. L.—the work alone tho' it must be constant & earnest, might be endured by gritting the teeth & moving on but when you add tó that the uncertainty, responsibility & anxiety, you find a burden such you might say with tears in your eyes the way of the law student is hard. From the foregoing sentences you will perceive that my life is such that it is a kindness to forbear complying with your request to give you an "account" of myself.

Sunday, I usually spend in town—everybody I visit is kind to me; especially are they so at Judge Robertson's and at Mrs. Sampson's I feel almost at home. But now she is gone & I thank God it is to a place where she shall have rest from the griefs that consumed her life here. To "suffer and be strong" must be *so* hard but women do it better than men. Men, when they suffer, are rather apt to want everybody to know it—rather mitigates the suffering. To resume where I left off—in town,

I think—I will bring myself again to the University where I find great pleasure in "dropping in" at Dr. Harrison's. Mrs. H. is such a kind, sweet woman. Wouldn't this be a bully world if it didn't have so many mean yukkum (not classic) in it? Well perhaps it would lack interest.

This summer? Well I shall spend it in King & Queen, & King Wm if the chills permit. I doubt not Uncle Walker will seriously object but I'll get over that by not saying anything to him about it. He wants me to spend part of it with him but the money is wanting. After the summer "then what?" is a question which perplexes me a good deal. Uncle Walker advocates San Antonio for my future home and I am inclined somewhat to it. I am prepared to go where I can make the mostest money in the leastest time. I *must* go where I can earn a subsistence pretty soon. I'd better stop for if I begin another page there's no telling *where* I would stop. Give my best love to Ma, the sisters & Wm. I shall be so glad to see you next summer.

Aff'ly Tom Haynes [31]

Columbia, Mo.
April 23, 1883

My dear Mother,

I have bought a lot in town with the view of building a home upon it. It is three acres, most beautifully situated back of the University campus and almost surrounded by the University grounds. The U. is only about a quarter of a mile away and I can return for lunch. I have decided to build about Aug. 1st.

Our plan is to let Belle and Mrs. Seddon and the children go to Virginia May 8th or 10th and I will follow June 1st, the evening of Commencement. This plan is best for *us* as my wife and children will have their usual summer vacation and I only three weeks less. Would this be more than you can stand along with the school at the same time? We are entirely willing to do what is best for the pleasure of the old Mother and the aunties who have all the trouble (to say nothing of Uncle Will).

[31] Tom Haynes married Bessie Maury, whom he met in Charlottesville, and established a law office in San Antonio, where his uncle, Walker Hawes, was practicing medicine.

When we return we will begin the house, which should be completed by Christmas.

Write as soon as you can collect your thoughts—

All send love,

Aff'y, F.

Arlington

Dear Cousin Lou,   July 24, 1883

Ma has been sick since I got home but she won't send for the doctor as she say she knows as well as he does what to do.

I saw Cousin David but he didn't recognize me, nor did someone I saw two weeks ago, she said I had fattened so. Corinne wrote, her relatives think she has improved so much in looks, thanks to Aunt Maria Louisa's sassafras tea.

Mother joins me in love to all of you.

Lou [Henley]

Lexington, Mo.

My dear Sister [Lou],   Sept. 6th 1883

I am torn between two decisions—Mr. McGraw, a large coal dealer here wants me to go to Texas and take charge of his coal operations there; or go to Washington Territory, the rising country now. If I go to the latter, I shall go to a place where I have friends who will do all they can to help me get started.

Tell Betsy not to regret anything, she can rest this year which is what she needs, and if need be can teach somewhere next year.

In the meantime, I shall wait patiently, feeling assured I shall be directed to the best place.

Best love to all,

Aff'y, D. W. Fleet

Montesano, Wash. Territory

My dear Brother [Fred],   Oct. 8, 1883

I arrived here a few days ago, having heard about this place and country shortly after arriving in Tacoma. Am going to open a Civil Engineer and Surveyor's office in connection with the real estate business.

Montesano is at the head of navigation of the Chehalis River which empties into Gray's Harbor about forty miles away. The nearest railroad is at Olympia and one will be built from that point to the mouth of Gray's Harbor in less than two years. The survey has been made and estimates sent to N.Y. for approval. There must be some outlet between Puget Sound and Gray's Harbor & I am watching for the terminus and there will terminate also. I came from Olympia on the stage and saw such timber I am afraid to describe as you may think I am exaggerating—cedars 8 feet in diameter at stump, 100 ft. high without a limb. Fir 10 to 12 ft. diam. & 200 to 250 ft. high. This section has the finest timber in the territory together with coal and iron beds—three tremendous natural resources and there must be railroads and some large town in this area. Montesano had only three houses a year ago, now it has 75 and 300 inhabitants. I did not come a day too soon and I shall grow with it. Two gentlemen—the proprietor of the hotel where I am staying at $6 per week, and the editor of the *Vidette,* have spoken to me about laying off a town site about 25 miles down the river and have promised me the selling of the lots. I have rented an office with an adjacent bedroom and will put out my sign in a few weeks. I shall write to Franklin in Kansas City for my money and have it to invest in the first opportunity I see. If you have any surplus, I think I can double or treble it in a short time, but I shall be very cautious with my own as well as other people's.

Have seen three sunshiny days since my arrival. The mornings are always foggy with fog from the Pacific. Send this home.

Best love to all,

Aff'y D. W. Fleet

Montesano, Wash. Ter.

My own dear Mother,   Nov. 15th, 1883

I feel happier and more contented than I have for several years. Am glad Will likes the gun and hope he brought in a good many sora with it. This is the greatest place for ducks & fish—salmon 6 to 25 lbs, the best fish you ever ate. They are so plentiful, people spear them. I think this will be great country in a few years.

Thank you for your letters. I am so glad to hear "Mahone was beaten, horse, foot and dragoon," for which I think all Va. should praise the Lord.[32]

I have been quite busy and everything is going smoothly. But for the wet weather and mud, this would be one of the most delightful climates I ever saw. I have laid out a townsite [33] about 14 miles below here which took about a week. I made a map of it, which some said was the nicest thing of the kind they had seen in this country.

I have not met any ladies since I came, don't visit unless I am invited specially. The town is growing slowly, but I expect a boom next spring, especially if the R. R. is built. Some are excellent people while others are rough. Those who have been here longer than 10 years are called moss-backs because moss grows on everything in that length of time because of the rain. What little land there is in cultivation (nearly all is in timber) produces marvelously 400 to 600 bushels of potatoes per acre. The butter and milk are superior to any I ever saw.

You have pleasant reminders of me do you little Mother? I wish you had more. I go to church every Sunday and use my voice, have been asked to lead the singing at the Congregational Church. And don't think you will never see me any more, of course I hope to come shortly when I can afford it.

Best love to all,

Aff'y David

---

[32] Gen. William Mahone, formerly of the Conservative party, presently headed the Readjusters, who advocated the repudiation of part of the state's huge prewar debt and were affiliated with the Republicans. The opposing Funders deemed the payment of the debt a matter of honor, however crippling it might be.

[33] David named the town Aberdeen for the Aberdeen Academy which he had attended in Virginia.

My dear Mother,   Columbia, Mo. Jan 12, 1884

I am greatly relieved at my lecture being over. I had it ready for the Curators at their annual meeting, and of course had the students and faculty present and a sprinkling of the citizens. It was not generally known because not advertised in the newspapers, & it has been suggested that I repeat it, which I will probably do. There is an idea too that plaster casts should be made of the tablet with its inscription [34] and presented by the University to each of the leading colleges of the State. In which case I may have to go & present it, "thereby doing honor to the memory of Mr. Jefferson," as Miss Randolph said in her letter. I carefully avoided any mention of myself in the transaction of which I was the *magna pars,* but made it all as impersonal as possible. Col. Switzler, editor of the *Statesman,* who has more self-assertion than anybody in town—or out of it, for that matter, told me I made a mistake in not telling what I had done and how I had done it. But I had the gratification of my own self approval.

Now as to your question about the baby's name—we decided to name him William Alexander. The Alexander, you see is a part of my name & that of a revered uncle as well as a common family name because of honored & distinguished kinsfolk on Belle's side.[35] William is a family name on both sides too, our

[34] The old granite monument, which for more than fifty years had marked the burial place of Thomas Jefferson at Monticello, with the accompanying marble tablet on which was inscribed the epitaph prepared by President Jefferson a short time before his death:

HERE WAS BURIED
THOMAS JEFFERSON
Author of the Declaration of American Independence,
of the Statute of Virginia for Religious Freedom,
And Father of the University of Virginia.
Born April 2nd, 1743. O. S.
Died July 4th, 1826

was given by Misses Mary B., Sarah., and Carrie R. Randolph, Mrs. Ellen W. Harrison, Mrs. Maria Mason, and Dr. W. C. N. Randolph, great-grandchildren of Thomas Jefferson, to the curators of the University of Missouri. A new and more elaborate obelisk had been erected by the U.S. Congress at Jefferson's grave, and since the Louisiana Purchase, from which Missouri was carved, was made during Jefferson's administration it was deemed fitting that state should have this memento.

[35] Adam Alexander (1772–1851), Presbyterian minister, president of Hampden-Sydney College, 1786–1801, and founder and first professor of Princeton Theological Seminary, 1812–51, was Belle's grandfather.

grandfather's, & your William's, the little fellows' beloved "Uncle Will", while Belle's Uncle William and brother Willie make it entirely harmonious.

All send love to all of you,

Aff. Fred

David was appointed civil engineer of the Northern Pacific Railroad in Washington Territory. One evening in the late summer of 1884, he came into the hotel in Montesano with his engineering party. Standing in front of an open fire with her back toward him was a very attractive looking woman. He turned to one of his companions and said, "There's a woman whom I want to meet." The next day from his place in the choir, he saw her come into the church with an older man and said to a friend, "There's the woman I'm going to marry." Later they were introduced at the hotel, where she was staying with her father, Nelson Waite, a lawyer who had come from San Francisco on legal business, bringing her along for the trip. After a courtship of a few weeks Lillian Waite returned to San Francisco to purchase her trousseau and furniture.

Montesano, Wash. Territory

My dear Mother and home ones,   Sept. 21st 1884

I went down to Peterson's Point and met my fiancée when she returned from San Francisco. We were married that evening, Thursday, Sept. 18th and today I am the happiest man alive. Our wedding day was the most perfect I ever saw, not a cloud seen the entire day, and if that is a favorable omen, our lives will be blessed and happy. I thought I had seen beautiful objects both in nature and art but all dwindled into insignificance when I beheld her on the night of our marriage. It was quite private, no one being present but her father and the family of the minister who performed the ceremony and in whose home it took place. As I wrote you he is my best friend here. She had some photographs taken in S. F., when they come I will send you one. She is intelligent, beautiful and good, and I know she can and will be a great help to me.

I shall not build until next spring. Everything is dull here but I hope will revive some after the Nov. elections. We are living at the hotel and will furnish our rooms with the furniture which Lillian brought in San Francisco, which is very beautiful.

Yesterday I was nominated at the Primary Democratic Convention for the office of County Auditor. That office is the best paying in the County, from $1500 to $2000 per year. If I can get it, it will ease me through these hard times wonderfully. Although the county is Republican, there is some hope of my election. It is an elective office for two years, at the end of that time I want to visit you all and bring my wife. Therefore, dear Mother, don't think you will never see me again for if our lives are spared, you certainly shall. Dear Sister's letter was a model one, just like her. Lillian wants to add a word. She was a Miss Waite.

Love to all,

Aff'y David

I want to love you for David's sake, and call myself
Your affectionate daughter and sister Lillian

Montesano W. T.
My dear Mother,   Nov. 10th 1884

I have just found out the official vote of the County and am glad to write you that I am elected. When I consider the odds that were against me, I am surprised that I was successful. Mr. Goodell and I were the only Democrats elected. I captured most of the temperance vote. Lillian has not been too well lately the election excitement being almost too much for her.

Hurrah for Cleveland & Hendrix. Can't hear certainly but it is very close and they are ahead. I have been congratulated many times that I, so new a man to the County, was elected to its best paying job. I feel sure of a living for the next two years anyway.

Best love to all,

Aff'y David

Montesano
Dear Mother and sisters,   Nov. 20, 1884

I feel very grateful indeed for the generous welcome you have extended to me as one of the family. It makes me realize how much David must mean to his mother and sisters. It is a source of regret that we should be separated by so many thousands of miles from such dear kindred. It is very pleasant to us away off here in little isolated Montesano—to remember we have dear relatives and friends, though so far from us, who live with us in thought and interest. However much we may miss the intellectual advantages, and feel the loss of mental stimulation with minds better stored than our own, we are happy, *very* happy. I think we are peculiarly congenial in every way and are companions in the true sense of the word.

I discovered before our marriage, David's tendency to be blue at times, and believe it was not so much his disposition, as that his life for years had been incomplete. He needed a home, a filling in between the active professional life and solitude, which the life domestic alone gives.

I know very little about housekeeping from teaching or experience, but I must have inherited the taste for it from my Mother. It is a pleasure to cook or do any work for David, he is so appreciative. He is very jubilant over the election of a Democratic President, Territorial Representative and County Auditor (himself). I am very thankful for the latter and believe it was in direct answer to prayer. Nothing less could have given him success here, I feel sure, with such odds against him.

David joins me in warmest love to all, and says, "Blaine ought to be tarred and feathered for his speech against the South." [36]
Your affectionate daughter and sister Lillian

My own dear Mother,   Montesano, March 10th 1885

Your and Sister's letter were received a few days ago. I am glad to write that Lillian is getting along splendidly since an abortion was performed just a week ago. We don't think she

[36] James G. Blaine (1830–1893), Republican candidate for president, had charged the Democratic party with trying to promote Southern political consolidation and thus defeating any rising spirit of national patriotism in the South.

could have lived if it had not been done, for the baby (five months) was dead and there was no telling how long it had been. I never saw anyone suffer as she has done for the last ten weeks.

No, I have not been able to attend to any business in that time and although my expenses have been very heavy, I hope with our good health in the future to be able to pull out before many months. You don't owe me anything but love, dear Mother, neither do the sisters, for they paid all when I married.

I think we have been drawn much more closely to each other in these our trials. It was the first real trouble I ever had and I thank God she has been spared to me. Thank you for your comforting letters,

Love to all,
Aff'y D.

Dear Mother and sisters,   Montesano, March 12th 1885

For the first time I am propped up in bed, and feel that I can attempt a letter to you. It seems almost like coming back from the other side to greet you and my heart is very full. To say the least it makes one feel very strange to have been so near death's door so many times. My heart is full of gratitude to God that he has spared me to live for David. Oh can a life-time of devotion repay such love, kindness and constant attention? Since I learned the depth and strength of his love for me, I determined I *would live* for his sake; and I believe that it, with prayer, has carried me through some of the crises. It has certainly been very surprising to see how kind the ladies of this place have been—nearly all have offered their services and for weeks until last Friday night, there have been night watchers, generally two. On the 27th of Feb. I suffered such a severe attack, Dr. Coleman said I couldn't live through another. David begged him to perform an abortion but he refused, saying I would surely die during the operation, admitting I would die anyway. So he was dismissed and Dr. French was called. Dr. French wanted Dr. Coleman to act with him, he taking responsibility for my life. Dr. C. refused on account of professional jealousy we think, so we had to wait until Sunday evening for Dr. Pearson from Aberdeen, one doctor not daring to act alone for fear of the trouble which might ensue, should I die. During this interim I was able to retain some beef broth and brandy stimulants—more than I had taken during the five previous weeks.

I will spare you the details of the operation which lasted most of the night but when it was over, one doctor collapsed as soon as he reached another room and was kept from fainting only by whiskey being poured down his throat. The other did not even attempt to leave the room but sank completely exhausted into a chair by my bedside. One lady was deathly sick but the other did not give up at all. She is a noble woman—the wife of a Methodist minister. She has been with me day times for the last three weeks and says she knows the good Lord gave her strength to get through *that* night, as it has been years since she has done anything of that kind. Truly God has raised up friends for us in our time of need.

I am reduced in flesh until I don't believe I would weigh 100 lbs. My hair was cut very short by the barber. The cropped hair with the pinched, sallow face and skinny body make me look quite unlike the girl David married—and yet—God bless him! he seems so inexpressibly happy now that I am out of danger, and we are making great plans for our summer's work together. The great trials we have been called to pass through have knit our hearts *so much* the more closely together, and brought us humbly to an appreciation of the goodness and mercy of our Heavenly Father.

You will pardon me, I trust, if I close abruptly now. Many thanks for your kind sweet letters and love from

Lillian

Montesano, Wash. Ter.

My dear Sister [Lou],   June 4th '86

We are getting along splendidly now, I have been enabled to get out of debt and start anew. We received all of your dear letters and expect ere this you have all of the little Missourians with you. I wish it were so that we could be with you all too. I do hope you will have the railroad and soon after it is built, we will come on it to the dear old home and you all. Dear little Mother, I have often told Lillian how active and industrious you were, that when you sat down to read, you always took your knitting in your hands and worked away at it. Some of the socks I have were knitted by your loving hands. Her eyes fill with tears and run over when a letter comes from you all with such loving messages to her.

    Love from us both,

Aff'y David

Dear Will,   11/6/86
    What is the matter with Va. to let the Republicans knock her down and sweep over her. And yet it is not so bad as if old Mahone had you by the throat. Don't you think you better move to "Old Reliable" Missouri? It used to be said if the Democrats would nominate a Comanche Indian he would be elected. For two years now divisions among the Democrats let in a Republican—but fortunately a very good man and many Democrats voted for him.

All well & send love,
Fred

Montesano, Wash. Ter.

My dear Sister [Lou],   Jan. 9th 1887
    Your letter acknowledging the receipt of mine with Christmas presents from Lillian and me gave us great pleasure to know you were all pleased. We felt it was more pleasant to give than to receive. Hope you took a trip and a nice vacation.

    Dear little Mother, it was just like her to give all of hers to "one of the children who could use it for some good purpose." I know there was never such an unselfish and devoted Mother.

    We are getting along nicely. A very happy and prosperous new year and much love,

D. W. Fleet

Montesano, Wash.

Dear Sister Belle,   Feb. 16, 1887

I received the parcel containing the slippers and am delighted with them. Thank you so much for your loving remembrance of me. Nothing could be nicer to wear during the convalescence than the slippers, if I am spared to wear them, they will cause many loving thoughts of the giver.

I have many times thanked our heavenly Father that in giving me such a kind, tender husband, He gave me also, loving relatives, who have one and all opened their hearts so cordially to the stranger. I do wish we lived nearer that we might at least once a year join you in the family reunion at Green Mount. It grieves me that our noble unselfish mother should be entirely deprived of the society of such an affectionate son. You do not know how much I reverence her and how much I would like to be with and learn of one who has given to the world such sons and daughters.

Mr. Fleet joins me in love to all.

Affectionately, Sister Lillian

My dear Grandma,

I haven't wrote to you for so long. Me and Henry are so glad we can be at dear old Green Mount. Mother and Father are going to Europe. We are mighty sorry to let them go but I expect me and Henry will have the best time of them all. I can bridle and saddle my pony so I can get a ride on Nina anytime. If I bring my skates will I have any skating and may I help you fill the ice house, I think it would be fun.

May I go out hunting with Uncle Will? What about Selim? is Uncle Will going to sell him? Please keep him for me to break.

Now goodbye, give best love to everybody from your

Aff. boy Sed

P.S. You are the best Grandma any boy ever had. We would like to bring the pony too.

Montesano, Wash. Ter.

My very dear Aunt Betsy,   May 1st 1887

Your letter and package were received a few days ago—the
first letter I ever received. Please accept my sincere thanks for
the beautiful and comfortable little bootees and sack; tell Grandmother Evelyn [Hill, a grandparent by affection] she has placed
her little grandson under lasting obligations to her for her nice
little present too. Tell her I am so glad she did not let my
dear Papa marry any of those Missouri girls, for if he had, I
would never have been born. My dear Mama and Papa say I
am growing like a little weed and am a smart little fellow. I
have bright blue eyes and dark hair, a nose rather inclined to
be pug, but will outgrow that soon. I am quite a high-strung
little fellow, but don't often cry.

I am so glad to hear that you are pleasantly situated and
your work is not too laborious. I trust I may have the pleasure
and honor of being taught some day by you and dear Grandmother Evelyn. I am quite a strong boy, I hold up my head
and it has never come near "dropping off" as my Papa says
some babies' heads look like they may do. I take lots of my
Mama's time now but soon will be able to save her many steps.
I am just two months old today.

Uncle Frederick sent Papa the picture of his three little men,
Seddon, Henry, and Will, said "Beat this if you can, dare you
to try it." They may be smart and fine looking children, but I
am going to be all that and *good* too.

Now dear Aunt Betsy, I must close my first letter, again thanking you and dear Grandmother Evelyn,

I am most affectionately your nephew,

Reuben H. Fleet [37]

My dear Mother,   5/3/87

I want to say a word about Bessie's being at home next year.
You must certainly have her. You need her yourself, as I don't
think at this time in your life you ought to be without her
help & comfort. Next year the children will be bound to give
you a great deal more trouble and care, and I would not be

[37] Reuben Hollis Fleet was born March 6, 1887.

willing to leave them unless I know Aunt B. would be there
to help you with them. She knows more about them & how
to manage them, and what they need than even little Grandma
[Seddon]. You know they are devoted to Aunt B., and they
will feel more like giving their mother up with her there. Belle
is weakening about going anyway when she thinks of leaving
the children and in case she declines, I sometimes fear my
courage will fail me. Then I expect to pay more than I thought
at first, for I want the little fellows to go to school regularly,
& I hope therefore you won't be so much pressed financially
as you have been this year.

I have been more fortunate with my Kansas City investment
than I expected and shall try to help Sister somewhat by $200
to $250 in her Education Fund for poor girls. I have not made
a fortune by any means but enough to go to Europe without
feeling strained. I am to give $1,000 to our new church building
here—rather more than my part, but I am willing to do it that
the work may go on.

We plan to come as soon as the University closes so Belle
and I may rest for two weeks before sailing.

Yrs. aff.,
A. F. Fleet

Bell's Valley, Va.

Dear Miss Lou,   May 22, 1887

Am truly sorry to hear of your being ill. Should anything
ever happen to prevent your leading the active life you lead,
your sweet influence would live on forever, that can never die.
I wonder sometimes if any school the size of G. M. has ever
benefitted the human race to the same extent as G. M. I believe
not. Having a peculiar aversion to even a semblance of flattery,
I seldom say all I feel. I know I appeared distant and cold at
times to both teachers and schoolmates when, could they have
looked in my heart, how surprised they would have been!

Have you ever read any of Father Ryan's poems? I have been
enjoying them so much.

Love to Miss Florence and Mrs. Fleet

Affectionately,
Lula M. Starke

My dear Lillian and David, August 28 '87

Never mind about staying on the line—I must write you that Reuben's pictures exceeded our highest expectations. I have looked at him long and lovingly, he has a fine head. You must take good care of him for he will be a big man some day.

Mr. Garlick came to see us yesterday & expressed some surprise at meeting Bess in the pouring rain. She was driving down to take some sponge cake & wine jelly to Mrs. Walker, who has been sick. I told him there was no turning back in my children.

We are getting on well with Fred's family and ours, if only you and the blessed baby were with us too! My dearest love to all three of you.

Your affectionate
Mother

Dear Miss Lou, Sept. 20, 1887

As another session begins, I shall take time to write what I have felt for so long—what a privilege it was to go to school in your home and to know your dear Mother. She culled the sweetest flowers from life's abundant thorns and laid them in our pathway, trying to make everything fragrant and beautiful for us. To know her was truly to love her and the home over which she presided.

Your devoted Aileen [Sinton]

Belona, Powhatan Co., Va.
My dear Friend, Dec. 8th 1887

I have felt very anxious to write to you all the session to thank you once more for your unlimited kindness to Eddy. She has mentioned so often since the beginning of the session how sweet & good you were to her & your continued interest in her studies. I feel more grateful than ever to you & your dear family but words are lacking to express my gratitude. I can only pray that your life may be crowned with heaven's richest blessing, & that others may add as much to your happiness as you have to mine. What an unspeakable comfort it is to have a dear friend to stretch out a helping hand in our hour of need. When I think of what my child may be because of your help & kindness, & what she would have missed without them—I realize that to you more than anyone else on earth do I owe my greatest pleasure, but I feel the Lord has put it in your heart to help her & others—that it is His Work in which you are engaged & His "Well done" awaits you when your work is finished here.

My thoughts are so often with you at Green Mt. that I feel almost as one of you. I share your joys & your sorrows, rejoice with you over the good news from the dear absent ones, sorrow with you over those who are sick, but hope you are all well at this time.

Remember me with love to each member of your household, & believe me ever

Yr. sincere friend,
M. D. Eggleston

In January, Betsy accepted a position to teach at the Miller School in Albemarle County. Mrs. Seddon taught her French class as well as participating in the Evergreen Society programs. The minutes record her reading, on one occasion, "a lovely little scrap" entitled "Contentment"; and again, Mrs. Seddon entertained the girls for a while by reading about the origin of the King's Daughters and an account of their work.

Both grandmothers taught Seddon and Henry. Will spent most of his time with his nurse and surprised the family sometimes by his remarks. His Fleet grandmother wrote his mother and father: "He was standing by the window one evening listening to the thunder. After a great rumble, he turned to me and said, 'Hasn't it got big wheels.' I said, 'It hasn't got any wheels.' 'Den how does it roar?' he asked. A question I couldn't answer."

The Evergreen Society record for January 11, 1888, contains the following postscript: "A letter has just been received from Father in Athens telling us of Mother's expected return to us and we are all delighted with the idea of having her back and I hope ere many more Society Meetings she may be one of our number. Minnie S. Fleet, Sec."

Anderson, S.C.
My dear Miss Lou,   Jan. 26, 1888

I know you will be more than surprised when you find this letter is from me. I think of you so often & as I have a writing fit on me, thought I would write to make you think of me.

I do wish you could come to see me and see what a pretty little home I have, everything so comfortable and cozy. But our baby boy beats it all, we named him Willett for Papa and he is something *wonderful.* He is almost two and talks so sweetly. Corinne wanted to know how many *children* I had. I told her I wasn't a rabbit to be having one every change of the moon. Just between us, Willett is more than we can manage.

It has been raining for three days and everything looks so gloomy but every now & then I fancy I can see you coming to the school room saying "Never mind, little children, sunshine & roses are coming." I have not changed a bit everybody tells me—the same old harem scarem Mamie—and my love and affection for you *all* could never change.

Affectionately,
Mamie

Richmond College
My dear Josie [Taliaferro],   March 4th 1888

I am very glad you are imbibing an atmosphere of such refinement, industry, neatness and sanctity as that which is diffused within and around your school. Much do I prefer it to a large pretentious and fashionable college where girls of every character are assembled if only they have the needed funds; and where little of real family and maternal influences can be exercised. I have long loved and admired Mrs. Fleet and all her daughters and sincerely believe they are doing modestly and thoroughly any amount of good which can only be recompensed in a better world than this! But, dear Josie, the greater the opportunity, the greater the responsibility! I shall expect when I see you again, to find an advance in everything good in your culture and manners and disposition.

Your affectionate grandfather
Robert Ryland

Montesano, W. T.
My dear Sister [Lou],   April 19th 1888

I got your letter and the book for Reuben—his first. He grows
more and more interesting every day. How I wish dear Mother
could see him for I well remember her fondness for babies,
especially fine looking, clean, intelligent ones.

We are building a nice little house in the most beautiful,
healthful location in town. When it is completed I will send
you a picture. It is on a high knoll and overlooks the whole
town and we own the land all around us.

Aff'y, D. W. Fleet

[Written on the back]
Dear Sister B.

I reached home safe & well about 6 P.M., the horses stood
the trip well. Mother took some Blue Mass last night which
did her a great deal of good. She is much better this morning,
up and stirring around. She says I must tell you the hen hatched
out twelve fine, hearty ducklings.

Sister is coming up to scratch manfully, she finds herself so
capable that she consulted me about having the "free school"
here next session. I voted *NO* long and loud. Don't mention
this in your letters, I will see to it.

Yrs. aff. J. W. Fleet

My dear Betsy,   May 31st '88

I must tell you about the last few days if I can collect my
wits sufficiently. Mother decided under the circumstances to
close the school a little early and notified the parents. Most
of them arrived by midday Thursday, and after a bountiful colla-
tion Mother spoke briefly—I copied her notes—"Girls, some
of you may teach and some of you may marry, in either case,
children will be very much a part of your lives. Some children
are like little human scrawl books, blotted all over with the
sins and mistakes of their ancestors. It makes a heaven-wide
difference whether the soul of the child is regarded as a piece
of blank paper to be written upon, or a living power, to be
quickened by sympathy, to be educated by truth."

She continued, "The true way to spell happiness is
W–O–R–K and always remember the most effective prayer of

a Christian is 'Thy will be done'." Belle didn't come down as she has been "invisible" for several weeks but moving about in her room. The last girl left Friday morning and that night Willie met Florence, who has been a calming influence and a great help. She found all the things in Richmond which Belle needed. Saturday Walter went to Hanover C. H. and brought Brother and all his trunks. He is well and so happy to see Belle. Minnie and Belle took great delight in unpacking his trunks and took armfuls of beautiful scarfs, sashes, fezzes, cricket caps, etc., etc. up to show their mother.

About dusk the Lord must have directed Lelia to send for Minnie and Belle to come and spend the night at Smithfield. She had some Aberdeen boys too so they enjoyed themselves very much. Soon after they left Willie went on horseback in one direction for Dr. Broaddus and Walter went in the buggy in another for his assistant, much to Mammy's disgust. Said Lucinda couldn't do nothin' she couldn't do. So thankful Belle's labor was short and a little boy was born early on "the Sabbath day." Both mother and baby got along well but we couldn't find the little trunk with the baby's clothes. Our Mother, usually so imperturbable under all circumstances, was dreadfully upset and said "My grandson, so naked and forlorn, and not a garment to put on him." Mammy ran to her house and got some old pillow slips, discarded for dusting rags, which was even more distressing to Ma, who said, "just like a little waif."

When Minnie and Belle returned Sunday, they uncovered the little trunk in the upstairs front hall where they had piled all the things from Jerusalem and Athens. When little Charles Preston was dressed in the exquisite little clothes which Belle and Mrs. Seddon had made for him, Minnie pronounced him a "beauty speck" and Belle a "little dandy," tho' Uncle Will said he looked a "little heated." Only the good Lord could have got us through it all.

All send love,

Yr. aff. sister Lou

The 1887–88 session ended the existence of the Green Mount Home School for Young Ladies, and the *Religious Herald* for September 27, 1888, carried a letter from a former pupil, which said in part:

Many Virginia girls will feel profound sorrow when they learn that the doors of this school are permanently closed, and the class rooms will never again be lighted by the countenance of faithful and loving teachers. I can scarcely realize that the sound of the teacher's voice is to be heard no more in the lecture room, that the tread of the pupil has died away into an eternal silence.

September, four years ago, found me one of an eager group waiting at our desks for the opening exercises to begin. "Dear Miss Lou" stated the principles on which we would be expected to deport ourselves and read a chapter from God's holy word, led in prayer to the "All-wise Father," invoking His blessing upon teachers and scholars, that they may be ordered and directed into an honest discharge of their respective duties. This was the plan for beginning each day's work. "Strength for to-day" was the burden of the prayer, and it was granted for no school was ever blessed with more faithful teachers. They loved their girls, studied their best and highest interests, and were their truest friends.

Of all the busy hours which passed in rapid flight, the one which brought peculiar pleasure to me was the "reading hour"—around which my thoughts cluster and cling—which will ever live in my memory. The work of the day had ceased and the night lessons had not begun. The shadows were growing upon the hills, and the soft kisses of nightfall were making melody through the treetops. As was the dew to the withered plant, so was this hour to our tired brains. Assembling ourselves in the schoolroom, one of the teachers would read some good interesting book. The literature selected was of the kind which always penetrated with a spirit of beautyfying purity—a sort of moral cleanliness.

The lecture room is silent, the faithful, loving teachers separated, the girls scattered, but the school has a record of honors won, of work well done. We hold a sorrowful farewell for those bright by-gone days. Teachers and scholars may not meet again this side of the river, but may we all meet in the "new city of delight" where perennial flowers bloom, where friendships are eternal.

III

"A lady's life"
1888–1900

After the Green Mount Home School for Young Ladies was closed, Lou continued to teach music to the pupils who came to her home. Betsy returned to Albemarle to teach in the Miller School, and Florence lived at Millwood, the Sizer home in King William County, where she taught the Sizer children and a few others in the neighborhood. Since by way of the Mattaponi bridge at Dunkirk, Millwood was only about three miles away, she came home on weekends.

My dear Bess,   Sept. 1, 1888

It was raining so hard this morning Will concluded not to go out, so we seized upon his leisure day—the first since you left, to clean out his office closet. We found things, new and old, we didn't know we had. We moved everything out and carried some of the rubbish up the garret. I found up there the body of one of Minnie's best fall dresses in the most out of the way place and will have to mail it to her.

I am as happy as possible having a chance to do these things and to lead such a lady's life. Though I enjoyed all the years of the school, I must say this respite is very welcome.

We haven't heard from Mo. but David sent us a descriptive catalogue of Chehalis County and Montesano which is so attractive, if I were younger, I would move right out.

Yr. aff. Mother

My dear little Betsy,   Sunday morning—Sept. 16th

The morning looked so unlikely I preferred staying at home and writing to you and reading to going to church, but if I could hear the sermon, I would go every Sunday.

I was never in better health and spirits than now that I am taking a little reasonable rest. My appetite is very good for

the little quiet contented meals we have. Willie got a barrel
of Graham flour from Mr. Sizer, which we enjoy. Florence is
contented and happy in her new home. Alice Campbell will
come tomorrow, that will be $400 for four scholars. Who is
doing any better? There may be others, but she is not worrying,
never does you know.

Do you read Fred's articles in the *Herald* and Dr. Dickinson's
flattering comments. As Fred is writing for fame, not money,
he is in a fair way to get it. We have not lost any time from
saving the peaches, pickling, preserving and canning—and the
last few days making peach leather and chips. Lucy and Maggie

Reuben Hollis Fleet

Walker came Wed. evening. Maggie hasn't found any school. I feel so sorry for poor girls who are anxious to work but can find nothing to do. They were so glad of some peaches.

Yr. aff. Mother

Montesano, W. T.
Sept. 21st 1888

My dear Mother,

A little girl baby came to our house this morning at 6 o'clock. Although L. was very low, she has revived now and both are doing as well as can be expected. I have been waiting this advent before answering Sister's last letter. Can you select a name for the little Washingtonian? [1] The little one comes at a very busy season but is most welcome, nevertheless.

We have good help, and L. shall have the best of care.

Love to all,
Aff'y David

Albemarle Female Institute
Charlottesville, Va.
Sept. 22, 1888

My dear Miss Lou,

You have no idea how I long to be at dear old Green Mount now instead of this horrible place. I ought not to say that I know because, no doubt, I'll like it very well after I begin to feel more at home. I felt at home from the first night I went to Green Mount but I don't here one bit. I came yesterday with Papa. Only a few boarders have come and most of them are so stiff and formal, calling each other Miss etc. I will have three room mates but only one has come and she is two or three years younger than I am.

Miss Lou, you can't image what a perfectly delicious time I had this summer, especially the time I spent at Green Mount. I think I can truly say I never enjoyed anything more in my life. Please give my best love to Mrs. Fleet and Miss Florence and kindest regards to Mr. Fleet. Write to me please Miss Lou. With the greatest quantity of love,

Your devoted friend,
M. S. S. [Mary S. Shelton]

---

[1] The baby was named Lillian for her mother.

Ballsville, Va.
Dear Miss Lou,   Sept. 26, 1888

You'll be interested to hear I have a position to teach this year and although I will never make a fortune in old Powhatan, I will be able to live at home.

How is Mrs. Fleet's health? I want to know *so* many things about you all. I shall never forget your kindness to me, though I was such a poor bashful creature I know I never showed it. I hope I have learned better now.

From what I hear it seems that Eddie has a shy notion of being "an old man's darling." I wrote her it was cruel of her to get married and leave me behind and she denied it.

I have written hurriedly so please excuse mistakes, with best love to each of you,

I am yours lovingly

Phoebe Hurt

Berryville
My dearest Cousin Lou,   Oct. 3, 1888

I am glad you like the change to teaching only music and hope it may be a comfort to Cousin Maria Louisa to have a quiet, peaceful home—but I cannot be reconciled to the thought of so many girls losing the benefit to be derived of a life at Green Mount to say nothing of the teaching. I would not be without my experience there for any amount of money. I can teach better day by day and be more patient when I remember how I was taught and just yesterday I was giving your rule for politeness.

My love to each one from your affectionate

Mamie

West Point, King Wm Co.
My dear Miss Lou,   Oct. 11, 1888

I know you remember how delighted all of us were last year to get a letter, and the one which came today is still dearer— the letter in the RELIGIOUS HERALD which Mrs. Abrahams wrote. It reminded me so much of last session, it was as much as I

Lillian Fleet

could do to keep back the tears. It seems so sad to think that the school at Green Mount is no more.

Father says "I hope your dear Mother has had better health since the school was dismissed for I know with her indefatigable nature she had a laborious time although her daughters assisted all they could."

Your fond friend,
Josie Taliaferro

Culpeper, Va.
Oct. 12, 1888

Oh! Miss Lou, I had so many fears about my ability to teach wisely and well, but from the first I adopted your rule—never to go into my school room without asking Divine guidance for strength during the day, and have been greatly encouraged by my success so far.

Give my love to your dear Mother, I have never seen anyone so guileless and full of love and kindness and yet so capable in coping with the difficulties which constantly confronted her. Unlike anybody else, she made me feel better just to come into her presence.

Miss Lou, you with your lovely flowers, your "sermons in stones and good in everything" and Miss Bessie and Miss Florence with their beautiful music, made it a rare privilege to be in your home and you have given me memories to brighten whatever dark days that may lie ahead.

I enjoyed Mrs. Abrahams' tribute to the Green Mount School, it was but a reiteration of what all your girls feel in their hearts. I know none of us thinks of the close of the school without a feeling of sadness.

Remember me affectionately to dear Miss Florence and with love for yourself I remain,

Your loving little Elizabeth [Watlington]

[Written on the bottom of the letter]
My dear Bessie,

These letters are so gratifying, I send them to you. Ma says there isn't an hour of the day or night when she is awake that she doesn't think of you and rejoice over your coming home so soon.

Love,
Lou

My dear little one [Betsy],   Sunday eve. Oct. 21st '88
    Last Monday I rose at five o'clock, had breakfast with Will and got him off to the Tappahannock Court, then little Waddell drove Florence and me to Mr. Sizer's about 9 o'clock. Florence opened her school and I spent a very pleasant day. I haven't been away from home for so long, everywhere I go people treat me with distinguished politeness. Bessie Douglas walked over to have dinner with me, looking as well as I ever saw her. They had ham and cabbage, bread, mill pond chub—no better fish—corn, Irish and sweet potatoes, butter beans, tomatoes, radishes, etc., then ice cream and cake. Florence has a very pleasant room and as pleasant a home as possible, comfortable and near home. Mrs. Sizer seemed so glad to have her, said she couldn't bear to trust anything as important as her childrens' education to a stranger.

Love from us all, yr. aff.
Mother

My dear little darling [Betsy],   Nov. 6th '88
    This is election day! Are any of you stirred up? I got up very early to get Will off to Clark's by 6 o'clock. The poll had to be opened at sunrise and he had to be there to swear in the commissioners. I made him a cup of coffee and boiled two eggs on the oil stove, all the time thinking, My Country 'tis *for* thee. Lou roused enough to say she would get up but she knew what a pleasure it was for me and would not deprive me of it. Did you read her latest effusion in the *Herald.* I tell her she must have a scrapbook for her pieces and Fred's. You don't know how much I enjoy being my own mistress and Lou does too. We are never idle or lonesome either. If you and

Florence were not happily situated, I should reproach myself
for leading a life of ease and you banished from home, but
as it is, I am just thankful all day long. No doubt Lou will
add enough to make this worth two cents.

Bless my darling child,

Yr. aff. Mother

[Lou added] Will and I have a reading hour together after
supper, go to his room and take turns until Ma is tired. We
are reading John E. Cooke's *Virginia* and enjoy it very much.
Don't you envy our quiet happy days?

Montesano, W. T.

Dear Brother [Fred]:   Nov. 8th 1888

I am defeated by the entire Republican majority, they made
a clean sweep of the County. I am taking it like a man, nevertheless. This is certainly an off year for Democrats.

Love to all, yrs. aff'y
D. W. Fleet

My dear Will,

I enclose this from D. It was no more than I expected after
the Republican cyclone struck the country. Did you ever see
anything like it? And that too when we thought about the time
of the Chicago Convention the G. O. P. had about gone up
the spout.

I hope D. is able to stand the loss of his office, & from what
Chamberlain told me I judge he is. Tell Mother I think she is
neglecting me in writing. Glad to hear the barrel starts today,
will let you know when it arrives.

Yrs. aff'y,
F.

My dear Grandma,   Columbia, Mo. Nov. 9, 1888

We all have got the blues because the Democrats were so
dreadfully defeated and we won't have any parade or fireworks.
Grandma was mightily taken back because she was so sure

Cleveland would be elected but she has heard since that Harrison is a good Presbyterian and she is a little more comforted.

Father has gathered his apple crop and after all that have specked, which Mother had cooked & what we have eaten—Selim ate nearly a barrel—he has about four barrels of good ones.

Thank you and Aunt Lou & Uncle Will for the good things you sent us.

Your loving boy,
Seddon

My dear Bess,

I send these notes. Ma & I have both written to David a letter of sympathy inviting him to come here with his wife and children next spring when his term is up. You must do the same. I hope something better is in store for him—I'm sure there is or he wouldn't have lost his place. Only three more Fridays, then I hope you'll come.

Devoted love from Ma and us all,

Lou

Staunton, Va.

My own dear Betsy,   Jan. 13, 1889

I hope you have put into execution the plan to close the school thus relieving your Mother of care and responsibility, and having your sweet home once more sacred in its privacy; though I know the loss it incurs to your pupils, who I am sure can never find another school with all its advantages. I am rejoiced to hear of your mother's good health. Can't you persuade her to make you a visit in the spring and both of you come to see us.

We went to Baltimore for business and stopped by Washington for pleasure. Attended one of Pres. Cleveland's receptions, and were glad to get back to our cozy little home.

A great deal of love from your true friend,

Julia K. Lushbaugh

Jan. 24th '89

Is it possible I haven't written to my dear little Betsy since she left? I knew Lou kept you supplied with the news and I have been busily putting together silk pieces with fancy stitches to make my grandchildren little quilts and knitting stockings and gloves for them.

You want to know how I am getting on leading "a lady's life" once more—Alice comes in about seven and makes my fire, and the one in the cellar and sets the table. Then Mary comes in with the bread risen in her house, and gets breakfast as soon as we want it. Alice washes the dishes and I tell Mary what I want for dinner. I go up and rarely ever go down again until it is ready, I tell her I am so glad to have a cook who knows more about cooking than I do. You would be surprised to see how Alice has "bloomed out" since Martha left. She told me in the most delighted way "Cousin Mary had promised to learn her how to cook." The result is that Capt. Smith told me I was looking younger and prettier that he ever saw me.

Mr. Lyne's place was sold the other day for $1500, about $2.00 an acre. Mr. N. Walker bought it for the wood.

Yr. aff. Mother

My dear Bessie,   Feb. 10, 1889

Alice has just come in to tell me Joshua has breathed his last. We have had little hope of his recovery for some days. He told me one day last week in his feeble stammering voice, "All my trust is in the Lord," so now we rejoice he is safe in his Father's house.

Lovingly,
Lou

My darling little Betsy,   Feb. 13th '89

Your letter came like a ray of sunshine to brighten up the day that had been made so dismal by Joshua's funeral. Mary bears it very well and so do the rest.

Lou coughed most of the night so I insisted that she stay in bed as she didn't have any girls to teach or children to amuse.

She took my advice & am sure will be well by tomorrow. Nobody can be as thankful as I that I don't have to be in two or three places at once. People who have never had a school don't know what it is to be divided in several parts.

Florence came Friday and told us what an elegant supper Mr. Sizer had on his birthday. There were eleven gentlemen and no ladies but those of his family. They had wild geese, old ham and scalloped oysters, bread, coffee, for the first course. Then three kinds of cake, jelly, ice cream & frozen egg nog. Col. Aylett asked Spotswood Pollard why he didn't celebrate his birthday like Mr. Sizer does. He replied he didn't have so much cause to be thankful for *being born* as Mr. Sizer has.

Yr. aff. Mother

My own dear Mother,   Montesano, Feb. 22, 1889

Your letter with the box of little things for the children came last night. Let me thank you for them; they are beautiful and Reuben says "pretty."

Your kind invitation came and we hoped we could accept it, but I shall be starting into a title abstract business. We are having a *boom* now that Washington has become a state and if I should leave even for a short length of time it might be ruinous to me. We want above all things to see you and have you see your two most affectionate and lovely grandchildren. We shall keep you before R's mind so he will be prepared to love you when he comes.

I am so sorry to hear about Joshua. Give my love to Mammy and Mary and tell them, they have my heartfelt sympathy.

God bless you all and best love from us all,

Aff'y, David

My dear Betsy,   Feb. 24th 1889

The thermometer was 4 below o this morning, and we hope to fill up with ice on Monday. We are so thankful the winter is so nearly gone before this bitter weather and we are so very comfortable.

Monday—We put in all the ice we could get today and the

house is not quite full, still it will be plenty I have no doubt if it keeps as well as usual.

Will had to go to Court and I went down to superintend it. I was very proud *to help* by cutting across the pond, it would not bear the weight of a man, but it would my ninety-five pounds, so I stood on the planks they put out and it really did help for me to set the large sheets afloat, I am afraid if you tell Miss Evelyn, she'll say again I ought to be put to bed. But I knew it wasn't deep enough to give me "a watery grave" and I haven't felt the slightest inconvenience except a little sore from the unusual use of the muscles in cutting. I didn't even get my feet wet or cold as I stood on planks all the time.

Mother joins me in love from your affectionate sister,

Lou

March 15th 1889

You have no idea, dear Miss Lou, how many times in my life when I have been uncertain how to act and what course to pursue, and I would be so much in need of good advice, some little opinion of yours, your Mother's or sisters' would come into my mind and decide me at once.

Lovingly,
Sallie Lee [Blount]

My dear child [Betsy],   March 17th 1889

I hope you will go to Staunton and to the University too to that concert. Why should you deprive yourself of such innocent pleasure and improving ones too—to save a little money. I, for one, don't feel nearly so poor as I did a year ago.

I hope Will can go to see you either the 13th or 20th of next month, depending on whether he can miss Essex or King Wm Court most conveniently. He gets a fair practice. What he makes I never ask him, but he is kept quite busy and is certainly in better spirits. He was made very glad last night by the advent of a little blaze face colt which we named Stella. Kate has a little male calf, a dear little creature and the fowls look well and happy.

Yr. devoted Mother

Miller School
My dear Sister [Lou],   April 7, 1889

I thought so much of you yesterday and wondered if it snowed as hard with you as it did here *all* day. Two peach trees under my window were full of pink blossoms which looked so pretty through the snow, but the hyacinths and brave little crocus were hidden.

Capt. Vawter never fails when I see him to say something about my misplaced sense of duty in leaving last year. He said, "we want you to stay here and take care of these children and never go off to take care of somebody else's."

Love to all from your affectionate sister,

Bess

Berryville, Va.
My dear Cousin Lou,   April 25, 1889

It is too great a pity for you not to have a large school to lead your students to higher thoughts and aims than they could ever have without your influence. Though I expect the quiet home and freedom of this year have been so delightful you will not give them up again for a teacher's life.

Yours always,
Mamie

My dear Bessie,   May 24, 1889

I have a sad piece of news to tell you. Josie Taliaferro is extremely ill. They telegraphed for her parents and they went at once. How can we ever be thankful enough that our school ended before any terrible calamity befell us! When I contrast our calm peaceful days with those of last year about this time I wonder how we lived through it. Only the omnipotent God could have upheld us.

The chickens wake me so early, I have to stop—with love from all,

Lou

My darling child, Lou starts me on the line and I hope I can stay on it to say don't get up to write home before breakfast.

I rather you should sleep and only send a postal to say you are well.

Your devoted Mother

My dear Mother,   June 7th 1889

The other two pairs of socks came and were exactly right and so comfortable. I shall never put them on without thinking how good you have been to me for the 48 years of my life and how your love and wisdom have guided and directed me.

I have more than a hundred letters to write regarding the school [2] and as I found it impossible to get an experienced stenographer, I dictate to one of our boys one or two hours a day and in two or three days he will get the letters out.

On my trip to Columbia, I rode down with Gov. Francis and he told me I would have his two oldest boys next year. He has six in all, & altho' I almost dread to take sons of prominent men, yet they must go somewhere and perhaps we can do as well for them as anyone else. It will be helpful to build up the school. I now have 3 sons of Supreme Court judges, one of an ex-governor and other state and county officials are among my patrons.

Love to all from us all,

Fred

Montesano, Wash.

My own dear Mother,   Aug. 21st 1889

Many happy returns of your birthday and may all those remaining be strewn with sweet flowers. Lillian and the children are in San Francisco, she will have their pictures taken and of course you shall have one. As to mine, I will try to have one taken when I go to Oregon next week to prove my timber claim. Times are dull at present but we are looking for better ones when the "Air line" RR comes in a month or two.

---

[2] A. F. Fleet resigned as head of the Greek Department at the University of Missouri and opened the Mexico Military Academy at Mexico, Mo.

I am glad Brother was not selected President of the University. It is a most responsible position and would cause him much anxious care, and his honors will come anyway in due time. Dear Mother, don't think I will ever run for Congress, we have men who are too talented for me ever to think of such a thing.

Most affectionately,
David

Columbia, Mo.
My dear Sister [Lou],   Aug. 22, 1889
Your welcome letter found us well and busy. I assign to the boys 20 panels of fence a day to whitewash, which they do in about two hours.

Minnie has enjoyed herself greatly this summer. It has been very gay for her set—too much so I tell her—six parties last week. Curious how young people do enjoy themselves with not more than a semblance of an idea in the whole crowd! And yet they can meet every day and not seem dull & stupid to each other. Minnie vows she will study this winter as she never did before. Belle is huge—mentally as well as physically, two inches taller than her Mother. Seddon and Henry are inseparable and devoted to each other, as are Will and Charlie, who play together.

Love to all, A. F. Fleet

My dear Will,   Montesano, Wash. Sept. 16th, 1890
Your letter of a week ago was just received in which you said Dr. Broaddus feared some internal abcess was forming. Poor girl, she seems to suffer more than her share.[3] I had hoped so much she was entirely out of danger. The care, trouble & anxiety to you all with her severe illness & away from me almost crazes me. I send you this money to help you pay for things

[3] Lillian, with her two children, crossed the continent in her traveling cape in midsummer to have her baby in Virginia. She lost the baby and was desperately ill at Green Mount.

you must need & if you need more, don't hestitate to call on me & I shall try to respond. If I could sell some property, I would come right on and stay until she is well enough to come home.

Poor dear Aunt Bess hasn't had much rest this summer & I do feel so solicitous about her—in fact about all of you. Please wire me how Lillian is.

God bless you all and a heartful of love from

D. W. Fleet

[Written in pencil on the back of this letter before it was sent on to Bess, who had returned to the Miller School]—We were so glad to hear of your warm welcome tho' it was just what we expected & what we think you deserve.

Lillian is improving & was able to eat some quail which Will got for her. Alexander came up today to bring her a partridge & Frank sent her another. Peachey sent her some squirrels, as you see she has been well supplied & enjoys the game more than any thing else. Millie Belle Dew sent her some wine which is very nice & wrote "if Mrs. Fleet likes it and if she is benefited by it, she is perfectly welcome to the rest I have. I will take pleasure in making anything she fancies—I have some brandy peaches and if you think she would like them, let me know."

Florence & I played all our duets for Lillian today & she enjoyed them, so did the children. She sees them now everyday. They spend some time in the garden helping? me & in the evening we have a fire for them to play by & we enjoy it too.

All send love,

Your devoted sister Lou

Indiantown, S.C.

My dear Miss Lou,   Oct. 2, 1890

I have heard from some of the girls of Mrs. David Fleet's extreme illness and loving sympathy for you all in the anxiety and care necessarily attendant thereupon, prompts me to write to you.

Miss Carrington, a friend of ours, saw Mr. & Mrs. Fleet some-where—on a ship, I believe, and said that they were the handsomest couple she ever saw. I thought how happy you would be to have them with you and was truly distressed to know she had been so ill. I know you of all people is submitting to His Will, for it is only by rebelling that the yoke is so hard to bear.

I am teaching in a "subscription school" now, then it will run as a public school for about three months. I clear about $20 a month while a private school and perhaps $26 when public.

We had an unusually gay and pleasant summer, which made it difficult for me to leave. Mother also opposed it strongly and the problem, "What is duty"? confronted me. I trust I decided wisely.

Nothing can efface from my mind the remembrance of the goodness, kindness and faithful instruction of my dear teachers and friends at Green Mount. I trust I will be a better woman all my life for that remembrance.

Much love to Mrs. Fleet, Miss Bessie, Miss Florence and my kindest regards to Mr. Fleet from your loving

Evangeline Pettus

Mexico, Mo.
Oct. 11, 1890

My dear Mother,

So glad to hear of Lillian's improvement and hope she is well enough to travel again.

Our school opened with 65 boarders and 90 day scholars. But we have had some trouble—four are no more—disobedience and falsehood, but we expect two others this week and are quite crowded. We have launched an extensive program of building and expect to have twice this number next year. This school has made a vast change in my life—from one of ease, quiet and restfulness, freedom from care and responsibility to one of anxiety, harassments and unrest. I have most of the administrative and all of the business affairs upon me, but I find excellent helpers in my Commandant of Cadets and teachers. I am a full-fledged colonel and wear the U.S. Colonel's uniform! Belle was mightily opposed to it at first, but has yielded to the logic of events. Would you recognize your son in the same uniform Sheridan wore when he came to visit you in '64?

Tho' I am often weary of the burden, I thank God for this measure of success in the enterprise I have undertaken, and to which I give my very best energies.

All send love,
Yrs. aff'y, A. F. Fleet

Mexico, Mo.
Oct. 20th '90

My dearest Grandma,

I have something dreadful to tell you. The other evening Henry and Seddon, thinking Selim was hungry too, took out to him a basket full of biscuits and they soured on his stomach and he died that night with colic. Just think of such a thing!! We are so distressed we don't know what to do. He suffered terribly and couldn't be relieved although everything imaginable was done for him.

I hope I will have better news next time, until then

Your devoted Minnie

My dear Bess,   G. M. Nov. 4th 1890

Ma & I rose early this morning so we could have breakfast with Will as he goes to Clarks to hold the election.

I hear our good Dr. Broaddus is extremely ill and pray he will be speedily recovered. Isn't it fortunate Lillian no longer needs his daily visits.

Now that it has turned cold we have given little Sister the little feather bed that belongs to her crib. When I put her to bed, she said, "Me want Aunt Bessie to lay by me in my little pillow bed." Showing that she remembers you and wants you to share all her pleasures. After her prayers, she remarked, "Me love God me want him to sit on my lap."

Friday, we had the parlour carpet and the ones in the office, dining room and chamber put down. In the midst of it, Reuben said, "Aunt Lou, don't you feel glad you are well." I am very well but too busy to gain any. I weight 101 and Lillian weighs 138, a gain of 17 pounds in the last two weeks. She has enjoyed the quail and sora which Will and friends have brought her.

We had our sweet potatoes dug last week & made a fine crop. Ma had three more barrels packed to send Brother.

Goodbye & God bless you.

Aff. yrs. M. L. F.

Miller School

My dear Mother, Nov. 10 '90

I miss your letters more than I can say but know the reason you don't write is because you can't see. Although it distresses me, I try not to grieve for I know how gracefully you submit to it.

I spent Saturday night at Capt. Vawter's and enjoyed Mrs. V's nice breakfast—hot rolls, fried chicken, rabbit, buckwheat cakes, fried apples, milk, butter, etc. Mr. Neve, from Grace Episcopal Church preached for us on Sunday. We are rejoicing greatly over the election and hope the Democratic gains will mean a Democratic President next election.

Not long before Christmas, so glad Lillian and the darling children will be with us.

Love to each one from Bessie

Florence was now teaching music and modern languages in the Durham Female Institute in North Carolina.

My dear Home-Ones, April 5, 1891

I didn't know Mr. Markham had written to you and feel much gratified at his opinion of me.[4] This week ends the third month of school. The children are progressing quite rapidly in their lessons as well as in their music. I bought some oranges yesterday, Mother, according to your instructions, treated the family and have enough to last the rest of the week.

I am so glad to have such good reports of Lillian and the children. It makes me so sad to think that the time is approaching for the parting at home and I wish I could be with you.

[4] John L. Markham was a member of the Board of Directors of the Durham Female Institute.

Dear, sweet, generous Brother David! How kind it was in him to send you that money, Mother. I hope you can make your arrangements to go to Baltimore when Lillian goes and the doctor can greatly benefit your eyes.

Dear Lillian, I trust you and the children will have a safe trip back to your far away home and you can take up the duties and responsibilities of your home life with renewed strength and energy.

Best love to all,
Florence

Montesano, Wash.

My dear Home Ones,   April 24th 1891 2 P.M.

We got here safely at 7 o'clock last night, gave our baggage in charge of a drayman and drove directly to the hotel where we had supper. I began to feel completely overcome with fatigue, so we hurried through and came home a little before eight. While Mr. Fleet [5] built up the fires, I got the beds in readiness and the children safely tucked in. I feel very thankful that we met with no accident and to find everything in the house in such good condition, and too, I am very glad it is raining hard for no one will be apt to come.

We took breakfast at the hotel and think we shall continue to board there for the fare is excellent. It is only two blocks and there is a good sidewalk so it will not be unpleasant going back and forth even in rainy weather.

Mr. Fleet is looking very well and says he feels he has commenced to *live* again. Poor fellow, I did not realize how hard it must have been for him to be so utterly alone all these months. He says we will never know how he has suffered. He has enjoyed the children so much and they have expressed so much love and affection for him.

People greet me very cordially & seem glad to have us back. Notwithstanding, I have cried nearly all day. I fear Mother will think I am sentimental and ungrateful, but I cannot help it.

[5] After Lillian's visit to Green Mount, she always referred to her husband as "Mr. Fleet," as was customary in Virginia.

It was very hard to give up all at once, Mother, sisters, and brother. I miss more than you can ever know, your loving care and kindness. Mr. Fleet promises that we shall go back in two years & I may stay as long as I wish, but that is a long time away. May God keep us all till we meet again.

Just at this point I heard someone at the door and you may be sure I was reluctant to admit them with my eyes so red and swollen. I found it was dear Mrs. Goodell, and she seemed to understand and sympathize fully when I told her I believed I felt much as a daughter would after she had first left the dear old home. She is the lady who took care of little sister the day after she was born when all others were so busy with me.

While she was here, Mrs. Devilbiss, the wife of the editor called so the rest of the afternoon was taken up with them.

Today, I have unpacked, everything came in good condition even the platter was not broken. Mr. Fleet says give you all his best love and tell you he is mightily obliged to you for giving his darlings up, that if business were a little better, he would be as happy as an angel.

I wish I could ride to the postoffice this afternoon with you, Uncle Will, I am so anxious to hear when Mother expects to have her eyes examined. Don't you think, Mother dear, you would be glad if Florence was with you. I do hope I shall get a letter soon, it seems so long since I left. Reuben just looked up and said "You got tears in your eyes, Mother, I don't want you to cry. You got me and sister and Papa." So I must try to be brave, but if you do love me, please write often.

Lovingly, Lillian

My dear Mother,   May 5, 1891

I have been feeling very far from you since you have been unable to write to me, I constantly find myself longing for one of your good letters, full of cheer and sympathy.

My health is better than it has been for years, I think it is due in large degree for the *hope* I have for the future. I complete my arrangements for the $30,000 loan from two banks for three years, to enable me to complete my building. This is the opportunity of my life and it seems best to avail myself of it. The Mexico people are very proud of the school and are doing all they can to help us.

Let me hear as often as you can,

All send love,
Yours, F.

My dear Brother [Fred],   May 26, 1891

We were very much pleased to get your letter and the one from little Belle. Tell her she would have been amply paid for her time and trouble if she could see how much pleasure it gave us all, especially her grandmother who has to be by herself so much now that I am well enough to work in the garden again. She sits at her knitting and thinks over and over again of all the children and of each saying of the little ones. She is as well as usual now and full of plans to can and preserve a large quantity of fruit for you. We never had so much before; but she is puzzled by one thing which you must lose no time in telling her. "How can all the fruit that we could preserve or can, help Fred with his 150 or 200 boys? Twelve dozen half gallon cans will seem such a drop in the bucket."

The cluster cherries will be ripe by next week, so you must write as soon as you get this to tell if we must proceed to can or preserve them. In one of my letters not long ago I asked if it would be possible for one of the mothers (Mrs. Seddon or Sister Belle) to come this summer and bring three of the children to help with the fruit, leaving one mother and the other three to help you, but you haven't taken the slightest notice of the invitation. We do want to see you all dreadfully, and we want to help you too if we can with the fruit. We have such an abundance of everything to eat—fruit, ice, fowls, milk, butter & vegetables that it seems a pity not to be able to share them with you and yours. We have such a good cook too in Mary's place, an excellent girl who is a great comfort with the work.

Mother is very much pleased to think your vacation is so near. She hopes it will bring some rest to Belle, even if it means only a change of work for you. She is delighted too with anticipation of the camping out for the boys, and says you must tell them it will then be in order to get boxes from home, with the best the mothers can send—do you remember? Of course those boys who are too far from home to get anything must share with those who do, I do trust nothing will happen to mar the record of the first year of the "M. M. Academy." Is your new building to be joined to the one you have?

I was greatly delighted with your discoveries about the Fleet ancestors. Only a few days ago, I read in Keane's *Handbook of Washington:* "In 1634 Henry Fleet, with a party of Calvert's settlers, visited the falls of the Potomac," and of course I wished I could know more of him and his voyages to Virginia. Where do you suppose Mr. Justice Winsor saw the "original narrative" of which you spoke.[6] Mother says I must tell you not to waste any time on your ancestry, it's not a question of are you *of* the nobility, but is there nobility *in you*. She thinks it was Napoleon who said "Be your own ancestor," and she doesn't think you will discover any Fleets who have done more good in the world than her children. You have no idea what aspirations and hopes she has for your children. "God grant they may be *all they ought to be,"* she says. You know she hasn't a particle of reverence and love for old things, which you and I have inherited from somebody. Though I made her acknowledge she would greatly prefer to know that Henry Fleet came over as he did, than to hear he had been exported for stealing as I have heard the ancestors of some Virginians we know were and whose descendants are still tainted every now and then with a streak of dishonesty. She prefers that her children should do noble things, rather than dream of what their ancestors have done and agrees with Tennyson, "Kind hearts are more than coronets, And simple faith than Norman blood." But I believe in "noblesse oblige" and think our kindred should be trained to feel themselves above doing anything low or mean.

---

[6] The "original narrative" was Henry Fleete, "A Briefe Journall of a Voyage made in the Barque Warwick to Virginia and Other Parts of the Continent of America" (1631), in the Lambeth Palace Library, London.

Mother says I must tell you she remembers whose birthday it is tomorrow and we will make all sorts of good wishes for our little Virginia boy.[7]

I hope you will tell us soon of the safe arrival of four pairs of socks she sent you. So you see whatever else may be failing her, her love for her children is unchanged and unfailing. It is such a pleasure that she can still knit and she does for each one of us.

With much love for each one from each of us, I am

Devotedly yours,

M. L. Fleet

My own dear Mother,   Montesano June 21st 1891

I was so glad of your little note—never mind about staying on the line—and to know the time has been long to you too and that you are planning and working for our coming next year. There will be one less at G. M. to welcome us and we shall sadly miss her dear old face for she was so much a part of the family. I shall never forget Mammy's coming to the road gate to take leave and seeing me so desolated, saying, "Put yo' head in the air and yo' trust in the Lord."

We received the Deeds of the Ocosta property from the Auditor's Office, all recorded and I enclose two for each one of you, except Will—his deed is for four lots. The two extra are given for the express purpose of helping to clear the debt when it comes due. Oh! Will, they may never be worth anything, but we hope in the next few years they may increase in value in the same ratio as have lots in the suburbs of Tacoma, heretofore the terminus of the Northern Pacific. If they do, there will be no happier people on the globe than we.

Today I was winding some saxony yarn when Reuben came in. "Let me do that," he said. "No," I answered without thinking. "Grandma used to let me wind *her* cotton. Grandma used to let me do lots of things you ought not to brought me away." We had a long talk about dear Grandma and tears were averted.

---

[7] Charles Preston Fleet, born at Green Mount on May 27, 1888.

I have never seen Montesano so dull nor money so scarce. We can't see the reason unless it is the general stringency of the money market and the boom in Chicago is turning away considerable capital from us. People are investing heavily there until World's Fair year.

Write as often as you can to your affectionate

Lillian

Mexico, Mo.

My dear Sister [Lou], 11/29/91

I am in no position to assist the boy whom you are interested in as there are still debts to be liquidated in connection with my school. I do not know him, nor can I take your judgment, for that is liable to error. It is not every boy it pays to help get an education—nor every girl either. If you had all that was due you for your wearing toil of 10 or 15 years in helping girls who have completely repudiated their obligations, you would be in comfortable circumstances the rest of your days. He can study at home where his brother can teach him and he can help his father. Do not perplex yourself further about him, if he really has merit, it will show itself.

Aff., A. F. F.

My dear Mother, 8/10/92 St. Louis, Mo.

I met Belle and the boys here. Thank you and all most kindly for taking care of them. Belle is greatly improved and can stand the strain, I trust, for another year.

Best love to all,
Yours, Fred

My dear Bess. Sept. 10th 1892

Friday we went to Bruington, Edward Pollard preached the sermon in the morning & his father made the address of the evening. Mag & Vic came home with us that night & went with

Minnie [8] & the Sizers & Marian & Garnett Ryland [9] to Farmington. Saturday evening Minnie came back here with them. Garland Pollard,[10] Frank Smith, William & Bessie Gwathmey &
Bessie Todd Fauntleroy were here also. All spent the night
but Frank and Garland. Mother keeps up very well but you
may know we miss you to help with all this company. I hope
you are having more rest than you could get here.

All send love,

Lou

My dearest husband [David],   Green Mount 7 June 1893
    I must tell you how often Mother says she wishes you were
here to enjoy the fruit. "Dear child, give him my best love,"
she says "and tell him I think of him everyday." How she does
love and admire the children! She thinks they are greatly improved in every way, dispositions and manners particularly. She
says, "Of course, they are *children*, Lillian, but they are remarkably *good children*—the best all round that ever came into this
house." If other people feel this way about them, we must try
to be more patient, loving and wise in our government, we
have only two—let us do as well by them as we can with God's
help.

Your loving wife [Lillian]

D. W. Fleet, City Clerk
                                     Montesano, Wash.
My dear sister [Lou],   July 19, 1893
    I received Lillian's letter saying she and Aunt Bess would
leave Monday for Chicago. Dear old girl, She is enjoying herself
so much and you all are so kind. The greatest temptation I

---

[8] Minnie was very pretty and witty and always had a train of admirers.

[9] Garnett Ryland was head of the Department of Chemistry at the University of
Richmond. The Garnett and Fleet families were very affectionate, the members always
calling each other "cousin." When asked how we were related, Professor Ryland said,
"the closest I can come to it is that my grandfather [Dr. John Muscoe Garnett] was
in love with your grandmother [Maria Louisa Wacker].

[10] John Garland Pollard became head of the School of Government at the College
of William and Mary and governor of Virginia, 1930–34.

ever had was to go to Chicago and meet them. It's too bad the World's Fair should have been held during a money panic. Never mind when I get rich I am coming to Va., buy a little farm and enjoy the rest of my days. Then you all shall come and stay some with me.

Give my love to dear Mother and tell her if I should have some unexpected windfall, I will run in some night and surprise her as of old.

Kiss the children for me & tell them to be good.

Aff'y, D. W. F.

Mexico, Mo.

My dear Sister [Lou], 3/18/94

I miss Mother's letters. Have you determined upon the date of her visit to Baltimore? I am very anxious about it. I trust the operation on her eyes may be safely and successfully performed.

All join in sending best love to all,

A. F. Fleet

Dear Bess, Sun. eve. Apr. 15, 1894

The day was so lovely, Willie took Mother out riding. Of course she could not see a thing in the bright sunlight but she enjoyed the pure fresh air and the little ride. Her eye is improving and yesterday she enjoyed knitting, isn't it fortunate she doesn't have to look at it.

Aff'y, Lou

Dr. Alfred Bagby asked Lou for a photograph and a sketch of Maria Louisa Fleet's life which he wanted to include in his history of King and Queen County. Part of her reply is given here.

We haven't a good photograph of my Mother. As you know, her beauty is that of the spirit which is nearly impossible to capture in a photograph.

John Seddon Fleet in 1894

John Seddon Fleet, A. W. Anderson, and P. E. Chapman at the Mexico Military Academy, 1896

For five years while the cataracts on her eyes were maturing, she was unable to read or write and she was too deaf to enjoy the services in the church she loved so well. Yet as each Sabbath came, she unselfishly urged all of her children to take their places in the Sunday School and church work. When we told her how much we hated to leave her, she said, "Never mind, you know I have my pleasant thoughts and happy memories and we are never alone when accompanied by noble thoughts." One day when I came home, I said, "Mother we are getting old, I am teaching the children whose parents I taught." She said, "Yes, dear, but we don't know it."

She conducted her school here for fifteen years and now our girls are scattered from New York to Florida, from California and Vancouver to Texas and South Carolina.

> "Time's restless billows ebb and flow
> and bear our barks apart.
> Love still abides, and evermore
> I hold them in my heart."

I follow them with my letters, scattered as they are, and sometimes I write them—My Mother's life is so "pure in purpose, so strong in its strife." I want you to take a lesson in patience from her crosses so bravely borne. All through life when her days were darkest and she has had some that were very, very dark, instead of useless repining she would count her mercies and blessings.

In the summer of 1895, Minnie, Belle, and the boys were sent to Green Mount to spend the summer with their grandmother, and their brother Reginald was born August 24 during their absence. Mrs. Seddon sent by them a little gift with this note: "For dear Mrs. Fleet, from her friend, Mary Alexander Seddon, with warm love and sympathy. Though we both have passed our three score and ten mark, we have health and dear ones about us and something we can still do to help in the little world we love. Content and thankful for countless mercies and blessings and happy in the nearing and precious hope of an infinitely more blessed home in our Father's house forever."

Their Aunt Lou held a "Literary Society" for the nephews, who

recited and read poetry and articles and took turns writing the minutes
of the meetings. Occasionally she added a note as she did on June
17, 1895.

We had a most delightful interruption of our daily meetings
in the visit of our beloved one, Col. A. F. Fleet, who paid us
a visit, all too brief on his way from Annapolis. He was appointed
by Pres. Cleveland as one of the Board of Visitors to the Naval
Academy. This brought him so near to Virginia, he had an
opportunity of visiting his childhood home.

He left for Baltimore June 13th accompanied by Minnie, Bessie, and our dear little Mother. Here she was fitted with some
glasses that enabled her to see better than she had done since
the cataract was removed.

Dear Bess,   Sept. 25, 1896
Last night we received a telegram "Our school and home
swept away by fire. Friends have opened their homes to us."

My first words were—What will Fred do with a large family
to be taken care of and educated. Ma didn't hesitate in saying,
"He will work hard and the Lord will help him." Will wired
him Mother's message and to come here and bring his family.

We are all well in spite of the dark shadow this has cast
over us. I must give this to Walter who is ready to go to the
mill.

All join me in love from your devoted sister,

Lou

My dear Mother,   Sept. 27, 1896
I have just received the following telegram from Mr. Henry
Culver: "You have the boys and no building. I have the building
and no boys. Let's get together." It seems such a logical arrangement, I have wired him we will come as soon as possible
and about eighty-five of our boys will go with me. Your message
in Will's telegram has been justified.

Love to all
A. F. Fleet

They arrived at Culver, Indiana, on October 10, 1896. The Culver School had some twenty boys, and the combined group was really the beginning of the Culver Military Academy.

456 Freemason St.
Norfolk, Va.

My dear Miss Betsy,   Sept. 17, 1897
   When I sent the telegram—"The end came at 2 o'clock before I reached here," I was so shocked and numbed with grief that I went through with the arrangements and the service with all the people, scarcely feeling anything. On my return from the cemetery, I found your dear letter in which you said "exceptional souls like your Father's and my Mother's are not extinguished when they vanish from our sight. They live on for us who knew and loved them—a precious legacy that cannot perish nor decay." This lifted me out of the morass of sorrow and now the thought of my beloved Father comes to me as a shining light to guide me throughout the days of my earthly pilgrimage. The thought of you, like a ministering angel to be there in my first days of sorrow to help through words, looks and deeds, gives me courage to return in a few days to the Miller School.

Your devoted friend,
J. P. C. S.[11]

Hotel Del Prado, Chicago

My dearest Mother,   Oct. 17th '97
   We had a good trip up this A.M. The Cadets came at 8:10 and just before them the Calvary and wagons, and by 8:30 we were off. The trainmaster was aboard and we made the run without incident in two hours. We took the suburban train to this Hotel and at 1:15 started to join the crowds to meet the President. We were the last in line but the first to pass in review by Pres't Harper's house.[12] The rain was coming down

[11] James Powell Cocke Southall (1871–1962) taught at the Miller School, 1893–98 and later became professor of physics at the Alabama Polytechnic Institute, 1901–14, and at Columbia University, 1914–40. He and Betsy Fleet were lifelong friends.
[12] Will Rainey Harper (1856–1906) taught at Yale University from 1886–1891 and was president of the University of Chicago until his death.

fast, but the boys were as steady as veterans and moved splendidly. Pres. McKinley raised his hat & smiled most approvingly & that paid the boys for the rain I'm sure. As soon as they passed, Maj. Gignilliat [13] brought them right here & had them change their clothes. I went to the reception where Mr. Harper greeted me very cordially and introduced me to Mr. McKinley, we had time for only a word. I then introduced myself to Mrs. Harper and she introduced me to Mrs. McKinley and after a few pleasantries, I bowed myself out. Mr. McKinley is very good looking, but not nearly so goodlooking as his wife! Mrs. Harper is fat and pudgy.

Unfortunately the Black Horse Troop had to go down town to be unloaded. They were blocked between two trains & were not able to be in the procession.

When I came back, I found the boys looking very dry and comfortable, but hungry! We had dinner at five for their benefit—a fine dinner—and you never saw fellows enjoy it more! I am writing this, Mother, because I know how you love and enjoy boys—and girls too!

Love to all aff.
Fred

Miller School

My dear Home-ones,   Nov. 22, 1897

I am so thankful to hear of Mother's continued improvement. Do you think the Major will meet Belle at Green Mount at Christmas? Mrs. Seddon intimated as much in her letter. It would be much less expensive for him to come to Virginia than to go to Indiana, if he sees Belle at Christmas. Bless his heart, I am very anxious to meet him.

It is time for the mail and I must stop with best love to each one.

Aff.
Bess

[13] Maj. Leigh Robinson Gignilliat was commandant of cadets at Culver Military Academy.

Maj. Kenneth Gordon Matheson, Belle's fiancé, was born in 1864 in Cheraw, South Carolina. He was educated at the Citadel and Stanford and Columbia Universities. The former commandant of cadets at the Mexico Military Academy, he was presently teaching English at the Georgia Institute of Technology. He was president of Georgia Tech from 1906 to 1922, when he became president of Drexel Institute. He remained at Drexel until his death in 1931.

David, spurred on by the stories of the gold strikes in the Yukon, got out his mining engineer's instruments and joined the prospectors.

> Gray's Harbor Abstract Co.
> Chehalis County, Washington
> D. W. Fleet, Manager

My dear Aunt Lou,   August 23, 1898

Your sweet letter of the 13th came Saturday, and in answer, I can tell you something of our plans. We received two letters from Mr. Fleet, in one of which he says he cannot possibly return before spring and wishes us to rent the house and start for Virginia the last of October.

Mr. Fleet's letters were both in journal style, telling of each day's happenings, so of course were intensely interesting to us. I shall bring them as you wish, dear Aunt Lou, to read to you. Dear old fellow, he writes so unselfishly—you can read more between the lines than in them, what he feels in having to decide not to return. He says it would be impossible to accomplish anything should he return this fall, but says it gives him unspeakable pain to tell us so. "Bear it manfully, darling, for it is no harder for you than for me." Aunt Lou, I can't write about it. His going has almost the bitterness of death in it for me. I don't know why I have felt about it as I have. God grant it is no prophetic feeling. Perhaps I shall be able to look at the matter differently before I see you all. I hope so for your sakes. If not I shall "bury my sorrow."

He says he is perfectly well, and although his plans have changed somewhat, he is not discouraged. They cannot go into Dawson on account of the extremely low water in the Yukon, so the Captain will land them at the mouth of the Kyukak River, up which they will pole 450 or 500 miles. He says the govern-

ment has recently established a post office at Koyuskuk and
the Laplanders will carry mail in all winter, so I have sent three
letters since Wednesday and will keep them going so he may
have that comfort. You might too, Aunt Lou, it would do him
so much good to hear.

Believe me, I appreciate the feeling you have about our coming and the loving thoughts you have so kindly expressed in
your letter. I am so glad Mother is so well and we shall see
her soon with arms outstretched to welcome us. She is always
the inspiration of those around her and I look forward to our
meeting lovingly and eagerly. The children are perfectly delighted at the thought of being with you again, and send quanti-
ties of love.

Write when you can to your loving sister

Lillian

[Written on the back of this letter]
My dear Bessie,

Myn had a letter from Sed in which he says he expects to
start to the University the 13th. I hope you and he can see
each other quite often, it will be a mutual help.

The weather has been so hot, we advised Myn and the Major
not to attempt to return their calls, & he seemed greatly relieved. They expect to leave Tuesday, I'll try to write more
after they are gone.

Love from all,
Your affectionate Sister Lou

Mary Seddon Fleet and Maj. Leigh Robinson Gignilliat were married
at Culver, August 2, 1898, and spent their honeymoon at Green
Mount. He was born in Savannah in 1875, was graduated from the
Virginia Military Institute, and received a M.A. degree from Trinity
College. He was commandant of cadets at Culver Military Academy
from 1897 to 1910, when he succeeded his father-in-law as superintendent upon his retirement. During World War I he served as a
brigadier general on Gen. John J. Pershing's staff. He continued as
superintendent of Culver Military Academy until his retirement in
1939. He died in 1952.

Maj. Leigh Robinson Gignilliat and his wife, Mary Seddon Fleet

My own precious Seddon,   C. M. A. Dec. 13, '98
    Belle [Fleet] expects to come to Green Mount for a few days
during the week you are there. She has sent all her invitations
and as her wedding day is only two weeks off, we are realizing
it more and more, and it gives us all the blues to think of it.
I do not see how we can get on without her. She had such a
satisfactory trip to Chicago, accomplished most of her shopping
and will have a pretty and complete outfit.
                         Your devoted Mother [Belle Seddon Fleet],

                                     Culver Military Academy
My dear Mother,   6:30 A.M. June 5, 1899
    I have been waking up at quite an early hour and with all
we have on hand with commencement, I find it impossible to
sleep, nor do I think there will be time to write later in the
day, nor for the next four days. I am very glad to say the Commencement Exercises have gone on very well, without a single
disagreeable or untoward circumstance. We have about fifty
visitors and I'm sure their number will increase to three hundred
as they are coming in on every train and the equestrian exhibition with the Black Horse Troop is very popular.
    And tomorrow is my birthday—I always think most of you
at that time, and I always feel like thanking you with all my
heart for having been such a good mother to me, and having
trained me so carefully. You know I have always given you
credit for almost all I have been able to do in life—however
little that may be!
    By the way, what would you think of my riding at the head
of the G. A. R. procession at Terre Haute, and being taken
all along the line for the Governor! That is what I did. The
Governor's escort goes before him and I was at the head of
the escort with two of my aides and thus I rode the whole
parade and received all the plaudits.
                         Best love, your aff. A. F. Fleet

My precious little Betsy,   G. M. Sept. 14, 1899

Lou has consented to be my amanuensis as I have a great many things I want to say to you. First, I want to tell you of our Wm's new honor. He was nominated in the primary to represent these counties in the Legislature. I tell him I hope he will always know and do what is *right.* Our old neighbor, Mr. Wilson, doesn't get around very easily now but he got someone to bring him to see me Sunday evening. He told me how proud I ought to be of my "Baby boy." He thinks all my children are doing well, but the youngest is most honored in being the first choice of all the people of this area for this responsible position. In his acceptance speech, Will asked his friends to stand by him if there were any opposition and Mr. Connor said, "There will be none." He bears his honors very modestly and I trust his head is too full of good sense to be turned by flattery. I want to say all my children have the been the greatest joy and satisfaction. I always said anyone who said children were no trouble were either lying or not doing their duty, mine have repaid me a hundredfold for all the trouble I took with them.

You must be sure to invite the boys to see you while the mountains are clothed in their autumn glory.

All send love to my precious child,

Yr. aff. Mother

In 1899 Henry joined his brother Seddon at the University of Virginia, and Will entered later.

My precious Henry,   Culver Oct. 25th 1899

We were glad of your letter and were especially amused by your account of your Indiana compatriot who wanted to meet someone from Indiana whom he would know how to talk to! I suppose as there are no class distinctions at the University, formality is used as a protection against too many acquaintances or any that might be undesirable, and it is clearly far more dignified and gentlemanly than the conditions that prevail at many universities and colleges and I like it on that account.

Maj. Kenneth Gordon Matheson and his wife, Belle Seddon Fleet

Tell Seddon Will appreciated his suggestion that he take German in Chicago next summer, but Father said he couldn't spare him from his office. I suggested possibly Miss Vonnegut might be induced to give him private lessons, she is said to speak remarkably pure German.

A heartful of love to you both,

Your devoted Mother [Belle Seddon Fleet]

Marjorie Vonnegut did give Will German lessons, and they fell in love; but saying she expected to love Will's kind in heaven, she went to New York, where she found a successful stage career and later marriage to Don Marquis. At the University of Virginia he won the first Rhodes scholarship to Oxford in 1904. While in England he became engaged to Cecil Lyall, daughter of Sir Charles Lyall, the Arabic scholar, and returned to the United States to teach at Princeton, "to prepare a place which I could ask her to share." Shortly after the outbreak of World War I, he returned to England, was commissioned a lieutenant in the Grenadier Guards, and they were married. After being at the front for about eighteen months, he was killed near Amiens in the Chemin des Dames offensive. Marjorie Vonnegut had a requiem mass held for him.

Dear Bessie,   Dec. 12, 1899

Can't you talk with Capt. Vawter and then with Seddon and Henry about the day you can meet at Hanover C. H. Fred and Will and Charlie will come there via Washington on Sat. the 23rd and I hope you can come too as it will be so much more agreeable for you to travel together. Our good faithful Walter has promised to go for you in the carriage and if this lovely weather continues, he will bring a saddled horse for the boys to take turns riding.

Willie will meet Belle and Reg in Richmond as there is a through train from Atlanta and that will obviate her having to change trains.

Willie has spoken to Mr. Ware about getting him a barrel of nice oysters and Sister and Hannah have made a beautiful fruit cake. Ma is anticipating so much pleasure in seeing all of you and is counting the days. She has finished the wool socks for Fred and the boys, (all I had to do was to turn the heels) and is busily knitting a beautiful zephyr scarf for Belle.

I trust you will all get here safely and will enjoy everything.

Love from all,
Aff'y Lou

House of Delegates
Richmond, Va.
My dear Mother,   Dec. 13th 1899

I reached here safely and well Monday. As the House adjourns for a day, I am going with a number of friends to Washington to the Masonic gathering.

I have written to Brother and will write to Seddon and Sister Belle and find out and effectuate their plans. I hope the weather will continue fine as it is now. Judge Blakey and I had a very encouraging talk with the railroad people last night. They assure us the road will be built.

I hope the home work is going smoothly,

Love to all,
Aff. J. W. Fleet

[Written on the bottom of the letter]
My dear Bessie,

I send you this letter and am thankful to say we are all well and I hope will be ready to enjoy a blessed holiday together. Tell Seddon and Henry they must bring their skates, we have such beautiful ponds, they can enjoy skating if the cold weather lasts long enough.

You must bring as many as you can of Albemarle's finest pippins. I want Brother to see that old Virginia can raise something besides broom sedge and pines. Mother is knitting by my side and wants me to tell you how happy she will be to see you.

Aff. Lou

After spending a happy Christmas in good health with all her children around her except David, Ma contracted pneumonia and died on January 6, 1900.

Green Mount
My dear Lillian,   Jan. 7th 1900

I know you will do all you can to cheer & comfort our precious David, in this hour of his bitter grief.

We must be thankful God took her home before her bright mind had failed, or her body became helpless from the weakness & infirmities of old age. She was always one of the very best of mothers & we can never outlive the feeling of her loss, but we can only bow in humble submission to our Father's will, & thank him for having given & having spared to us so long such an unselfish noble Christian Mother.

I will try to write often and all of you must too.

Your loving sister Lou

Col. A. F. Fleet, Supt.
Culver Military Academy
Culver, Indiana

My dear David,   1/9/1900

I presume W. wired you Saturday the 6th as he did me— "Mother died this morning. Funeral Monday 2: o'clock P.M." And altho' I have for years been thinking that such a message might come at any moment, I was greatly shocked and grieved to hear it, and feel we have all suffered an irreparable loss.

As you know, perhaps, Belle had been in Atlanta with little Belle for a month or more and she came from Richmond; Bessie, the boys and I came from Hanover Court House to meet at Green Mount and spend the Christmas with Mother. The arrangement was perfect. We went down Sat. P.M. and stayed until the next Friday, enjoying greatly the sight and association of all the dear ones. Mother was looking better than I had seen her for a long time, altho' of course more feeble with the weight of increasing years, and very cheerful and bright. This time there were no tears when we parted but she expressed only serenity and peace.

We often spoke of you and Lillian and the children and if you could have been there, her cup would literally have been overflowing. Hence it was a great shock to hear the sad news so quickly. But she certainly fought a good fight, finished her course, and kept the faith.

Surely children never had a better Mother—so brave, so unselfish, so anxious for their highest temporal and spiritual good. The old home will never be the same without her and I don't know that I want to go back there again.

Good bye, best love,

Yrs aff'y A. F. Fleet

Green Mount

My dear Brother David: Jan. 11, 1900

I know you will want to hear all about our dear Mother's funeral so I will try to write of it to you tonight. Monday Jan. 8th was an ideal winter's day, beautifully clear and the thermometer ranging from 50 to 60 degrees. At one o'clock the people commenced coming, and by two, I think there were between four and five hundred here. We knew it would be too great a trial for cousin Alex to conduct the service, as he looked on her as a second mother so Will got Frank Beale to take his place. The casket was placed in the front hall near the back door, and the people were assembled in the office, parlor, dining room and porches. Will and we three sisters stayed over the parlor where we could hear very well. Mr. Beale stood in the parlor door, and as he spoke loudly and distinctly I think everybody could hear him. The first hymn was "Rock of Ages," which perhaps you remember was one of our Father's favorites, and was sung at his funeral. Then followed some beautiful Bible verses, and a most comforting prayer. The next hymn was "How Firm a Foundation," and then a five minutes' talk.

The pall-bearers then bore the casket to the grave. All these were her nephews:—cousins Robert Ryland, Wm Haynes, Alex Bagby, Willie Bagby, Jimmie Fleet and Frank Smith. We thought it best not to go to the grave as Sister and Willie both faint so easily; so we didn't hear the concluding prayer offered by Mr. Long, the Bruington minister. The hymns at the grave were, "O God our help in Ages Past," and "Abide with me." The hymns were beautifully sung and so comforting. There were four white and four colored ministers. Although there was such a crowd here of both white and colored, everything went on without a thing to mar the sweet and solemn services. The flowers were beautiful, especially a wreath of white japonica sent by Bessie Aylett.

I can hardly realize we shall never see her again on earth but feel perfectly resigned to God's will. She had dreaded outliving her usefulness and being a burden, so we must be only thankful she didn't have that trial. Our friends have been so good and sympathetic, I think we have received at least a hundred letters. It was Mother's wish that we shouldn't wear mourning for her, so we have decided not to do so.

Now, dear Brother, I must close, praying God's blessing on you and yours, and hoping to see you all again some time soon. Kiss dear Lillian and the darling children for me, and believe me always,

Your devoted sister,
Florence

Miller School
Jan. 12, 1900

My dear Bro. David,

I came back to work yesterday and have met with much sympathy and consideration. The kind sympathy of our friends and kindred is soothing but in my heart there is an aching void which never can be filled.

I trust you and all the dear ones are well. I am—except tired, but I hope that will pass.

In looking over Mother's little knitting box which always stayed at the foot of her bed, I found your last letter and am sure she had read it over and over with great pleasure.

With best love for each one—we must love each other better than ever before because *she* always wanted us to do that.

Your devoted Betsy

After it was all over, Lou also wrote to her absent brother.

My own precious David,

I know you would want to hear of the last days when our darling Mother was with us. She was taken sick the day after Brother and Sister Belle left. We thought at first it was an ordinary cold and fever, but it developed into pneumonia and weakened her very rapidly.

She was always so bright and cheerful we could never realize how ill she was. Wednesday morning she sat up a little while, and persuaded Will that she was well enough for him to leave her for his duties in Richmond, but Bessie stayed to help nurse her. Thursday morning she read some in the *Christian Herald* and said, "I hope Lillian has gotten her paper and the book you ordered for her." She asked me to have the *Christian Herald* and "How to make Home Happy" sent to Lillian. She was so anxious to have you all here again and help you train the dear children for the greatest usefulness here and the highest happiness hereafter. But she is not lost to you or to them, her precepts and her example will be an inspiration to us all as long as life shall last. I believe your letter with the gift of money was the crowning joy of her happy Christmas—to hear you were all well and your business was prospering again.

She was unconscious for almost twenty-four hours so she could not send her absent loved ones any message. But so often I have heard her say the last words she wanted to speak to us would be, "Children, *love* one another, and help each other all you can."

"God's finger touched her and she slept." I flew to her Bible for comfort and my eyes rested on a page she had turned down for me, I know, and marked it with a lock of her hair—"Thou wilt keep him in perfect peace, whose mind is stayed on thee: because he trusteth in thee. Trust ye in the Lord forever; for in the Lord Jehovah is everlasting strength."

Knowing how lost we would feel without her, she had written on the margin of the page, "You cannot grieve for me for I am with your father and our Father in Paradise."

Epilogue

Col. A. F. Fleet was superintendent of Culver Military Academy until his retirement in 1910. Of his sons:

John Seddon received B.A. and M.A. degrees from the University of Virginia; he became head of the Peacock-Fleet School in Atlanta, Georgia, but he returned to Culver where he was headmaster and Latin teacher until his retirement.

Henry Wise/Wyatt attended the University of Virginia for two years when (according to Seddon) he sold his books for new. He joined the army; after duty in the Philippines, he served in France during World War I as a colonel of infantry and was sent to the National War College. Later he was in charge of the ROTC at Amherst College, where to his amusement an honorary degree was conferred on him for his contribution to the college.

Charles Preston received a severe injury in school football and died shortly afterwards.

Reginald Scott was graduated from Georgia School of Technology and served as a captain of artillery in World War I. He was an investment banker in Atlanta until World War II, when he went to San Diego to join Consolidated Aircraft Corporation.

Lou lived at Green Mount and taught her music pupils. She played the organ and taught in the Sunday school at St. Stephens Church for more than fifty years. On Sunday afternoons she held a Sunday school class for children, black and white, in the nursery during the winter and in the yard under the trees when the weather was warm.

David did not strike gold in Alaska; he and Lillian lived in Aberdeen, Washington, after his retirement as auditor of Che-

The Fleet boys in 1902: (seated) Henry Wise/Wyatt, Reginald Scott, John
Seddon; (standing) Charles Preston and William Alexander

halis County, where he was affectionately called "Daddy Fleet" by everyone in town. Of his children:

Ma's admonition to Lillian about Reuben, "Take good care of this child for he will be a big man some day," was justified, for on the plaque below his portrait in the International Aerospace Hall of Fame, 1965, San Diego, California, is the inscription:

REUBEN HOLLIS FLEET

Pioneer Military Aviator—Aviation Industrialist—Philanthropist—Patriot. . . . Maj. Fleet organized the first U.S. Air Mail Service May 15, 1918. Formed Consolidated Aircraft Co. 1923, later the great Convair Corp. Under his leadership were produced 18,000 of the famous B-24 Liberator bombers, and the PBY Catalina flying boats which played major roles in World War II, a production miracle made possible by his genius for organization and innovative methods. His post-industry years have seen him intensely devoted to public service and philanthropic projects

Mrs. James William (Nannie Burke) Fleet

for the underprivileged and the community and the promotion of love of country among the young.

He was enshrined in the Aviation Hall of Fame, Dayton, Ohio, posthumously, November 22, 1975.

Lillian married Edward K. Bishop, banker and lumberman of Aberdeen and Seattle. He always attributed his success in business to his "partner," and together they engaged in a myriad of social, civic, and philanthropic affairs.

Florence and Betsy continued to teach and survived their mother only a few years.

William remained at Green Mount with his sisters. In 1903 he married Nannie Burke, and they maintained Ma's tradition of hospitality to family and friends. When the office of county judge was discontinued, he was elected attorney for the Commonwealth and held that position as long as he lived.

Appendix
Students at Green Mount Home School for Young Ladies

Session 1873–74

Acree, Page
Bagby, Hannah
Bird, Mattie
Dew, Lelia
Fleet, Sallie Browne
Jones, Ellen (Nellie) Brooke
Ryland, Ida

Day Students

Councill, Mary Brooke
Fauntleroy, Claybrooke
(music)
Fauntleroy, Ella
Smith, Lelia
Smith, Sallie Brooke

Session 1874–75

Acree, Page
Baylor, Charlotte (Lottie)
Bird, Mattie
Dew, Lelia
Fauntleroy, Claybrooke
(music)
Fauntleroy, Ella
Fleet, Sallie Browne
Jones, Nellie
Leigh, Manie

Session 1875–76

Acree, Ella
Acree, Page
Bagby, Hannah
Baylor, Charlotte (Lottie)
Bird, Mattie
Caldwell, Rosa
Councill, Mary Brooke
Davies, Mary
Dew, Lelia
Evans, Emma
Fauntleroy, Claybrooke
(music)
Fauntleroy, Ella
Fleet, Kate
Fleet, Sallie Browne
Gwathmey, Emilie
Gwathmey, Rosalie
Jones, Nellie
Latané, Lizzie
Leigh, Manie
Nason, Belle
Pollard, Carey
Pollard, Mollie

Ryland, Alice
Smith, Kate
Smith, Lelia
Smith, M. S.
Smith, Sallie Brooke
Washington, Mary

Session 1876–77

Acree, Page
Baylor, Charlotte (Lottie)
Bird, Sue
Caldwell, Mr. (music)
Caldwell, Rosa
Crump, Minnie Belle
Davies, Mary
Evans, Emma
Fauntleroy, Claybrook (music)
Fauntleroy, Mattie Kate
Fleet, Sallie Browne
Gwathmey, Emilie
Gwathmey, Nettie
Harwood, Mattie F.
Jones, Nellie
Latané, Lizzie
Leigh, Manie
Nason, Belle
Pollard, Mollie
Pollard, Sallie
Ryland, Alice
Ryland, John (music)

Session 1877–78

Bagby, Hannah
Bird, Mattie
Bird, Sue
Blount, Sallie Lee

Brown, Mabel
Crump, Minnie Belle
Evans, Emma
Fauntleroy, Mattie Kate
Fleet, Emma
Garlick, Attie
Garlick, Ellen
Gatewood, Ellen
Harwood, Mattie
Jones, Nellie
Latané, Rosa
Morrison, Sallie
Smith, Sallie Brooke
Todd, Bessie
Walker, Betsie Todd
Westwood, Ida
Wright, Belle
Wright, Lelia

Session 1878–79

Bagby, Nellie
Bagby, Virginia
Bird, Mattie F.
Bird, Sue
Blount, Sallie Lee
Carlton, Bettie Lee
Crump, Minnie Belle
Fauntleroy, Mattie Kate
Fleet, Lucy
Fleet, Sallie Browne
Garlick, Ellen
Jones, Nellie
Latane, Rosa V.
Lee, Bettie
Nipe, Alice
Sinton, Aileen
Ware, Kate

Westwood, Ida
Wilson, Essie
Wright, Belle
Wright, Lelia

Session 1879–80

Bagby, Virginia
Blount, Sallie Lee
Carlton, Bettie Lee
Fauntleroy, Mattie Kate
Fleet, Lucy
Fleet, Sallie Browne
Henley, M. Lou
Latané, Rosa V.
Reynolds, Mary
Smith, Lelia (music)

Session 1880–81

Blount, Sallie Lee
Fauntleroy, Mattie Kate
Fleet, Lucy
Henley, M. Lou
Sale, Nannie F.
Starke, Loulie

Session 1881–82

Chidester, Kate
Henley, M. Lou
Jeffress, Corinne
Sale, Nannie F.
Steel, Janey P.
Westwood, Mattie L.
Williams, Loulie
Williams, Mary

Session 1882–83

Chidester, Kate
Gresham, Julia T.
Hall, Florence
Henley, M. Lou
Hoge, Cassie
Hoge, Marian
Jeffress, Corinne
Prevost, Mamie B.
Starke, Loulie
Steel, Janey P.
Vest, Mary B.
Westwood, Mattie
Williams, Loulie
Williams, Mary

Session 1883–84

Barber, Anna C.
Campbell, Mag
Chidester, Kate H.
Gresham, Julia T.
Hall, Florence
Harrison, Laura
Harrison, Mary
Hoge, Cassie
Hoge, Marian
Jeffress, Corinne
Leigh, Lottie
Love, Grace
Prevost, Mary B.
Reese, Kate
Vest, Mary B.
Walker, Maggie
Williams, Lucille
Williams, Robbie

Session 1884–85

Barber, Anna C.
Campbell, Netta
Gregory, Lenora
Gregory, Lizzie
Harrison, Laura
Harrison, Mary
Love, Grace
Morrison, Rossie
Pettus, Evangeline
Smith, Evelyn
Walker, Maggie

Session 1885–86

Barber, Anna C.
Campbell, Mag
Campbell, Netta
Eggleston, Eddie
Harrison, Laura
Harrison, Mary
Morrison, Rossie
Pettus, Evangeline
Walker, Maggie
Watlington, Lizzie

Session 1886–87

Barber, Anna C.
Campbell, Mag
Eggleston, Eddie
Fleet, Minnie Seddon
Hancock, Cabell
Lipscomb, Mary
Martin, Mamie
Morrison, Rossie

Session 1887–88

Averell, Mamie
Biscoe, Sadie
Eggleston, Eddie
Fleet, Belle Seddon
Fleet, Minnie Seddon
Hancock, Cabell
Hurt, Phoebe
Littlepage, Lucy
Moore, Victoria
Morrison, Rossie
Ryland, Maggie
Shelton, Mary
Taliaferro, Josephine
Walker, Maud

Jacob David Wacker m. Maria Pollard William Fleet m. Sarah Browne
1781–1829 1817 1796–1831 1751–1833 1795 1776–1818

Maria Louisa Wacker Benjamin Fleet
1822–1900 1818–1865

m.
1842

Alexander Frederick Benjamin Robert Maria Louisa David Wacker Florence Betsy Pollard James William
1843–1911 1846–64 1849–1917 1851–1937 1852–1903 1854–1904 1856–1927
m. 1871 m. 1884
Belle Seddon Lillian Waite
1851–1940 1858–1939

Reuben Hollis 1887–1975
Lillian 1888–1971

Mary Seddon 1873–1952
Alexander Frederick 1875–76
Belle Seddon 1876–1969
John Seddon 1878–1964
Henry Wise/Wyatt 1880–1945
William Alexander 1883–1918
Charles Preston 1888–1930
Reginald Scott 1895–

Green Mount Black Family 1813–1899

Milly (Mammy) Diggs m. Joshua Gaines
1813–1891 1813–1889

Harry Gaines Mary Washington

Caroline Harry Isabel Lorelle Martha Ann m. Richard Baylor
b. 1855 b. 1857 b. 1859 b. 1860 b. 1864

Harry Richard Hugh Major Gignilliat
1894–1974 b. 1896– b. 1899–

Index